Archaeology from Art

Exploring the interpretative potential of British and Irish Neolithic rock art

Edward Evans

BAR British Series 363
2004

Published in 2019 by
BAR Publishing, Oxford

BAR British Series 363

Archaeology from Art

© Edward Evans and the Publisher 2004

ISBN 9781841713557 paperback
ISBN 9781407320052 e-book

DOI https://doi.org/10.30861/9781841713557

A catalogue record for this book is available from the British Library

This book is available at www.barpublishing.com

BAR Publishing is the trading name of British Archaeological Reports (Oxford) Ltd.
British Archaeological Reports was first incorporated in 1974 to publish the BAR
Series, International and British. In 1992 Hadrian Books Ltd became part of the BAR
group. This volume was originally published by John and Erica Hedges in conjunction
with British Archaeological Reports (Oxford) Ltd / Hadrian Books Ltd, the Series
principal publisher, in 2004. This present volume is published by BAR Publishing,
2019.

BAR
PUBLISHING

BAR titles are available from:

BAR Publishing
122 Banbury Rd, Oxford, OX2 7BP, UK
EMAIL info@barpublishing.com
PHONE +44 (0)1865 310431
FAX +44 (0)1865 316916
www.barpublishing.com

TABLE OF CONTENTS

List of figures...iii
Acknowledgements...v
Preface...vi

CHAPTER ONE
An appropriate subject? Ideology, aesthetics and the rock art of the British Isles and Ireland.................. 1

1.1   Introduction 1
1.2   'Palaeo-mythology'.. 1
1.3   Palaeolithic hangovers, the other side of paradox 2
1.4   Marginality, insularity and mantra 3
1.5   Methodology: The power of precedent 3
1.6   Interpretative Mantra.. 4
1.7   The magic circle 5
1.8   Passage tomb art and the archaeological context 5
1.9   Changing paradigms?... 6
1.10   Creating context 7

CHAPTER TWO
Study parameters and contextual connotations.. 10

2.1   Introduction.. 10
2.2   The abstract rock arts of early agricultural Europe 10
2.3   The content and context of European agricultural rock art 11
2.4   A single tradition or divergent trajectories? 13
2.5   Connoting Contexts.. 14
2.6   The distribution of British and Irish rock art 14
2.7   The connotative spectrum of rock art and landscape 14
2.8   Case study analysis and the specificity of connoted effect 18
2.8i   Kealduff and Coomasaharn: The rock art of the Inveragh Peninsula, southwest Ireland...... 18
2.8ii   Glen Lochay, Perthshire.. 21
2.8iii   Loch Tay, Perthshire 23
2.8iv   Castleton, Larnarkshire 26
2.9   A polysemous context?... 27

CHAPTER THREE
Spectrum saliency. Connoted effect and the monuments of the British and Irish Neolithic....................... 28

3.1   Introduction.. 28
3.2   The *power-full* allure of procession.. 28
3.3   The causewayed enclosures 30
3.4   The Cursus Monuments 33
3.5   The Henge Monuments 34
3.6   The monumental spectrum 39

CHAPTER FOUR
Watery graves and high spirits. Rock art and the passage tombs of Ireland... 40

4.1   Introduction.. 40
4.2   Landscape art and the passage tomb: A single tradition or separate strategies? 41
4.3   Rock art and passage tombs: A convergence of repertoire?... 42
4.4   Image concealment and the altered state 44
4.5   Loughcrew: A conflation of worlds 48
4.6i   Inside-out at Newgrange and Knowth: Newgrange 51
4.6ii   Inside-out at Newgrange and Knowth: Knowth 53
4.7   Art and the 'dead' 55
4.8   From houses of the dead to embodiments of the spirit world.. 55

4.8i   Death and Identity 58
4.8ii   Life after death and the materiality of the spiritual 59
4.9   Critical connections 59

CHAPTER FIVE
Tracing trajectories. Image redeployment in the final Neolithic and early Bronze Age 62

5.1   Introduction 62
5.2   Spectrum continuity 62
5.3   The Clava Cairns: A change of direction 64
5.4   Spectrum change 66
5.5   Strategies of early Bronze Age image redeployment 66
5.6   Western Ireland 66
5.7   Western Scotland: The Kilmartin valley, Argyll 67
5.8   Northeast Scotland 68
5.9   Central Scotland 68
5.10   Northeast England 69
5.11   Northwest England 69
5.12   Strategies of early Bronze Age image redeployment 69
5.13   Cornwall and the southwest of the British Isles 70
5.14   Regional patterning in strategies of early Bronze Age image use 70
5.15   From Neolithic to early Bronze Age 72

CHAPTER SIX
Discussion. An interpretation of the rock art of the British Isles and Ireland 73

6.1   Introduction 73
6.2   Cultural selection and the 'specificity' of carving 73
6.3   Conceptual ambiguity and image formulation 75
6.4   Alternative strategies, parallel realms 75
6.5   Diagnostic and undiagnostic expression: accessing the spirit world 78
6.6   The significance of final Neolithic-early Bronze Age image redeployment   80
6.7   Conclusion: history from art 82

AFTERWORD 84

REFERENCES CITED 85

LIST OF FIGURES

Figure 1.1: The tabularisation of rock art design elements...4
Figure 1.2: The principal passage tomb at Newgrange..6

Figure 2.1: Valcamonican rock art in tabular form..11
Figure 2.2: The 'swastika' 11
Figure 2.3: The labyrinth motif and its distribution..11
Figure 2.4: Galician deer..12
Figure 2.5: The Goats Crag 'deer' 12
Figure 2.6: The distribution of British and Irish rock art..14
Figure 2.7: The 'intermediate zone' north of Loch Tay..15
Figure 2.8: Castleton 3, one of the four carved ridges of this site. 16
Figure 2.9: Flora regrowth at Kealduff...17
Figure 2.10: Cairnbann West. The use of natural surface features is indicated by dashed lines. 18
Figure 2.11: The Behy Valley, Inveragh. 18
Figure 2.12: This distribution of rock art at Kealduff and Coomasaharn. 19
Figure 2.13: The Kealduff ridge 19
Figure 2.14: Kealduff 3. 19
Figure 2.15: Kealduff 2. 20
Figure 2.16: The loosely pecked 'linking' cruciform motif of Kealduff 5. 20
Figure 2.17: The enclosed, grouped cup-marks of Kealduff 1. 20
Figure 2.18: Kealduff Cliff...20
Figure 2.19: the 'vertical' radials of Coomasaharn 1. 21
Figure 2.20: The distribution of Scottish Case study sites..21
Figure 2.21: The distribution of rock art in the Lochay Valley. 22
Figure 2.22: The approach to Glen Lochay 2. 22
Figure 2.23: Glen Lochay 2..22
Figure 2.24: The surviving imagery at Glen Lochay 3..22
Figure 2.25: Views to the mountains from Glen Lochay 3..23
Figure 2.26: The carved ridge of Glen Lochay 5...23
Figure 2.27: Image 'panels' from Glen Lochay 5. 23
Figure 2.28: The distribution of rock art along the northern shore of Loch Tay 24
Figure 2.29: Duallin 24
Figure 2.30: The valley south of Duallin...25
Figure 2.31: The east-west alignment of imagery at Edramucky 2 25
Figure 2.32: The massive ridge system at Cragganester seen north-to-south. 25
Figure 2.33: The large outcrop of Craggantoul 26
Figure 2.34: The cup-marked summit of Craggantoul...26
Figure 2.35: Views south over Loch Tay. 26
Figure 2.35: The intra-ridge outcropping at Castleton...27

Figure 3.1: The chronology of redeployed rock art in the British Isles and Ireland. 28
Figure 3.2: Henges as pathways 29
Figure 3.3: Patterns of rock art intervisibility approaching the Milfield Basin 29
Figure 3.4: The M3 through Twyford, Hampshire 31
Figure 3.5: The Loughcrew cairns in their hilltop location. 31
Figure 3.6: The causewayed enclosure in its clearing location..32
Figure 3.7: The Dorset Cursus...33
Figure 3.8: The Rudston *Cursus monuments*...34
Figure 3.9: The bank / landscape relationship at Avebury 36
Figure 3.10: Stonehenge as it appears today. 38

Figure 4.1: The 'long barrow' at Fortingall..41
Figure 4.2: The cup-marked boulder associated with the Fortingall barrow 41
Figure 4.3: The double-spirals at Achnabreck..42
Figure 4.4: Newgrange kerb 17 42
Figure 4.5: Cup-and-ring style art at Loughcrew cairn V..42
Figure 4.6: A cup-marked orthostat from Loughcrew cairn T. 43

Figure 4.7: Newgrange Kerb 95 43
Figure 4.8: Orthostat L1 Loughcrew cairn T..43
Figure 4.9: The distribution of passage tombs and rock art sites...44
Figure 4.10(a): Rock art site '1' at Carnbane East 44
Figure 4.10(b): *Rock art site '4' at Carnbane East* 44
Figure 4.11: Hidden imagery from Newgrange..45
Figure 4.12: The diagnostic content of rock art in the British Isles and Ireland. 45
Figure 4.13: The signs of all times. 46
Figure 4.14: Dronfield's diagnostic entoptic forms 46
Figure 4.15: Orthostat C9, Loughcrew cairn U: an example of Integration 47
Figure 4.16: An example of pick-dressing: Orthostat L19 at Newgrange 48
Figure 4.17: The distribution of 'complex' imagery as defined by Thomas (1992) for Loughcrew cairn T. ...49
Figure 4.18: The distribution of landscape-like imagery at Loughcrew cairn T..49
Figure 4.19: The construed left foot of Loughcrew cairn T..51
Figure 4.20: Key kerb stones at Newgrange...51
Figure 4.21: The roof-box and hidden art at Newgrange...52
Figure 4.22: The distribution of curvilinear imagery at Knowth 54
Figure 4.23:The Knowth mace head...55
Figure 4.24: Passage tomb 'grave goods'...56
Figure 4.25: Angular passage tomb imagery and decorated pins 57
Figure 4.26: Rock art therianthropes 57
Figure 4.27: Possible processions at Knowth 59

Figure 5.1: Bronze Age barrows in the Stonehenge landscape..62
Figure 5.2: The decorated stone circle at Croft Moraig...63
Figure 5.3: The wedge tombs 63
Figure 5.4: The Clava Cairns..64
Figure 5.5: The redeployment of rock art in the British Isles 67
Figure 5.6: The engravings at Chapel Stile 69
Figure 5.7: Redeployment strategies in Britain and Ireland 71
Figure 5.8a: The 'cove-like' arrangement of the Chapel Stile rock art site...72
Figure 5.8b: An example of the internal settings at Avebury 72

Figure 6.1: Kealduff 1. 77
Figure 6.2: The Braes of Taymouth..79
Figure 6.3: Neolithic time-line 83

ACKNOWLEDGEMENTS

A great many people have been of great help in the production of this thesis. None, however, should be held responsible for any inaccuracies in its content. The first word of thanks goes to the landowners of Inveragh and Loch Tay, too numerous to list but without whom the collection of data for this research would have been impossible. In this context, thanks must also go to Steve Boyle of RCAHMS for his kind provision of the Loch Tay data base and Richard Bradley for his list of contacts in Strath Tay.

Many colleagues have been instrumental in discussing the ideas presented in this thesis. Simon Crook, Ken Lymer, Kate Rochester, Robert Wallis and Alex Woodcock, all took time out of their own research for my benefit. In particular, I would like to thank Darren Glaizer for his assistance during fieldwork. Liam Galvin also deserves special recognition for his library searches and introduction to the Clare Historical and Archaeological Society. The Society also receives my thanks.

Technical help has been offered and gratefully received. Thanks to Amanda Craine and Richard Busby for their assistance with digital photography. Philip Evans made the illustrations for this monograph possible: thank you for your patience and the teaching skills you never knew you possessed.

More personally I would like to thank Joy and Roger - mum and dad - for their encyclopaedic brains, constant supply of books, wine and support on my return to university. Hedge End Cricket Club also warrant mention, particularly Steve Allen, Ramesh Kolli and Neil Rushden: thanks for keeping me sane during the summer and giving me something to look forward to through the winter.

Two people remain, each deserves special mention. Firstly, Thomas Dowson, the ever patient supervisor. Thank you for both carrot and stick, advice, assistance, direction and, most importantly, friendship. Last - but true to the cliche - no means least, Netty Galvin: emotional prop, ever ready ear, financier, fieldworker, artist and partner; without you, for so many reasons, this work would never have been produced.

This monograph is based on a doctoral thesis generously funded by the AHRB. In this context, thanks must also go to Mark Edmonds and Colin Richards for taking the time to read and examine my thesis. Both made valuable and insightful comments which I hope I have done justice to in this monograph.

THANK YOU

Edward Evans June 03.

PREFACE

This monograph represents the outcome of three research projects investigating the Neolithic rock art of the British Isles and Ireland, a series begun as an undergraduate in 1998 and culminating in 'this' doctoral thesis. During the initial collection of data for these studies I was struck by the similarity evident in the methodological position taken by a then recent publication - Beckensall and Laurie's (1998) *Prehistoric rock art of County Durham, Swaledale and Wensleydale* - and a series of articles published in the *Proceedings of the Society of Antiquarians of Scotland* dating to the latter half of the nineteenth century. A further review of the literature revealed a widespread commonality of approach - the compilation of lengthy gazetteers - suggesting the existence of a methodology that had dominated British and Irish rock art research for over 100 years. As a tradition of research this methodology systematically ignored what had initially interested me in rock art - questions of interpretation and meaning - yet these aspects were discussed with increasing frequency in the literature of other artistic traditions located around the world (e.g. southern Africa). British rock art research appeared to be isolated from the theoretical and methodological advances being made internationally and there seemed to be little overlap between the ideas I wished to pursue and those which dominated the domestic discourse. Concomitant to this 'artistic' isolation, the discourse of Neolithic archaeology in Britain makes very little reference to the practice of rock carving. It appeared to me as if neither domestic rock art research, nor archaeology, was particularly interested in engaging with the interpretative potential of the rock art. I felt, that should research into this body of art look beyond the confines of its immediate discourse the interpretative power of the imagery could be released and the schism between art and archaeology closed. Taking an analogy from Neolithic archaeology: the problem was not a paucity of evidence, but determining what was relevant and what this relevancy meant (Thomas 1999a:2).

At this point I was presented with a coincidence which offered a way to proceed. This coincidence came from my reading of two books published in the same year, 1998: Richard Bradley's *On the Significance of Monuments* and Alfred Gell's *Art and Agency*. Bradley's book establishes the existence of a widespread circular archetype common to many monuments of the Neolithic and early Bronze Age, into which he draws the circular components of the cup-and-ring repertoire. The extent to which this perimeter form is manifest in the monuments of this time implies that Bradley's observations *are* indicative of a meaningful correlation, but Barrett's (1994:91) intimation that "architecture will mean little if we only view it in terms of the allocation and ordering of space" and the contention that monuments refer to something bigger than themselves (Thomas 1999a:46) suggest that the significance of this archetype lay beyond the circle itself. It was here that Gell's work became, to turn a highly appropriate phrase, *salient*. Gell talks at great length about the psychological saliency of an artist's *œuvre*: the multi-directional interconnections which allow disparate individual works to be recognised as the products of a single person or school. This suggested to me that if a commonality of

perimeter form existed between the monuments of the Neolithic perhaps they, and the rock art, could also be understood as an œuvre and the complex multi-directional relationships which hold this construction together explored in the search for explanatory patterns.

The synergetic combination of Bradley's and Gell's work provided a framework through which to assess the saliency of the Neolithic œuvre. To be explanatory, however, it remained necessary to come towards some conception of how this saliency was made meaningful. Lewis-Williams and Dowson (e.g. 1990) have long emphasised the constraining materiality of image support in their interpretations of southern African rock art. Coupled with recent sensory analyses of art located in other geographical regions (e.g. MacGregor 1999) this approach suggests that meaning resides as much in the materiality of an art object as its visual imagery. In this context, the existence of a Neolithic œuvre leads neatly into Lewis-Williams' (1998) conception of focussed polysemy: the dynamic refocusing of an image's associative spectrum, and consequently meaning, according to its contextual constraints. From here, it became possible to re-conceptualise meaning as social engagement with the connotative effect of rock art and monument materiality and explore how this effect was further informed through the juxtaposition of these material items against a series of recurrent topographical correlates. In this way the distribution of meaning over the œuvre could be explored and the relationship between art and monumentality examined without creating tautology. The analysis of these connotative juxtapositions is not the same as the search for a metaphysical entity underlying all Neolithic life (see Thomas 1997:58), but the equivalent of theorising the imagery in its local and regional context (see Yates 1993); a means to extend enquiry beyond the mass collection of data characteristic of established research trajectories and turn this same data into the interpretative schemes which had first interested me in rock art research.

The structure of this monograph closely mirrors the development of these thought processes. The first chapter begins with an exploration and critique of traditional approaches to British and Irish rock art and concludes with the theoretical structuring of an alternative methodology. Chapter two is concerned with the definition of study parameters. Within this broad structure, a combination of literature synthesis and case-study fieldwork are used to identify saliency in the rock art repertoire and the structure of spectrum composition. The following chapter explores the pervasiveness of this saliency in, and the applicability of the devised methodology to, the monuments of the Neolithic: an exploration ultimately resolved into a series of monument type - and site specific - interpretations. Chapter four considers the practice of Neolithic image production and consumption in the passage tombs of Ireland. In particular, emphasis is placed on this imagery's relationship with the carving and consumption of landscape art. Consideration of the redeployment of rock imagery in monuments of an early Bronze Age date brings a temporal extension to chapter five, allowing the trajectory of a number of regionally identifiable decorative strategies to be traced through time and an examination of the distorting impact of history on the meaning of 'Neolithic' rock art. Finally, chapter six offers a detailed interpretation for the open-air rock art of the British Isles and Ireland, both in the Neolithic and early Bronze Age. It is these interpretations which ultimately comprise a history of the Neolithic written through its art.

CHAPTER ONE
An appropriate subject?
Ideology, aesthetics and the rock art of the British Isles and Ireland.

For generations, the open-air rock art of the British Isles and Ireland has been denied a role as meaningful archaeological evidence. Generally, beyond the compilation of lengthy gazetteers this rock art has either been ignored and marginalised or used as supporting evidence for other archaeological concerns; concerns which predetermine judgements relating to the legitimacy and interpretation of the imagery.

1.1   Introduction

When looking at rock art ... everybody must agree that its most important aspect is its meaning (Malmer 1989:91).

To ask "what does it represent?" and be satisfied with a single answer is not the same thing as asking "what does it mean?" (Duff 1975:15).

The perception of the open-air rock art[1] of the British Isles and Ireland is subsumed in a series of paradoxical relationships which espouse a language of myth, prejudice and marginalisation. The persistence of ideas perpetuated by this language has created blinkered methodologies which in turn propagate particular intellectual discourses. The source of these discourses lies outside this body of art and can be found in the cave art of the European Palaeolithic. The prominence and authority accorded to select images from the Palaeolithic of western Europe owes little to the role of prehistoric art in the prehistoric world. Rather it is about prehistoric art in the modern world (see Chippindale 1985). The discovery, seizure and re-definition of these images has led to the creation of sustained methodological and conceptual prejudices which are difficult to escape. These prejudices have their roots in the very birth of rock art research, through the classic stories of discovery surrounding such sites as Altamira and Lascaux. The narratives which accompany this period of discovery are so full of drama that they immediately confirm all presuppositions relating to the origins of art (Davis 1993:327; see also Root 1996:73) and its power of legitimisation. The early 'heroic' explorers of the European Palaeolithic caves carried with them the self-image of the art-historian, dedicated to the recovery of significant works of art; they disregarded countless artefacts in their search for "les belle pièces" (Viewpoint 1994:249; Conkey 1996:292). Although such practice is no longer considered acceptable, many intellectual strategies continue to be embedded in the understandings of this time of discovery (Conkey 1996:288).

1.2   'Palaeo-mythology'

---

[1] Throughout this monograph, terms such as rock art and petroglyph refer to the materiality of the 'support' as much as the imagery itself.

Creative human behaviour, specifically art, is often perceived as an activity ultimately less important than the primary forms of material production. Varying degrees of marginalisation consequently characterise the study of prehistoric art in many areas of the world. This situation is repeated in microcosm within rock art research. Investigation of the French Upper Palaeolithic has long been regarded as a special case on both historical and logistical grounds, accepted as mainstream and attracting specialists of status and standing. Bednarik (1993a:207) contends that much of this prominent research has been conducted in an emotive and jingoistic manner that, for "a full century" has allowed Eurocentric scholars to present "a largely unsustainable model which greatly over emphasises the role of south western Europe in bringing art, language, religion and culture to the world" (Bednarik 1992:264; Conkey 1996:288; Dowson 1998a).

This geographical focus is accompanied by a misrepresentation of prehistoric art in favour of naturalistic depictions of large animals (Tomaskova 1997; Dowson 1999a, 1999b). The Palaeolithic corpus, however, contains over 500 depictions of human beings, whilst, within the Franco-Cantabrian region, non-figurative images out-number figurative by a ratio of five to one (Bednarik 1993b:1). Overemphasis on animal depiction diverts researchers' attention away from the potentially significant question of what is implied by the stylistic differences between these image types (Conkey 1996:298), an example of the misconceptions which inhibit the formulation of discourse.

Much preconception is rooted in traditional understandings of the aesthetic (see for example, Heyd 1999:451). Haberland (quoted in Shiner 1994:225) contends that "our main obligation ... is to convince art historians that the art of Aboriginal north America [for example] is 'Art with a capital A'". This stance compels the researcher to appraise non-Western images, including those of prehistoric Europe, through modes of seeing characteristic of modernity. Such time-travelling empathy is only possible by concurring in the constructs inherent in the paradoxical relationship the Western world holds with the concept of 'primitive' art: a relationship centred around the equally paradoxical construct of the 'great family of man'. These constructions project a universality of brotherhood, complete with sibling rivalry, in which it is art which fulfils the role of "great unifier", functioning as "the most obvious outpouring of the linking humanism of feeling between peoples" (anon. quoted in Price 1989:29). It is the belief that aesthetic values are retrievable independent of context that allows them to be posited as the "impossible link" (Davis 1993:327-31), implying that "we should be able to understand

1

something that formerly was opaque to us" (Heyd 1999:452-5). Hidden within this understanding of rock art are the power relationships which allow the Western world to assume the mantle of the 'philanthropic' big brother, whose broad mindedness and largesse allows 'him' an enlightened appreciation of other cultures (Price 1989:25-6), an ability denied to the younger ('primitive') sibling. This insistence separates the 'civilised' from the 'primitive', allowing the latter to be seen as both brother and other (see Price 1989:37).

Prehistoric art falls either side of this lingering binary. It is the difference in both the conception and the traditions of prehistoric art, however, that support this contradiction. Only when the language of high culture is employed can prehistoric imagery be drawn into the same interpretative frame as the art of modernity (Tomaskova 1997:266). For this to be accepted as natural and unproblematic it is necessary to cleanse prehistoric images of their social and cultural context, asserting a deeper correlation between object and viewer through the aesthetic. The contextual cleansing of art objects suggests that they are valued above the people who produced them; they are effectively dehumanised in a process analogous with the West's de-contextualisation of contemporary indigenous arts (see Root 1996).

Here the power of myth overcomes a further paradox. The academic study of Art traditionally focuses upon the life and work of the named artist as creative individual. The impossibility of this process with regard to prehistoric imagery, however, is essential for the continuance of myth. It is the very anonymity of these images that allows them to be appropriated into the rubric of Western artistic history. In the absence of a named individual, those who produced these images are presented as figures simply fashioning artefacts in accordance with inherited and prescribed rules: interchangeable technicians of a mythical, continuing, and unchanging artistic spirit. As such, aesthetically valued 'primitive' art objects are abducted into the 'protective custody' of Western mentality (see Price 1989:37; Morphy 1994:258), and the cave art of the European Palaeolithic posited as the beginning of all artistic practice (Bednarik 1992:32; Soffer & Conkey 1997:3); Lascaux effectively becomes the "figure 1" of art history (Davis 1993). The pervasiveness of these ideological constructions is often all-encompassing, so that even an archaeological forum dedicated to the critique of aesthetics in archaeology (Viewpoint 1994) begins its introduction, if not with Lascaux, then with Altamira, juxtaposed against Tutankhamun's death mask: itself a celebrated icon of civilised cultural achievement.

The contextual cleansing of this process, however, renders prehistoric imagery worthless to the archaeologist who, after all, should be concerned with people. Consequently, it will never be possible "to elucidate the meanings of ... visual imagery if we focus ... on what is familiar to us from the traditions of Western art" (Conkey 1996:246). Such modes of thinking perpetuate the idea that the "existence of simple imagery, such as the representation of hands, next to more elaborate representations of emus, kangaroos, flying foxes, and human beings makes it apparent that, at least occasionally, rock art was made by the relatively unskilled" (Heyd 1999:455). It is not necessary to expand on how reductive this view is, how much significance it ignores by holding on to the traditional tenets of Art History. This quotation does, however, raise the question of what becomes of prehistoric art which falls outside the aesthetic ideal, outside the vocabulary of Art History; imagery such as that of the British Isles and Ireland. According to the same ideological concerns which privilege Upper Palaeolithic parietal art, non-figurative motifs can only be placed on the primitive side of the primitive/civilised divide. There is, however, much self-deception at work here as history is reduced to selective and sanitised ancestors, an uninformative and universalised bloc.

1.3   Palaeolithic hangovers, the other side of paradox

The role aesthetics play in according pre-eminence to Upper Palaeolithic imagery not only privileges the questions asked of the art but the methodologies proposed to answer them. Methodological dogma, derived from both archaeological orthodoxy and the tenets of Art History, decrees that the basic problem with rock art studies is a lack of control over time (see, for example, Franklin 1993:1; Hesjedal 1995:200). Placing such importance on the dating enterprise creates a precedent which often precludes the development of effective research strategies and undermines the status of rock art as meaningful archaeological evidence. Smith (1992:399), for example, claims "rock art was not considered an appropriate medium for testing the theory ... [of information exchange] ... because there is little information on the dating ... of rock art within Australia".

For Upper Palaeolithic art, however, science has brought the hope of secure dating (Clottes 1993:20). This security brings both archaeological and Art Historical respectability, further strengthening the internal prejudices of rock art research. Bahn (1996:1-3), speaking of the "revolution in analysis and dating", suggests that "thanks to the introduction of detailed analysis of pigments and of direct dating, the last few years ... [represent] the most exciting and important phase in Ice Age Studies since both the phenomenon was first discovered and authenticated" (but see Clottes 1993:24; Zilhão 1995; Zilhão et al 1997). The use of the words "discovered" and "authenticated" convey the same rhetoric of Art History which suggested that chronology was of the upmost importance to begin with.

Despite numerous difficulties and contradictions, through the scientific and ideological endeavours invested in them, the motifs of the European Palaeolithic are continuously fore-grounded in the consciousness of both researchers and public alike. Consequently, with regard to the rock art of the Irish and British Isles, Frodsham (1996:131) suggests "the development of an acceptable chronology ... should be regarded as a priority". Unfortunately, this has not been forthcoming, with Beckensall (1997) recently positing "a chronological nightmare" echoing the concerns of Graves who, as far back as 1876, frustratedly declared that the "age of the cup and circle marks ... [is] still undecided". Consequently, although the prospect of the salvation of science has been held out for the art of the Upper Palaeolithic, the techniques and methods of this salvation seem to be inapplicable to the rock of the British Isles and Ireland: little brother desires the respectability of his older sibling, only to be shown that imitation is not merely impossible but actively distancing.

Refined chronologies can assist the interpretative enterprise, but to marginalise and denigrate the value of an entire artistic trajectory on chronological grounds is reductive in the extreme: image content deemed irrelevant in deference to age There is, for example, a widely accepted broad chronological frame for the rock art of the British Isles and Ireland. Instead of reiterating what may often be seen as a statement of 'failure', working within this it is possible to develop alternative methodological and conceptual strategies which can release the archaeological value of the art. If research continues to defer addressing these issues, then Frodsham (1989:16) will have cause to remark again that "our ignorance ensures that their ... significance continues to elude us" leaving not archaeological evidence but a "bewildering profusion of multiple ring markings, cups and grooves" (Ritchie & Harman 1985:146).

1.4   Marginality, insularity and mantra

It is impossible to deny that innumerable authors have offered as many interpretations for the Neolithic rock art of Britain and Ireland. But, following on from Ritche and Harman's (1985:145) contention that "probably more has been written about the 'purpose' of such markings than any other archaeological imponderable", it must be noted that these interpretations have done much to enhance the imponderable and little to resolve the purpose of this abstract, open-air rock art. Moreover, as noted above, research on the apparently more spectacular rock art of Europe and Africa, and the well-established methodologies developed in those regions, has greatly enhanced the enigmatic status of the so-called 'cup and ring art'. Recently, some academic attention has been paid to this imagery, but rock art still remains peripheral to mainstream discussions of prehistoric Britain: sustaining its enigmatic status and perpetuating an insular tradition of study which inhibits understanding.

1.5   Methodology: The power of precedent

The inscriptions ... were discovered ... near Ballynasare bridge ... They are two in number, and, like those of Staigue bridge, are cut upon the surface of the natural rock ... Whilst all the circles on the rock at Staigue are perfect, several of those at Ballynasare are incomplete. Sometimes a short and slightly curved line, drawn from a small hollow outside the circle to the central cup, passes through the open part of the circumference (Graves 1876-8:286).

The second cluster lies ... northeast end of a row of grouse butts ... A low flat rock has a cup and two concentric rings, cup and three rings, divided by a channel midway across the rock ... The third has seven cups and linked channels on a flat slab (Beckensall 1999:65).

Although separated by over 100 years of research - and obvious reductions of more extensive works - these two quotations illustrate the emergence and continuation of a traditional methodological approach to British and Irish rock art research: the compilation and repetition of lengthy, descriptive inventories. To emphasise description at the expense of more critical engagement enhances the apparent intractability of meaning, and reaffirms the enigmatic status of the art. In the face of an 'intractable' enigma, subsequent investigations have become inseparably tied to the sanction and legitimacy of precedent and the production of inventories has taken on a self-sustaining trajectory. The prevalence of this approach is clearly illustrated in that 71% of over 100 publications reviewed include a gazetteer of this kind, often forming the principal part of the work. The necessity of data collection is beyond dispute, but the value of exhaustive, mass collection for its own sake is illusory (Lewis-Williams 1983; Clottes 1995:38-9), even misleading (see below). To simply repeat what has been done for the past 100 years will not bring us any closer to understanding this body of art.

Traditional reliance on gazetteer description has created an overwhelming surfeit of information which, in more recent years, has engendered a parallel approach to British and Irish rock art. Control has been sought over the "bewildering profusion of multiple ring markings, cups and grooves" (Ritchie & Harman 1985:146) described by the gazetteers through the dismemberment of 'compositions' into their constituent 'design elements'(see, for example, Morris 1981; Van Hoek 1987; Beckensall 1991; figure 1.1). These strategies may often be designed to explore image variation on a region by region basis, but – in conjunction with a common measure of complexity defined by an increasing number of concentric rings (e.g. Bradley 1997) - involve so much simplification that their classifications become meaningless, as a rigid adherence to sets of arbitrary characteristics forces the data into preconceived types: converting a 'bewildering profusion' into a homogeneous artistic tradition characterised by a series of dots and circles.

Over familiarity with the outcomes of these methods inevitably informs interpretation. Gazetteer descriptions - providing directions of how to find each site and emphasising the current physical characteristics of the landscape – for example, predetermine how the relationship between imagery and setting is understood, whilst interpretation of the imagery itself becomes intimately tied to the apparent pre-eminence of the circle.

3

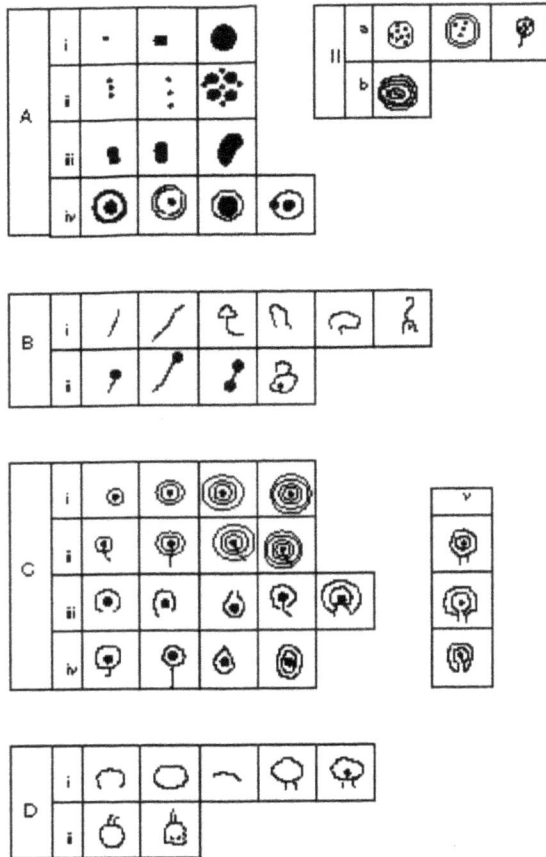

Figure 1.1: The tabularisation of rock art design elements (after Van Hoek 1987 with modifications).

1.6   Interpretative Mantra

A survey of the literature concerning British and Irish rock art reveals a series of interpretative *mantras*; the repeated discussion of one 'interpretation' or another with minimal development of thought, over and over again: paralleling the insularity evident in method. Taking just one example from amongst many, the coastal location - and prominent viewpoints - of many art sites have been used to support theories of diffusion (Raistrick 1936; MacWhite 1946; O'Kelly 1958; Davis 1959), migration (Young 1937-8) and invasion (Cowling & Hartley 1959). As products of their own time there is nothing intrinsically wrong with these ideas and their presence in the discourse of British and Irish rock art research mirrors that of the archaeological literature. It is their continued repetition beyond this particular time-frame (see, for example, Anati 1963; Morris 1966, 1967; Burenhult 1979; Fett & Fett 1979; Van Hoek 1993,1997) which has restricted understanding of the art. This is not to suggest that more recent authors have *directly* repeated the arguments of the mid 20th century, nor to imply that the patterns which underlie their interpretations are in no way meaningful. Rather, to make use of such an explicit diffusionist framework predetermines the boundaries of interpretation and recursively sustains the same intellectual mantra which suggested that diffusionism was an appropriate approach to begin with.

In many ways it appears appropriate to attribute the formulation of interpretative mantra to the academic separation of archaeological and rock art research in the British Isles since the early-mid years of the 20th century (see Bradley 1997:34). The absence of an interchange of ideas between these two pursuits has promoted the recursive emulation of strategies which, at one time or another, have been 'successful' in interpreting the apparent enigma of the art. Consequently, interpretative schemes no longer seen in other areas of Neolithic archaeology have retained their currency in British and Irish rock art research. Moreover, alongside this broad trajectory, it is not unreasonable to suggest that the longevity of diffusionist explanations is interwoven with production of gazetteers. As noted above, these gazetteers implicitly reinforce a particular way of engaging with the relationship between rock art and topography, promoting a very ordered way of moving though the landscape which readily 'becomes' evidence for structured migratory routes.

Although placing great emphasis on the apparent correlation between image location and viewpoints, Bradley's (e.g. 1997) interpretation of rock art distribution as indicative of well-established route-ways directing a dispersed population towards major ceremonial complexes, marks a significant intervention in the discourse of British and Irish rock art research. Bradley's work can be distinguished from its predecessors in that he takes a descriptive observational mantra and turns it into an interpretative device which seeks to explain the significance of the art's location in terms other than those made familiar through established discursive trajectories. Consequently, Bradley's substantial contribution cannot be considered mantra; but, his interpretation does carry certain implicit understandings which have important implications for the reception and subsequent development of his work.

Like the diffusionist explanations of preceding generations, Bradley's work - whether one accepts his interpretation or not - successfully controls the enigmatic connotations of the art. Given the discursive history of British and Irish rock art research, it is not surprising that his interpretation has also been subject to recursive emulation. Moreover, although grossly underestimating the sophistication of his argument, Bradley's interpretation retains the familiar – and, therefore, highly reproducible - correlation between route-ways and gazetteer description; whilst, in writing from the position of Neolithic archaeologist, his argument is further legitimised by the prevalence of interpretations which seek to explain the monuments of this time in terms of choreographed procession (see Evans 2003:111-4). Consequently, Bradley's scheme has begun to take on the appearance of an immutable framework, in which almost all subsequent studies - including those which raise mild critique (e.g. Beckensall 1996:140) - take the same terms of reference to engage with the art: a concern with viewpoints, patterns of intervisibility and route-ways (see Beckensall 1997, 1999; Van Hoek 1993, 1997; Purcell 2002, for example). This produces an homogenisation of thought which rules out alternative ways engaging with - and interpreting - the imagery (but see Waddington 1996, 1998;

4

below). As such, what was once innovative and challenging has had its critical foundations stripped and is in danger of becoming mantra.

1.7   The magic circle

The Literature of British and Irish rock art research also exhibits a number of interpretative mantras which actively eschew history. Commonly, amongst this type of mantra the imagery is assessed as having "some magical or religious significance" (Shee 1968:145; see also Edwards 1934 for example). Although pagan orators, druidical altars, witchcraft, sacrificial victims and cults of the natural world (e.g. Romilly-Allen 1881-2:81-95; Browne 1899-1900:297; MacKenzie 1899-1900:330; O'Sullivan & Sheehan 1993:81) are regularly used to bring colour to such accounts, the grounding assumptions of these interpretations remain the same. Religion is again cited to account for the cessation of carving; be this the advent of a new religious impetus such as Christianity (see MacKenzie 1899-1900:327; Edwards 1934:125) or the decline of established belief systems (see Beckensall 1998:8; Beckensall & Frodsham 1998:55).

Although religious motivation may constitute part of a credible interpretation, to simply claim this through mere citation and without interpretative rigour forces the petroglyphs into preconceived primeval constructions attendant to the concept of 'primitive' art (Evans 2003:17-27). The use of such vague and descriptive language implicitly holds with the idea of an 'other' who is free from the shackles of civilisation and comes complete with a rhetoric of "fear, darkness and eroticism" (Bihalji-Merlin in Price 1989:62). This rhetoric gives rise to sweeping generalisations which obscure the peculiar characteristics of the art and, once again, asserts a homogeneity which divests the imagery of its interpretative potential. Moreover, van Hoek's (1997:16) suggestion that there are "several instances [which] ... suggest that cup-and-ring art represents a complex body of magical and socio-religious rituals of migrating peoples" demonstrates how two intellectually unrelated mantras, which have no reason to be drawn together other than their common citation, can be sustained in parallel.

Methodology interacts with this rhetoric to produce a particularly 'British' - and specifically Neolithic - other, whose stereotypical characteristics underpin further mantra-like interpretations. On this occasion, however, it is the dismemberment of imagery into its constituent 'circles' which provides the basis for interpretation, and 'the Neolithic'[2] its context. Interpretations of the circles commonly adopt the same high level of generality evident in magico-religious explanations of the art. Often, the circle is interpreted as representing "wholeness and harmony, its form symbolically emphasising cyclical space and time" (Harding 1998:221), or that it depicts the "phenomenological cycles of nature": the circles of life and fecundity (Waddington 1996:161-2). Such rhythms, however, "are to time what sex is to gender" (Gosden 1994:9). The same methodological impetus sustains comparable interpretations of a broader range of Neolithic imagery; so, although in "a strong sense it is quite impossible for us in the present to attribute particular meanings to these motifs, ... it is not too far fetched to imagine that the spirals, concentric circles, facets, lozenges, chevrons, zig-zags, parallel grooves and lattices ... [refer to] worldly phenomena like water ... rain, wind, clouds, vegetation, sun and moon and the human body" (Thomas 1996:158-9).

Although the authors who produce these interpretations do not suggest that the imagery merely constitutes a naive mimicking of nature with no conceptual engagement, by implication interpretations which emphasis worldly phenomena reduce the creators of these abstract images to a "primal state of natural aesthetic innocence" (Taylor 1994:255), perpetuating the myth of an unspoilt culture at one with, and analogous to, its environment. In many ways, the position taken by these authors unconsciously replicates the West's paradoxical relationship with ancient art. Greek art, for example, "is said to find power in reason and embody it in the human form", whereas 'primitive' art is described in terms of "the powers central to human life" which are embodied in "natural metaphors like breasts" (Shiner 1994:232). With more specific regard to the Neolithic of Britain and Ireland, this implicit understanding of 'primitive' art evokes the rural idyll and golden age of Albion; the semi-mythical British past of literary anthropology in "which folk-tales and legends become part of an unlocalised, unhistoric past ... which make the land and the people a scene and characters into which anything could be projected" (Williams quoted in Evans 1993:432-3).

Such understandings emerge within the discourse of 'the Neolithic' precisely because this concept has decreed that the rock art of the British Isles and Ireland is not archaeology; it lacks the defining characteristics of archaeological evidence: a readily recognisable context and secure chronology. Consequently, without context all that is left to the scholars of 'the Neolithic' is the familiar rhetoric of the Neolithic other. In this context, it appears as more than coincidence that it is the unexcavated, unexplored and undated monuments of Albion which have traditionally been the inspiration for so much literary projection (Evans 1993:434).

1.8   Passage tomb art and the archaeological context

Recent attempts to draw rock art research into the archaeological mainstream have sought to make rock art the equivalent of archaeological data (Dowson 2001:317). This is exemplified by the scientific endeavours invested in the cave art of the European Palaeolithic. The techniques and methods of this endeavour, however, have been suggested as inapplicable to British and Irish rock art, leaving it without a

---

[2] This 'contextual' understanding of the term 'the Neolithic' is derived from Thomas' (1993) discursive analysis of how this area of British archaeology has come to define its structuring objects of knowledge.

scientific discourse. Despite this, the strategy of turning art into archaeology is prevalent in the discourse of 'the Neolithic'. This is due to the existence of another tradition of image making in the British and Irish Neolithic: the art of the passage tombs. The historiography of passage tomb art is not without its mantras, gazetteers and literal interpretations; it has also, however, "been described as a war of ideas" (Brennan 1983:62).

Figure 1.2: The principal passage tomb at Newgrange

The placement of art on readily recognisable archaeological features, features that can be examined through devices other than the art alone, supplies the contextual and chronological security demanded by archaeology. This makes models that appear to resolve the relationship between these phenomenon highly attractive. Consequently, a research trajectory which posits open air carvings as later derivatives of passage tomb art has become well established in the discourse of British and Irish archaeology (see, for example, Childe & Taylor 1938-9; Davis 1959; Van Hoek 1987; Bradley 1997 amongst many others): moving the open-air art from Albion into 'the Neolithic'.

Although intended to make art, archaeology; this approach further denigrates the interpretative potential of the imagery. Certainly it is important to explore the relationship between art and archaeology, it is, however, the manner in which this relationship is studied which can be problematic. It is often suggested (e.g. Mithen 1989:670-78; Donta 1992:11) that the role and meaning of a body of art should be assessed first through its archaeological associations and only then through images themselves, implying a descending order of importance which posits rock art as mere "*supporting evidence*" (Mithen 1989:678, my emphasis). This kind of approach imposes an externally defined, *a priori* context on the imagery, within which the art is denied its own reality (Dowson 1998:71-2) and manipulated to support potentially erroneous archaeological theorisation.

The export of interpretations derived from neuropsychological investigations of the passage tombs (e.g. Bradley 1989; Lewis-Williams & Dowson 1993) to the open air corpus (e.g. Frodsham 1996:134; Bradley 1997:51; Beckensall & Laurie 1998:17) provides a recent example of how this understanding

of context can influence the interpretation of landscape art. The logic which links passage tomb and open air art suggests that if the imagery of the former is demonstrably connected to the entoptic phenomena experienced during altered states of consciousness, then so to must the latter. Although restricted in its range of enquiry (see Jones 1999), Dronfield's (1996) methodology for the identification of diagnostic entoptic forms suggests that such logic values the 'context' of the passage tombs above the intellectual tenets of the method. That is, unlike the passage tombs (see Dronfield 1996), the open air art (see Evans 2003:163) - by-and-large - lacks images which are exclusively of the altered state, suggesting that the direct transposition of interpretation from passage tomb to open-air context is inappropriate. Despite this, it is possible to account for the stylistic differences between these two contexts of image deployment by positing a temporal and ritual move away from the immediate impact of the altered state and the tombs (see Bradley 1997). This explanation, however, uses the proposed neuropsychological connection to override significant chronological evidence (see Waddington 1996), validating a well-established – but largely undemonstrated – archaeological assumption. There may well be a neuropsychological link between the art of the passage tombs and that of the landscape, but this needs to be critically demonstrated – and, certainly, neuropsychological research provides us with a number of ways to think critically about this relationship – not simply apportioned by writ of providing landscape art with an archaeological context (see Evans 2003:146-209 & 251-69).

1.9   Changing paradigms?

Analysis of the historiography of British and Irish rock art research reveals a discourse inhibited by the weight of tradition and established ways of doing things. This sustains concretised modes of thought whose resultant literary mantras fail to unveil the archaeological potential of the art and, consequently, feedback into the academic marginalisation of the imagery. Moreover, failure to recognise the interpretative potential of the imagery has - in the face of an ever-increasing scientific knowledge of the monuments of this time - unwittingly posited rock art as a new cornerstone in the maintenance of a familiar Neolithic 'other'. If British and Irish rock art is to attain the same academic status as traditions of image making in other areas of the world - a recognition that rock art does offer a valid way of investigating the past - it is necessary to actively encourage different forms of engagement with the imagery.

The important research of Richard Bradley in the 1990s almost single-handedly reintroduced an archaeological respectability to British rock art research. Bradley's work, however, retained a number of well-established discursive tenets, which helped facilitate the kind of stereotyped response that ultimately becomes interpretative mantra. Despite interpretations which evoke the phenomenological properties of the circle, Waddington (1996, 1998) offers a way of engaging with the rock art of the British Isles which moves further beyond the established traditions of discourse. Waddington constructs a model of image production and consumption grounded in a specifically local landscape study. In so doing, his work avoids the predetermining topographical assumptions engendered by traditional methodologies and escapes from the monolithic interpretative mantras that have traditionally subsumed the entirety – and diversity – of the corpus. One scholar, however, does not constitute a change of paradigm, and there *are* ways to interpret the art which do not rely upon the circle.

It is in this context, I argue, that rock art can be deployed as a means of writing an alternative archaeology for the Neolithic, one that, although it acknowledges the importance of established thought, does so a critical manner that challenges rather than reinforces mantra. This involves the creation of different theoretical and methodological approaches to the art. Rather that positing rock art as supporting evidence for other archaeological concerns, it is possible to explore archaeology through the rubric of the art, giving equal interpretative weight to each. This is not so much an archaeology of rock art as a history of the Neolithic written through its art.

1.10   Creating context

Much modern anthropology of art suggests that image comprehension is often unconscious, embodying "relationships which the people themselves do not, possibly can not, formulate in words but are of prime importance for an understanding ... of their art" (Firth 1992:25), relationships which are "palpably *felt*" (Morphy 1994:666, original emphasis). Such imagery summarises the "unsummarisable" and expresses the inexpressible (Lewis-Williams 1998:88). The lack of recognisable visual cues in abstract arts is commonly believed to exacerbate this apparent opacity. British and Irish rock art, for example, is widely considered intentionally ambiguous, purveying many meanings. Analogical allusion to the multitude of values inherent in contemporary understandings of the cross swiftly follow, but little is said regarding the specific body of art. The assertion of many meanings, therefore, has become as much a matter of avoidance as an attempt to elucidate meaning. Rather than attempting to reformulate specific meaning this monograph considers how rock art and its locale connote inference to produce visual and cognitive effect.

An effective understanding of prehistoric imagery can be approached through analogy with what has come to be known as New Genre Public Art. This is an art form whose self-image is one of social planning and active intervention, in which

> *For the past three or so decades visual artists of varying backgrounds and perspectives have been working in a manner that resembles political and social activity but is distinguished by its aesthetic sensibility. Dealing with some of the most profound issues of our time ... [they have] developed distinct models for an art whose public strategies of engagement are an important part of its aesthetic language* (Lacy 1995:19).

If this concept is accepted, then prehistoric art must be recognised as a system of action which, rather than encoding the symbolic properties of the world, intends to change it (Gell 1998:6). Much has been written about how material culture is active and how this translates into conceptions of agency (Lewis-Williams 1997; Dowson 1998b; Last 1998; Gosden 2001; Pollard 2001). Although Gell's (1998:11) theorisation of biographical space goes someway to broadening the applicability of these concerns, the other inter-penetrative side of this duality, the institution, is less often explicitly considered. The institution remains an off stage presence, only obliquely referred to. It is, however, a construct no less explanatory than an active conception of material culture.

It is the apparent repetitiveness of action that Giddens (1984) posits as the material grounding of social institutions. As such, institutionalism acts to bind the fleeting encounter to the longer term mechanisms of social reproduction. In specifically artistic terminology, it is this which enables individual works to be subsumed into a class of common attributes, or style. Repetition, in such circumstances, appears as the memory of art works (Gell 1998:162 & 235). Memory, however, can be selective or even deliberately forgetful, possessing an ability to eschew history (Douglas 1995:13-5). This dialectic of remembering and forgetting suggests that "repetition will contain the very differences that serve to work the present as a site of conflict ... In each instance there is a juxtaposition or a constellation that breaks the effect of continuity" (Benjamin 1994:245). Rather than the great unifier of art history, tradition must be considered inauthentic, betraying what it hands over through its incompleteness (Caygill 1994:8-22). This understanding of tradition creates an imperfect history in which rock art trajectories, for example, are characterised as much by intervention as repetition. Such punctuation is most obviously manifest in the deployment of idiosyncratic images. Motifs deployed as innovative interventions, however, simultaneously become part of the institution, re-affirming its apparent 'fixity' whilst, at the same time, significantly altering it. In itself this tension constitutes of a strand of evidence (Lewis-Williams 1995a:5).

Through interpreting variation in the self depiction of shaman Dowson (1994) writes an alternative history for the Bushman of southern Africa in just this manner. Style, in Dowson's account, is simultaneously processes and product (Lacy 1995:46; Roe 1995:28; Voss & Young 1995:77), the dynamic interplay of innovation and tradition manipulated for political ends (Geary 1993:89; Neitzel 1995:396). Gell's (1998:76-7) conception of abstract arts, in which he attributes internal agency and the perception of effect to part-to-part and part-to-whole relationships, extends the possibility of writing such a history for the rock art of the British Isles and Ireland. According to these same relationships of innovation and institutionalisation divergent trajectories emerge within the traditions of the British and Irish corpus: a suggestion substantiated in the pronounced regional patterning of this rock art (Evans 1999). Many accounts which attempt to address corpus variation amongst abstract arts, however, do so through the individualisation of standardised motifs (see above). Consequently, the integration of visual pattern and 'texture' (see Gell 1998:76-7) is lost and the internal agency of the imagery denied.

An alternative approach to abstract arts can be derived from the development of Dowson's (1994) analysis, namely, to see corpus variation as the writing of history. Effective engagement with this history is attainable through addressing the *saliency* of the corpus. The understanding of saliency developed here reworks that postulated by Gell (1998:157). Gell defines saliency as a psychological entrapment by the 'aesthetically' significant attributes of a series of art works, which holds the viewer's attention across the entire corpus. The identification of saliency implies that a series of recurrent, prominent and noticeable features are extant across a body of art. Within this, however, it is possible to distinguish two kinds of saliency: the material and the social. Amongst rock carving traditions, material saliency is revealed by the interaction of content and placement, the latter further subdivided into two types: site characterisation (earth-fast boulder or glacial pavement for example) and topographical position (riverside or mountain top location amongst many others). It is how these recognisable physical recurrences allow for our engagement with the rock art that gives access to the imagery's meaning, purpose and significance: its social saliency. That is, it is the construction of social saliency which allows rock art to operate as informing context. Before specifically identifying the saliency of British and Irish rock art (see chapters 2 and 3) it is necessary to explore the wider applicability of this concept and how it can be deployed to reveal meaningful information.

In a manner analogous with the internal dynamics of abstract decorative strategies, different institutions are sustained in conjunction with each other (Giddens 1984:18). Within Gell's thesis the concomitant existence of different institutions translates into a highly relational understanding of context, with art objects occupying a socially defined slot appropriate to receive them. To apply this conception of a slot to prehistoric images carries with it the danger of subsuming the legitimacy of the imagery within a preconceived relational structure in much the same way as accounts which uncritically deploy decorative strategies as supporting evidence for preassigned archaeological suppositions. A more constructive response to the theorisations of Giddens and Gell is to recognise that the functional interdependence of art and other cultural components does exist, and suggests that what is detected in one 'institution' may also be detectable, to a greater or lesser degree, in another (Darvill 1997a:173; see also Chapman 1997:31). It is the connotations of synecdoche (see also Gell 1998:159-60) inherent in these remarks which are of greatest relevance. If style is something which enables an art work to be compared to a whole body of work, then axes of coherency may exist between decorative strategies on the one hand and monumental manifestations on the other. Indeed, Gell (1998:95) himself proposes a "synergy between art forms and modalities of expression which conventional aesthetics tries to deal with separately, because they give pleasure to separate senses ... If we can see visual patterns as frozen traces of dances, so we can see dances as being half-way to music, which normally accompanies them".

To conceptualise Neolithic material culture in this way it is necessary to take a macroscopic view of art and architecture; to perceive each manifestation as part of a single indivisible work, or *œuvre*, rather than an aggregate of fragments (see Gell 1998:220-35). As such, contradictory details and variations of form between institutions can be studied in terms of balance and how this balance is temporally and spatially transformed. It is the inherent shiftiness of balance which introduces discontinuity into tradition. This is not too dissimilar to Thomas' (1999a:119) commentary on the decorated media of the British Neolithic in which he contends that "rather than a transfer of symbols from a parietal to a mobiliary media, we should envisage the formulation of a set of signifiers which were used in different ways in different regions". In this way, rock art as institution presents the archaeologist with an opportunity to explore long term histories of cultural continuity and change through the persistence, or lapsing, of social practices over generations (Braun 1995:129-30). Alternatively, rephrased in Gell's terminology, trace a structural invariant under salient morphological transformation and demonstrate how each component of the œuvre is ancestral to, and descends from, other works through a multiplicity of multidirectional mutual referencing.

To an extent, the circular archetype common to "[v]irtually all the ceremonial monuments constructed in Britain and Ireland between 3000 and 1500 BC" (Bradley 1998a:132) goes someway to demonstrating the appropriateness of this theoretical construction. Of greater significance is the observation that under critical evaluation the circle itself becomes indistinct, obscured by the myriad of idiosyncratic perimeter forms which make up its more general usefulness as a classificatory tool. It is this very indistinctness and blurring of the edges (Bradley 1998a:132) which is potentially most informative. Brophy (2002) in a recent analysis of "the quest for causewayed enclosures" notes a similar muteness in the typological identification of this monument type. Something more is at work than a commonality of perimeter form, something beneath the surface of the circle which defies archaeological classification but suggests that a 'homology' exists. As such, both art and archaeology can be explored under the rubric of the other without subsuming the imagery in inappropriate constructions of context or eschewing archaeology altogether.

Material saliency is intimately connected to social saliency and, as noted above, it is this which gives interpretative access to purpose, meaning and significance. Lewis-Williams (1990:129-30, 1998:88-9) suggests that the images he identifies as "key symbols", those art works which lie at the heart of a belief system, do not exhibit a specific meaning. Rather, they articulate a broad range of associations and connotations which make up the images' semantic spectrum or, perhaps as Gell would phrase it, spectrum of effect. The dominant component of this spectrum constitutes its focus, the remainder an illusive, but meaningful, penumbra. For Lewis-Williams (1998), speaking of the Bushman imagery of southern Africa, it is the shamanistic context of the art which generates the penumbra,

8

within which shamanic components bring a resolution of focus. Significantly, the recent theorisation of sensory approaches to art (see MacGregor 1999, for example) suggests that the same analytical processes are as applicable to attributes of rock carving - such as the materiality of surface (e.g. Lewis-Williams & Dowson 1990) - as image content.

Rock art, however, does not exists apart from the wider landscape. Consequently, fluctuation in the polysemous balance of the imagery operates in conjunction with that evoked by a range of associated landscape features (see chapter 2), to produce a web of context parameters which can be traced through the wider Neolithic. In so doing, further levels of polysemous variability and focus are revealed through the shifting circumstances in which the effect recognised in the rock art is deployed in the construction of different monument types. It is how the spectrum slips into and out of focus - how it

is constantly re-balanced and yet remains intimately conjoined - that is potentially informative. Such interplay is to consider art as context and reveals the saliency of the Neolithic œuvre.

The use of rock art as context allows for the meaningful investigation of imagery formerly considered to be opaque. It is an approach which moves research beyond the imposition of predetermining models or the necessary generalisations involved in the comparison of perimeter form. The archaeological value of the British and Irish rock art can therefore be re-asserted, and research into this decorative strategy need not remain a marginal concern. To focus on the inferential and connotative may appear unnecessarily obtuse, but perhaps all that is left to the archaeologist concerned with prehistoric imagery is how these art works can be *felt*, at least by us.

CHAPTER TWO
Study parameters and contextual connotations

The rock art of the British Isles and Ireland connotes saliency at a number of different conceptual levels. This translates into pronounced spatial patterning which presents the rock art of Britain and Ireland as a distinctive, but internally coherent, unit of analysis and defines the geographical scope of this investigation. Saliency is manifest in the connotative juxtapositions of rock art content, materiality and landscape correlates which inform each other to produce a spectrum of effect with clearly identifiable and recurrent characteristics.

2.1 Introduction

if specificity is lost ... any generalisation becomes so general as to be useless, ... if too much specificity is retained, then establishing its meaning by relating it to events or cases of a similar class becomes impossible (Rowlands quoted in Harding 1997:291).

The Galician group is derived, ultimately perhaps from the East Mediterranean, but immediately from the northwestern part of the Iberian peninsula, where it appears to be mixed with epi-palaeolithic survivals. From Ireland, most likely from Kerry, these carvings spread to North Britain (MacWhite 1946:75).

Positing the polysemous connotations of rock art as context allows for strategies which seek to explore the effect, meaning and purpose of the cup-and-ring marks. Attendant to this, however, are less abstract concerns, concerns which define the parameters of study in terms of the geographical distribution of the evidence (comparable temporal considerations are addressed in chapters 3-5). Just as strategies are needed to construct the context of analysis, so they are required to engage with these more prosaic concerns.

Previous research (Evans 1999) suggests a local origin for spectrum focus. It is also, however, suggestive of concomitant generic understandings of the imagery. Indeed, Neolithic deployments of rock art may be considered operative at three interdependent 'levels' (see below). As such, to focus solely on the local is to ignore important, and relevant, evidence. Consequently, rather than considering how meaning and purpose are revealed, this chapter begins with consideration of where, in geographical terms, it can be sought, and concludes with the identification of connoted context and spectrum composition.

2.2 The abstract rock arts of early agricultural Europe

Rock art associated with the early phases of agriculture is found in many regions of Europe, including, Britain, Ireland, Iberia, Scandinavia, Switzerland, northern Italy and southern France. Traditionally, the rock art of England, Scotland and Ireland is considered "virtually identical", part of a single distribution (Johnston 1989:130-5; Davis 1959-62:624). MacWhite's influential article, *A new view on Irish Bronze Age rock*

scribings, published in 1946, raised what is now one of the most commonly discussed 'features' of rock art distribution (see Davidson 1950:40; Anati 1963; Shee-Twohig 1981:97; Van Hoek 1987:42; Bradley1997a; 1998b; with Valcarce 1998) in extending this proposed intimacy to Iberia. Within this scheme the coastal bias evident in rock art distribution (MacWhite 1946:62; Morris 1979, 1981; Van Hoek 1993:23) and prevailing topography of Atlantic Europe readily suggests nautical modes of transmission. Indeed, the concentration of rock art along the peninsulas of western Ireland (Johnston 1989:41), the deeply penetrating estuaries of the Dee (Kirkcudbright) and former shoreline of the Firth of Forth (Bradley 1997a:134-5), among other sites, echo the informal landing places identified by McGrail (1987:267-9, 1993:199) as characteristic of prehistoric seafaring. Informal landing places, however, have their own significant attributes and other factors may be at work in the creation of this coastal bias (see chapter 6; also Helskog 1999 for a discussion of the *"shore connection"* common to Scandinavian rock art).

A number of scholars extend this apparent zone of artistic interaction further north into Scandinavia (Van Hoek 1987; Walderhaug 1995:171; Sognnes 1996:15). On reaching Scotland from the Iberian Peninsula, van Hoek (1997:7), for example, postulates the divergence of well-established migratory routes, the most easterly of which followed the eastern coast of the Scottish mainland before - via Orkney and Shetland - moving on to Scandinavia. Similarly, citing a distinction between the rock art of western Norway and the rest of Scandinavia, Fett and Fett (1979) propose direct contact between this area and the western islands of Britain which then, following the arguments of Beltran, is extended to encompass Scotland, Ireland, Galicia and the Canary Islands (see also Burenhult 1979:92). Connection to the Alpine regions, Carschenna in Switzerland, Valcamonica in Italy and Mont Bégo in southern France is then proposed through reference to common circular imagery transmitted along inland waterways. Ultimately MacWhite's influential article has created a long-lasting impression of an international artistic tradition whose apparent standardisation at a super-regional level (Harding 2000:346) implicitly underpins the idea of a common symbolic system (see McMann 1980:140; Johnston 1989:308-11; Jackson 1995; Van Hoek 1997; Bolin 1998).

Generally, accounts which 'successfully' demonstrate direct interconnection between the rock art trajectories of Atlantic Europe do so by emphasising the recurrent appearance of standardised individual motifs in each region (see MacWhite 1946; Fett & Fett 1979). Taking the rock art of Valcamonica as an example, and referring to figure 2.1, the methodological frailty of an approach that isolates specific, and common, elements is demonstrated. Figure 2.1 indicates the presence of concentric circles, accompanied by a central cup-mark, in northern Italy. If similar charts are produced for the other regions of early agricultural Europe with traditions of rock carving the same basic motif recurs, allowing the imagery of almost any area to be drawn into a single common trajectory. These standardised motifs, however, "are common goods decoratively, the presence of which in two different areas hardly provides definite evidence of a connection" (Malmer 1989:96-7; see also Ashmore 1986:59).

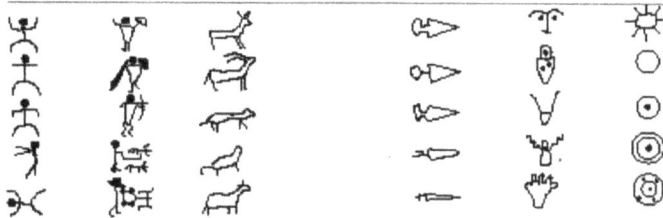

Figure 2.1: Valcamonican rock art in tabular form (after Anati 1994 with modifications).

With comparable ideas in mind, Marstrander (1979:99) suggests that "complex figures weigh more in the scales of evidence than elementary motifs". The validity, or otherwise, of this statement is easily assessed by returning to the rock imagery of Valcamonica. The whirligig, or 'swastika', motif found here immediately recalls that located on Rombalds Moor, Yorkshire (figure 2.2). Jacobsthal (1938:68) contends that "the identity is striking, even the filling dots and the 'tail' are the same in Italy as in Yorkshire; the only difference is that the Italian pattern whirls clockwise and the English counter-clockwise". According to Marstrander's scheme, the presence of similar swastikas at Pubble (Fermanagh) (Johnston 1989:90), Bohuslän (Fett & Fett 1979:84) and Os Campos (Rozas 1999:116) offers some validity to the identification of a single widespread decorative strategy in early agricultural Europe.

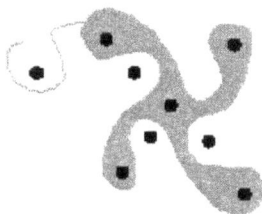

Figure 2.2: The 'swastika' (after Jacobsthal 1938).

Comparable evidence is found in the distribution of the labyrinth motif. This motif is found throughout western Europe, at Ausevik (Scandinavia), Newgrange and Hollywood (Ireland), Tintagel (England), Boddington Mains (Scotland), Valcamonica, and Galicia. Broadening the field of enquiry, however, reveals two near identical motifs in Arizona (figure 2.3). Clearly it would require extreme pleading, and a highly imaginative interpretation of the evidence, to propose a sustainable artistic relationship between these two continents during this period of prehistory. If this is accepted then, by the

same logic, the 'evidence' provided by the distribution of the labyrinth within Europe must also be questioned.

Figure 2.3: The labyrinth motif and its distribution (after Pena Santos & Varela 1979).

Comparison of isolated individual motifs, no matter how complex, must therefore be considered methodologically inappropriate for assessing the affinities between rock art traditions. Image composition, however, suggests an alternative approach. Bradley (1995b:92), defining composition as numerate frequencies of concentric rings, demonstrates a statistically defined correlation between the concentric characteristics of rock art found in Donegal, mid-Argyll, Northumberland and Galicia, suggesting close artistic affinities between these regions during prehistory. The methodological prerequisites of this approach, however, concern themselves with an art composed of dots and circles, obscuring the idiosyncrasies and regional patterns which also characterise this distribution. Consequently, in some respects Bradley's analysis, despite its statistical qualifications, follows the approach critiqued above in deliberately looking for similarity at the expense of difference. Consideration of composition, however, is potentially informative: analogous to the identification of the multiple levels of saliency at which the rock art of the British Isles and Ireland is operative. This relies upon a more self-consciously visual approach to the art, a more subjective engagement which allows for the exploration of effect.

2.3   The content and context of European agricultural rock art

Depictions of cervids appear in 124 panels of Galician rock art, 50% of which also exhibit abstract motifs. The relationship between animal and abstract depictions is often manifest in an

11

intimate conjoining of different image-types (Walker 1977:455; Bradley 1997a:42; Rozas 1999:120-3; figure 2.4) which suggests contemporaneity.

Figure 2.4: Galician deer (after Pena Santos & Varela 1979).

Animal figures are also found amongst the rock imagery of the British Isles. Four are located in the rock shelter at Goats Crag (Northumberland) (Waddington 1999:108; figure 2.5), three at Ballochmyle (Ayrshire) (Beckensall 1999:96) and one in Argyll (Feather 1964-5:316; Fett & Fett 1979:87). The final example is the unique depiction of a deer at Eggerness (Garlieston Bay, Scotland) composed of, and integrated with, more familiar abstract imagery. Beckensall (1999:90-2) identifies two further deer at this site, but chronologically places them in the Iron Age because of the unusual nature of the depiction. Whilst there are difficulties in assigning a later date to these images, immediately designating them as contemporary with the wider rock art repertoire is equally problematic and, consequently, they are excluded from subsequent analysis.

Figure 2.5: The Goats Crag 'deer' (after Waddington 1999).

It is noticeable that these isolated depictions of deer are far from the consistent feature cervids represent in Galician imagery, whilst none at all appear in Ireland. Moreover, the British depictions are highly stylised and roughly shaped, no more readily identifiable as deer than as any other quadruped. Neither, with the exception of the three cup-marks at Goats Crag, are they associated with any form of abstract art. Unlike the deer of Britain, those in Galicia exhibit great variety in size, style and detail, generally being markedly more naturalistic.

Stags, for example, may be carved with detailed antlers, internal designs or engaged in active 'scenes' which bring a sense of mobility to the Galician imagery absent from the British quadrupeds. More generally, within the Iberian corpus, the infilling characteristic of British depiction is rare and, instead, the numerical bias greatly favours outline alone.

Human figures and depictions of metalwork extenuate the sense of difference engendered by the differential manifestation of animal carvings in the rock art of these areas. Evidence for any form of human image is questionable within Britain and Ireland. The Fetts' (1979:86), for example, were only able to identify a single "doubtful" human figure at Wemyss (Fife). Although footprints are more common, they remain rare (Forde-Johnston 1957:34; Beckensall 1999:86). Moreover, with the exception of the Cochno stone (Scotland), the deployment of the foot motif occurs only in a burial context, within areas devoid of landscape art. Clear examples of human figures are, however, seen in Galician rock art. Although these images are primarily restricted to 'stick-figures', like the cervids, they are portrayed in animated 'poses'. Footprints also appear, but rather than being deployed in a grave context they are found, either singularly or in pairs, as integral components of the open air corpus.

A limited, and qualified, correspondence, however, does appear to exist in depictions of weaponry (see Bradley 1995b:94, 1998b:141). Although there are no hard and fast rules pertaining to the deployment of weapon imagery in Galicia, certain patterns are observed. As is the case in Britain, depictions are rarely found alone, only 11% of daggers and 5% of halberds are deployed singularly. Moreover, the placement of these images on vertical, and physically 'accessible' surfaces, recalls the decoration of the Badbury cairn and lower reaches of the Stonehenge uprights (but see also Scarre 1997 regarding the 'box-buckler' symbol of stone 57).

There are, however, a significant number of differences that override this tenuous correlation. In Britain the unhafted axe head predominates: in Galicia it is the hafted axe, daggers, swords and halberds which are most common (Bradley 1995b:93, 1998a:130). Although lacking the realism of Valcamonican weaponry, this Galician imagery allows for the identification of type; very few of the rougher examples characteristic of British depiction are encountered. Moreover, like depictions of cervids and humans 50% of these weapon images appear alongside abstract motifs (Bradley 1998b), a situation only encountered in the Kilmartin cist burials within the British Isles. The most significant point of divergence, however, is found in the context of image deployment. As noted above, depictions of weaponry in Galicia are found in the open-air, whereas in the British Isles they are restricted to monumental contexts: contexts which are also associated with the dead. It is significant that in both contexts the weapons shown are of Bronze Age date and that the British monuments can be similarly dated. Clearly this has important chronological and social implications for interpretative schemes which see the open-air rock art of Atlantic Europe as an unified entity (see

12

below and chapters 5 & 6 for an interpretation of 'Bronze Age' rock art in Britain).

The intimate integration and contemporaneity of Galician figurative and abstract components suggest that, although consistencies are seen in the 'circular' imagery between regions, when the entire abstract repertoire, the corpus as a whole, composition and context are taken into account - the rock art of Galicia exhibits as much difference from, as similarity to, that of the British Isles and Ireland.

Despite the arguments of the Fetts (1979), neither the hunters' nor the farmers' rock art of Scandinavia appears to have much in common with the open-air imagery of Britain and Ireland. Certainly, as in virtually any case, a number of superficial similarities are apparent (see Sognnes 1996:21; Coles 1995:182). Perhaps the most striking point of divergence, however - solely in terms of abstract imagery - is its rarity in Scandinavia. Weaponry also serves to distance the rock art of this area. Like Galicia, although depicting different types, these images can be identified as caricatured classes. Other similarities to the Galician corpus can be found in their disregard for scale in relation to other motifs, most notably boats and humans. Although rare, Burenhult (1979:94) suggests that the axe blades of Simiris 19 (Scandia) recall those of Stonehenge, an argument that again ignores different contexts of deployment and consumption. Difference from Britain, Ireland and Galicia, is again asserted through animal depiction. Despite occurring on the same panel as abstract motifs, the intimate inter-connection between figurative and geometric motifs commonly seen in Spain is absent, whilst type and detail distinguish the Scandinavian from the British examples. Human depiction occurs with a greater numerical frequency in Scandinavia than Galicia, whilst in contrast to the predominance of paired footprints in Spain, 70% of Scandinavian foot motifs follow paths perpendicular to the rest of the imagery (Bradley 2000a:142). Many more are shod, in a further expression of intra-regional idiosyncracy. It is the prevalence of boat depiction, however, that most clearly reveals the distinctive character of Scandinavian rock art.

The rock art of the Alpine regions, Valcamonica and Mont Bégo, appears at odds with the imagery discussed above and is probably somewhat later in date (data derived from Anati 1994, 1995; Barfield & Chippendale 1997; Arcà 2000; Bevan 2000; Harding 2000:336). Significantly, however, many of these carvings appear to contain depictions of weaponry and other items of personal apparel: the 'spectacle-spirals' of Ossimo I, for example, recall the dress adornments of the Fulda-Werra group. As such, it does not appear unreasonable to follow Yates' (1993) interpretation of Scandinavian rock art and suggest that the imagery of Valcamonica and Mont Bégo - and possibly also Galicia - reveals a concern with expressing the creation of personal identity through the depiction of certain sets of material culture: a concern absent from the rock carving communities of the British Isles and Ireland.

Somewhat surprisingly, it is the engravings of Carschenna (Switzerland) which initially appear to demonstrate the closest superficial convergence with the rock art of Britain and Ireland. These 10 engraved rocks are almost entirely composed of cups surrounded by a number of concentric rings (Zindel 1970:142; Sauter 1976:111). The art, however, generally lacks the more idiosyncratic imagery, complex inter-linking and embellishment characteristic of Britain and Ireland. Moreover, the location of the imagery in the high mountain passes of the Alps, again places the art in a very different context of consumption to that of the main study area.

2.4   A single tradition or divergent trajectories?

Taken as a totality, there appears to be little evidence to support the idea of a direct - and sustained - connection between the artistic trajectories of early agricultural Europe beyond their immediate regions. Leaving aside the petroglyphs of Carschenna - because of their limited sample size and context of deployment - if British and Irish rock art holds affinities anywhere it is with Galicia, but this, in itself, is questionable. That which initially appears to suggest unity, the 'circle', ultimately demonstrates divergence through its myriad of associations. Where convergence is seen amongst the decorative strategies of mainland Europe - in their common concern with the creation of personal identity (?) - it further serves to separate these trajectories from those of the British Isles and Ireland, at least until the early Bronze Age (see chapters 5 and 6).

It is not just their separation from the rock engravings of Atlantic Europe that suggests that the rock art of Britain and Ireland constitutes a coherent unit of analysis, but also the internal 'consistency' of the corpus. In the broadest sense, imagery of the British Isles and Ireland is manifest as *standard*: the carving of a central cup-mark, surrounded by a number of concentric rings. This range may be *elaborated* into a series of regionally identifiable characteristics, through which the standardised components of the repertoire are brought into composition. Where such elaboration is absent, this, in itself, is indicative of specific regional patterning: the domination of cup-marking around Loch Tay, for example. Integrated within these broader trajectories, numerous *idiosyncratic* motifs appear: images which are unique to a particular locale and suggestive of the work of a single artist, or the manipulation of a locally significant decorative theme (Evans 1999). It is this complex interplay of standardised, elaborated and idiosyncratic motifs which gives both local difference and unity to the rock art of the British Isles and Ireland, a unique combination of interaction which gives these images an internal agency not encountered elsewhere in Europe.

2.5   Connoting Contexts

The literature of rock art research is littered with phrases that profess to link imagery and landscape. Authors recurrently suggest that "the art was united with the land" (David & Lourandos 1998:195); that rock art invested the landscape with symbolic meaning (see Zvelebil 1997:39); or that the art represents the first step in the humanisation of the landscape (Sognnes 1996:22). By virtue of its materiality, rock art *is*

13

intimately connected to the landscape, but this statement cannot be allowed to stand as an interpretation in its own right. Rather, specific exploration of the relationship between image materiality and landscape provides one means of intellectually constraining the potentially infinite multiplicity of connotations which make up the rock arts spectrum of effect. What the contents of this spectrum are and the mechanisms by which it operates constitute the remainder of this chapter. Data provided by general syntheses is juxtaposed against that derived from specific case studies, and ultimately resolved into an informing context for further analysis.

2.6   The distribution of British and Irish rock art

Figure 2.6: The distribution of British and Irish rock art.

Rock art is primarily confined to the northern reaches of the British mainland, above a line connecting the Peak District and Yorkshire. Within England, a numerical bias falls to the east of the Pennines, a distribution which is reversed in Scotland (Walker 1977:458; Van Hoek 1997:13). These divisions are by no means absolute. Cumbria, for example, exhibits rock art of a highly idiosyncratic character and predominantly monumental context (see chapter 5). Similarly, in Scotland petroglyphs are found in the Edinburgh (Clyde-Forth) area, Tayside and the extreme northeast. In general, however, rock art is concentrated in Yorkshire, Durham, Northumberland, Galloway and Argyll. Current research is both extending the range of these concentrations and identifying additional clusters. Tayside, for example, may come to be regarded as one of Scotland's major sources of evidence (see below).

Rock art is found in over half of the 32 Irish counties (Johnston 1993a:146, 1993b:258). Despite this impression of widespread distribution, the art is again clustered into three major

concentrations: the Cork-Kerry group to the southwest; northeast Donegal, notably Magheranaul and Doagh Island; and the only major concentration in the east: Louth (Shee 1968:144; Lacy 1983:98; Van Hoek 1985:123, 1987:23-5, 1997:12; Johnston 1989:42; Harding 2000:341). Within this the numerical balance of distribution is heavily weighted in favour of the Cork-Kerry group (Johnston 1989:19) (figure 2.6).

The identification of pronounced clustering at a national scale is about more than simply plotting dots on maps and reinforcing what has been presented on innumerable occasions. It demonstrates a distinctive characteristic of British and Irish rock art which leads into questions of analytical strategy and the creation of interpretative context (see also chapter 6).

2.7   The connotative spectrum of rock art and landscape

Within their regionally defined groupings, more localised clustering is also apparent (Johnston 1989:239; Bradley 1995c:108). Taking just a few examples from amongst many: Waddington (1998:37) identifies three discrete rock art clusters in the Milfield Basin; Bradley (1997a:90) the restricted Pennine distribution of the Yorkshire engravings; Beckensall (1999:75) a focus on the Wharfe watershed; whilst Morris & Bailey (1964-5:154) illustrate similar patterning throughout southern Scotland.

There are a number of often unasked questions to be considered before these observations can be accepted as meaningful. The first is of geology. The most fundamental requirement for the deployment of rock art is the availability of a suitable surface. If such surfaces are restricted to specific areas then clustering should be expected and geology, not cultural selection, would determine distribution. Within the British Isles, however, Bradley (1997a:90) demonstrates that rarely do rock art spreads occupy the full extent of the parent rock. Johnston (1989:257, 1993b:260) points to comparable patterns in the Irish evidence. Case study fieldwork undertaken at Kealduff and Coomasaharn, on the Inveragh Peninsula (Co. Kerry), and Glen Lochay and Loch Tay (Perthshire) conform to this general pattern, but micro-topographical considerations suggest that other factors are at work in determining local distribution patterns (see below). Fieldwork results from Castleton (near Stirling, Lanarkshire) are very different. Although this site is located in an area of intensive arable agriculture, within which a high number of clearance cairns may obscure 'true' distribution, the deployment of imagery is restricted by the availability of a particular kind of surface (see below).

Obscuration of distribution patterns may also be derived from modern research strategies. Prior to the first season's fieldwork (summer 2000) Dowson (pers comm) commented on the correlation between local clustering and the modern road network in the case study areas of Inveragh and Glen Lochay, suggesting that distribution may be as much to do with convenience and expediency as any prehistoric reality. Exploring beyond recognised clusters and road systems, however, failed to uncover any new carving sites around the

Irish cases studies, but did reveal a huge amount of uncarved rock. Investigation in Glen Lochay revealed much the same pattern. In this latter instance, however, although many uncarved rocks were found, a number of stones exhibiting a low number of cupules (usually one or two) were located: notably on the slopes below Glen Lochay 2 (see below). Fieldwork undertaken along the north shore of Loch Tay (RCAHMS spring 2001, Evans summer 2001) illustrates that existing distribution maps for this area are far from comprehensive. Between the farmlands of Morenish and Shenlarich (see below), 118 petroglyph sites were located where less than two dozen were known before (Steve Boyle (RCAHMS) pers comm). Significantly, although the number of known sites and their recognised distribution subsequently increased, each new find is located in the same zone of topographical preference exhibited by known sites, whilst uncarved rock continues to predominate.

Johnston (1989:10) finds further consistency in the association of specific motifs - five concentric rings for example - with particular types of topographical features, such as 'table-top' outcrops, within Ireland. This correspondence is not seen in either the rock art of the British Isles nor that of Inveragh. Instead it is immediately local topography, rather than feature type, that has the greatest influence on distribution (see Evans 1999). What does recur, however, is the repeated situation of rock art in landscapes of rapidly changing topography - areas such as valley headlands, watersheds, marine beaches and lower hill slopes - locating them in a topographically defined intermediate zone at the "outer limits of the prehistoric landscape" (Bradley 1997:100) (figure 2.12).

Figure 2.7: The 'intermediate zone' north of Loch Tay.

Unfortunately, this categorisation of landscape implies marginality, a concept grounded in the assumed binary between centre and periphery which renders communities bounded and isolated (see Young & Simmonds 1995:7-10; 1999:148). Placement of imagery at the boundaries of these isolated entities serves to separate the art from those who produced and consumed it, implying that it is only possible to study the engravings in isolation, abstracted as a category of analysis with full methodological resonance (see chapter 1).

The inappropriateness of placing the rock art in a marginal intermediate zone is illustrated through the characteristics of the art itself. Although only one site within Britain exhibits associated artefacts (Bradley 2000a:73), in itself something which may be attributed to a lack of interest and excavation, the differential weathering of motifs suggests a temporal engagement with rock art contrary to academic placement outside of main activity areas[3]. Bradley's (1997a) analysis of image location in terms of audience composition, however, suggests that such a critique is - in many ways - inappropriate. Indeed, what follows is not so much a criticism of Bradley as a re-evaluation of the connotative significance of the so-called intermediate zone and the role this plays in the evocation of the imagery's effect.

It is not necessary to view the contradictory landscape of the intermediate zone as a series of oppositions. More profitable is to write of something made complementary; a 'paradoxical' overcoming and bringing together of difference within a tangible sense of contrast. This understanding of topographical difference finds resonance in, and is perhaps only realisable through, the juxtaposition of petroglyph materiality and landscape characterisation. In their contradictory 'boundary' location, the majority of carved surfaces do not give their location away (Christison 1903-4:143; Beckensall 1997:10, 1999:7; Beckensall & Frodsham 1998:51). Few are visible from a distance, their identification involving "a strong sense of knowing where to look" (Beckensall 1995:9). In effect, the rock art is 'blended' with the contradictions of the landscape in such a way as to suggest both an acquiescence to topographical contrast and a negation of it. This, however, is not to deny any relationship between image location and conspicuous topographical features. The location of carved surfaces, such as those at Rowter Rocks (Derbyshire), Caller Crag, Robin Hood's Stride (Northumberland) or Glen Lochay 2 and 3 (Perthshire) for example, adjacent to highly visible outcrops, again suggests paradoxical relationships of advertisement and concealment. The carvings are not hidden but nor are they easy to find: neither a highly public statement nor an evocation of secrecy (see also Johnston 1989:50-1).

These contradictory characteristics are replicated in the micro-topographical relationships of imagery deployed along prominent rocky ridges. Ridge systems once again locate rock carving in an area of abrupt topographical change. Rather than simply being enhanced by positioning on these rocky promontories, each decorative component is simultaneously obscured by its positioning on the rock face, set back from the crest and camouflaged by the sheer mass of rock. This relationship is exemplified by the Castleton (Lanarkshire) engravings (figure 2.8) and replicated in the ridge systems of

---

[3] The accumulation of detritus and flora regrowth at a number of rock art sites, however, suggests that differential weathering is a rather problematic measure of the longevity of a locales use-life (see below).

Kealduff, Glen Lochay 5 and the massive outcrops of Cragganester and Craggantoul on the northern shores of Loch Tay. As such, although contrast is apparent between the connotative mechanisms of these ridge systems and the 'blending' of smaller outcrops, the connotative effect of these site types is, in many ways, comparable. It is the material ambiguities of rock art and landscape juxtaposition, in whatever specific formulation, which appear most significant: the resistence to being classified or pigeonholed which is integral to their materiality.

Figure 2.8: Castleton 3, one of the four carved ridges of this site.

Through the simultaneous creation and negation of difference, the rock art connotes *tergiversation*. The use of a political term such as tergiversation may appear out of place. Alternative terminology - such as transgression- however, disrupts the paradoxical balance of art and landscape juxtaposition. By contrast, the connotations of subterfuge and shiftiness inherent in the term tergiversation, and the political position of the quisling - or tergiversator - effectively serves as an analogy for the 'dual' nature of rock art and landscape blending. That is, the quisling simultaneously occupies a position on 'both' sides of a political divide and, to maintain this position, must *work* for both. Consequently, tergiversation, as applied in the context of the rock art, expresses the sites' resistance to classification and allows the contradictions inherent in the relationship between art and landscape to remain visible and to inform each other. Ultimately, this paradoxical construct is the most recurrent of all connotative devices and lies at the heart of the imagery's focussed material polysemy.

Effect is more fully connoted - and specifically enacted - through the interconnection of the paradoxical materiality of tergiversation and the connotative values of a wide range of recurrently associated landscape features. Each of these variables simultaneously enhances focus and provides penumbral understanding. For example, numerous authors have noted a correlation between rock art deployment and bodies of water. Johnston (1989:244-5) suggests that 85% of all Irish engravings (excluding the Cork-Kerry group which are not included in her analysis) lie within 50 metres of water. O'Sullivan and Sheehan (1993:81, 1996:79) note a similar distributional bias on the Inveragh Peninsula and propose a cult of water sources as explanation.

Rather than subsuming the evidence in blanket cultic explanations (see chapter 1), the correlation between rock art and water suggests that it may be more profitable to explore the relationship between art and settlement (see Waddington 1996:150; Bradley 1995b:94; 1997a:152, 2002:7). Within Ireland, support for this suggestion is found in Johnston's (1989:260-7) contention that the topographical and environmental associations of 97.8% of rock art sites are indicative of ideal settlement conditions. A comparable correlation is made for the British Isles (Bradley 1997a:92; Walker 1977:464). To simply posit a connection between rock art, water and settlement, however, is no more explanatory that a generic water cult.

An alternative approach to the recurrent association between rock art and water can begin to be discerned in Waddington's (1996, 1998) suggested convergence of art, water and subsistence strategy in the Milfield Basin. There is a good deal of evidence to conclude that the practical landscape simultaneously constituted the ritual landscape, and vice versa, during the British and Irish Neolithic (see, for example, Swartz & Hurlbutt 1994:15; Zvelebil 1997:36; Cooney 2000:21). Waddington's identification of inscribed grazing areas as a peculiarly local manifestation of this convergence provides a causal explanation for the location of rock art in close proximity to water. There is, however, an intimacy in the relationship between art and water that is not fully captured by Waddington's model: an intimacy very much tied to the contradictions of tergiversation.

Like the relationship between landscape topography and image materiality, it is not the immediate physicality of these associations which is significant, but the convergent metaphorical connotations evoked by their physical properties. Water, for example, is also a polysemous thing, interacting with the connoted effect of the rock art at a number of successive and mutually sustaining levels. It both creates a physical boundary and simultaneously offers opportunity for passage. From source to sea, rivers cross-cut a range of landscape zones (Richards 1996a), overcoming and evoking topographical contrast. Water also reflects, and falls from, the sky, transcending its apparent physical 'limitations'. It can change colour or physical properties according to light or temperature, both gives and takes life, destroys crops and leaves rich soils. Water is both change and transformation, controllable and uncontrollable: in essence "metaphorically and physically contradictory" (Brophy 1999a:71, 2000:52-4).

The connotative saliency between this list of characteristics and those derived from the material juxtapositions of the rock art is self evident, but more immediate conjoining is evident in the carvings' capacity to retain rainwater. The processes of evaporation and drainage ensure that this is a temporary, or transgressive, intimacy which again evokes tergiversation; it is also an intimacy which 'naturalises' the juxtaposition of natural and engraved surface markings (see below). [These connotative associations may also be manifest in forms not immediately recognisable from the rock art context. The recurrent deployment of water-rolled stones in the construction of different monument 'types', for example, not only architecturally articulates the contradictory properties of water but also suggests further levels of material ambiguity and the transmogrification of substance. Moreover, many of these stones are quartz, a material which instigates a complementary inferential trail of tergiversation, transformation and transgression (see chapters 4 & 5)].

The substantial dimensions of many carved outcrops allows Waddington (1998:35) to suggest that the 'original context' of the rock art was the woodland glade: a context which does much to enhance the connotative effect of the rock art. It does not seem unreasonable to suggest that these clearings constituted substantial landscape features in their own right, enhancing the impact of the imagery in a manner analogous to the visual contradistinctions of flint mines, stone quarries and freshly cut earthen monuments (Edmonds 1995:59; Bradley 2000a:87). Forest clearings and natural openings, however, would have been common landscape features during the early Neolithic (Brown 1997:139, see also Groenman-van Waateringe 1983; Tolan-Smith 1996), part of a world view which involved practical engagement with the forest (Evans et al1999:241; Topping 1997:113). This implies that, rather than being a stage for the extraordinary, the clearing would have featured in the ordinary daily lives of Neolithic communities. This is not to suggest that Neolithic settlement was consistently located immediately adjacent to the rock carvings; indeed, the absence of material culture spreads in such locations would argue against such a correlation (but see above). What is significant about a clearing location is that it places the rock art in a locale whose physical characteristics and conceptual associations, if not the specific site itself, would have been intimately familiar to the people of the Neolithic as part of their day to day existence.

As well as being simultaneously familiar and unfamiliar, clearings evoke the exposure of forest 'edge' and the juxtaposition of very different landscapes. These are dynamic environments subject to regrowth and retreat with or without anthropomorphic involvement. Consequently, this edge is far from static; it shifts, merges and shifts again: transgressing, ameliorating and enhancing landscape difference through its essential fluidity (see Moore 1996; Simmons 1996; Brown 1997; Tipping 1996; Topping 1997; Thomas 1999a for discussions of the Mesolithic-Neolithic landscape). This suggests that the location of these engravings in clearings was not merely the product of accident or opportunism, but an evocation of further levels of recurrent connotative effect.

Moreover, as a consequence of their horizontal plane and clearing location, these images are likely to have become obscured by the accumulation of detritus, soil and subsequent flora regrowth. This is clearly demonstrated at the case study sites of Castleton and Kealduff (figure 2.9). The fluidity evoked by flora regrowth mirrors that inherent in the exposure of forest edge, suggesting that at intervals the rock art was of, or apart from, the forest. Further levels of connotative effect are apparent in the floral obscuration of rock imagery along the northern shores of Loch Tay. A number of carvings located by

RCAHMS in the early spring of 2001 could not be found at the height of summer when the annual phase of regrowth is at its peak. This is suggestive of a seasonal engagement with the imagery during spring, autumn or winter. It is significant that two of these seasons, spring and autumn, are liminal times of year, facilitating the passage from winter to summer or summer to winter, whilst simultaneously demarcating each: in effect, temporal periods of tergiversation. One can only surmise that location in a wooded environment would accelerate detritus accumulation, suggesting that regrowth and subsequence clearance played a significant role in the understanding of the rock art and the rites associated with it: performative displays of tergiversation analogous to the transgressions of surface and removal of debris encountered as part of the 'original' engraving (see chapter 6).

Figure 2.9: Flora regrowth at Kealduff.

The material attributes and associations of carving itself are suggestive of further connotative tergiversations most immediately expressed through the breaking of surface. More significantly, in his 1994 publication *The discrimination of rock markings*, Bednarik contends that "visual ambiguity is a fascinating, multifaceted subject for rock art students which has been inadequately explored". Whereas Bednarik is concerned to discriminate between the artificial (art) and the natural, to preserve the integrity of the database, when it comes to the rock art of the British Isles and Ireland such discrimination is not only unnecessary but actively misleading. Carving is applied to the rock face in a manner which does not 'detract' from the outcrop itself. The imagery fits within the existing order of the surface in a "veneration" of the outcrop that complements its natural 'aesthetics' (Waddington 1996:159-60, 1998:46) and liberates the "forms which adhere in the uncut stone" (see Gell 1998:30). At Dod Law, for example, the composition of the imagery pays careful attention to the zoning of the rock created by a series of natural cracks and steps. Similar patterns are observed at Achnabreck (Beckensall 1999:20-5). More intimate associations are seen in imagery which emphasises existing surface features or incorporates natural irregularities into composition (see Buckley 1992:21; Shee 1968:145; Beckensall 1998:8; Beckensall & Frodsham 1998:51). At the sites of Chatton Park, Weetwood and Amerside Law (Northumberland), for example, natural basins are enlarged and long radials attached (Beckensall 1999:26). Similarly at Ballingloughan, Tankards Rock and Drumgonnelly (Louth) solution holes form the central cup-mark around which concentric rings are arranged (Clarke 1982; Buckley & Sweetman 1991:84; Johnston 1989:70). Both suggest a

17

particularly local take on more widely manifest practices, a pattern repeated in case study analysis.

Frodsham (1996:130) suggests that the intimate relationship between carved and natural markings results from a copying and elaboration of natural prototypes. The same argument is used by Steinbring and Lanteigne (1991:23) to account for the world wide distribution of visually similar carvings. To account for the presence of rock art as a simple copying of the natural world, however, is not satisfactory (see chapter 1). Alternatively, Bradley (1997a:158) suggests that natural markings may well have been understood as the remains of older carvings whose significance was renewed through the application of 'fresh' art. There is some merit to this idea but, given the propensity for connotative tergiversation evident in the material associations of the art, it is perhaps more satisfactory to suggest that amongst this body of art the ambiguity created by the juxtaposition of natural and artificial surface markings was integral to meaning, an active and intentional device which deliberately resists categorisation. Coomasaharn 3 suggests that this connotative relationship was very specifically worked out. The natural markings incorporated into this panel did not suggest the overall form of the design; rather they have been deployed in a manner which intentionally brings spatially 'distant' motifs into the composition. It is the link, the interconnection and physical transgression which is implicated by this use of natural 'imagery'. Similar concerns appear to be at work at Cairnbaan West (figure 2.10).

Figure 2.10: Cairnbann West. The use of natural surface features is indicated by dashed lines.

From the subtle juxtapositions of image content, through topographical correlates and on to national distribution, the core connotative concept of tergiversation is repeated throughout the corpus. Case study analysis further reveals how these components were manipulated to connote peculiar effect and idiosyncratic roles for particular images within this wider connotative saliency.

2.8 Case study analysis and the specificity of connoted effect

Despite the range of common characteristics, the practice of rock carving in the British Isles and Ireland is far from stereotypical. Each carving demonstrates a specificity of spectrum focus in which connotative components are

differentially balanced. Although the presence of each case study site is acknowledged through the use of distribution maps, attention is focussed on those sites which expand understandings of the connotative matrix. Consequently, the presentation of data gives the opening pages of this section a rather descriptive feel. As discussion develops, however, further levels of recurrent patterning are revealed and the argument takes a more coherent analytical direction. As such, the remainder of this chapter is not about constructing specific interpretations, but instead extends the range of observations from which interpretation can be derived (see chapter 6).

2.8i Kealduff and Coomasaharn: The rock art of the Inveragh Peninsula, southwest Ireland

Rock carving on the Inveragh Peninsula makes up the greatest concentration of landscape imagery in Ireland (figure 2.17). The peninsula, measuring 60 by 30 kilometres, is characterised by a number of mountain ranges, orientated northeast-southwest, and intervening valley systems which extend to an indented coastline (O'Sullivan & Sheehan 1993:75, 1996:1-9). The art is primarily found on boulder-strewn peaty slopes and ridges located in valley headlands: an area embodying the connotative characteristics of the intermediate zone. Although many areas are devoid of imagery, the rock art represents the predominant archaeological feature of the peninsula, consisting of 119 panels from 43 locales (O'Sullivan & Sheehan 1996:78-97).

Figure 2.11: The Behy Valley, Inveragh.

The sites of Kealduff and the adjacent townland of Coomasaharn are located on either side of the Behy valley's southwestern headland (figures 2.11 and 2.12). A small lake and a number of streams lie between the two concentrations of imagery. To the south, east and west, the valley is contained by a horseshoe of high, sharply rising mountains, but open towards Dingle bay in the northeast, the most obvious point of access to the valley. Weather patterns are highly localised, alternating in a matter of minutes, although fore-warning is given by the skyline over Teermoyle mountain to the southwest.

18

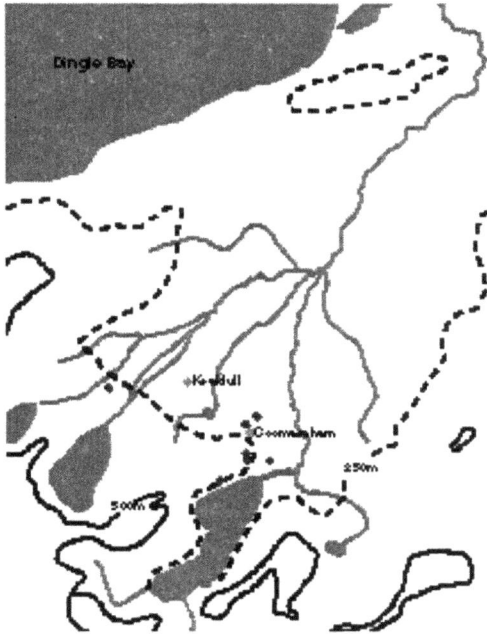

Figure 2.12: This distribution of rock art at Kealduff and Coomasaharn.

Figure 2.14: Kealduff 3.

height of the stone is greater than the horizontal carved surface. Kealduff 6, for example, consists of a small table-like boulder, its horizontal surface exhibiting a single motif consisting of a central cup-mark, concentric circles and a meandering radial. Kealduff 7, by contrast, consists of a large sloping boulder with highly eroded, loosely pecked imagery virtually invisible even in oblique sun light.

The Kealduff complex is composed of a cluster of 17 petroglyphs arranged on, and around, a prominent rocky ridge which forms the northeast edge of a stoney plateau (figure 2.13). Towards its southwestern extreme the ridge rises gently and seamlessly 'flows' into the plateau above. The plateau is also the driest area of the valley, draining through the ridge on to the lower lying ground below. As the ridge swings towards the north its gradient sharply increases, forming a 'cliff' face that runs south-west to north-east before abruptly terminating. Interestingly, this orientation mimics that of the peninsula's dominant valley and mountain systems. With the exception of Kealduff cliff (see below) this is the most prominent topographical feature of the valley headland.

Figure 2.13: The Kealduff ridge (indicated by out-cropping rock in the mid-ground).

Three instances of carving are located on the valley floor below the plateau. The most visible of these, Kealduff 3, positioned at the foot of the ridge, is clearly part of this larger feature. Indeed, this engraving resembles those of the ridge in both materiality and motif characterisation (figure 2.14). The remaining lowland sites are located in close proximity to each other, some distance to the north-east of the 'cliff' face. These sites are significantly different from those of the ridge itself. Although of differing dimensions, in both cases the vertical

Almost every exposed outcrop associated with this ridge has been carved. This distribution, the absence of imagery on the plateau above and highly discriminatory engraving of rocks on the plain below suggest that the ridge itself was identified as appropriate for ornamentation: clear evidence of cultural selection (but see chapter 6). All the engravings associated with this ridge are immediately accessible, particularly when approached from the south-south-west, from the mountains to the ridge crest. From the north and northeast access is more difficult. This, however, is the only direction from which it is possible to enter the valley and, as such, is probably the 'accepted' direction of approach. Although from this side the ridge is at its most imposing, most of the art is not immediately visible. Rather it is set a little way back towards the plateau. It is only on its more gently sloping areas that carving is integrated with the 'facade' of the ridge, a pattern which is repeated in all case studies. Consequently, almost all the imagery remains hidden when approached from the northeast until the ridge has been climbed. As such, movement around and over the ridge is an integral part of experiencing the art, a physical transgression of the topographical and conceptual connotations of tergiversation which reiterates the significance of location and is implicated in the rites performed at these carving sites (see chapter 6).

19

Figure 2.15: Kealduff 2.

Figure 2.17: The enclosed, grouped cup-marks of Kealduff 1.

All the carvings at Kealduff present unusual features, either in terms of the motifs depicted or the techniques employed. As noted above, Kealduff 7, for example, is composed from a series of individual peck-marks, similar in technique to Kealduff 5, the vertical section of Coomasaharn 3, and in technique and content to Kealduff 2. At both Kealduff 2 and Coomasaharn 3 (figure 2.15) these areas of loose pecking appear on the rock surface below motifs executed in the more typical manner, occupying atypical 'vertical' surfaces and performing a 'linking' function. A similar picture arises with regard to Kealduff 5. Although no variation in surface gradient is apparent in this latter example, the loose pecking again acts as an inferential 'link' between adjacent panels carved in the more typical technique. Image content is also suggestive of connotative convergence and interconnection, once again emphasising a peculiarly local preoccupation with the cruciform.

The cruciform motifs of Kealduff 3, 5 and 8 are unique amongst the rock art of Ireland and the British Isles. In no sense, however, are all three identical. Each exhibits a different number of arms and associated arcs. The precision inherent in their organisation, general shape and restricted distribution do, however, mark them as a single type: perhaps the work of an individual artist or the manipulation of a highly specific meaning in an equally specific place. Regardless of questions of specific meaning, this imagery again signals the significance of the ridge area: a significance enhanced by the idiosyncrasy evident in the gapped spirals of Kealduff 3 (see O'Sullivan & Sheehan 1993:81) and grouped cups of Kealduff 1 (figures 2.16, 2.17). This multifaceted idiosyncrasy is not unique to Kealduff. The same pattern (but different motifs) is repeated at Mevagh in Donegal, a place of comparably distinctive topography (see Van Hoek 1987:36).

Figure 2.16: The loosely pecked 'linking' cruciform motif of Kealduff 5.

Although situated only one kilometre to the southeast, the Coomasaharn 'complex' exhibits a striking difference to that of Kealduff. O'Sullivan and Sheehan (1996:81) identified fifteen rock art sites around the spur of Teermoyle Mountain, the northern face of which is demarcated by Kealduff cliff (as distinct from the ridge discussed above) (figure 2.18). Five carvings are located in the fields south of the spur, four on its crest and five along its northern base, whilst the one remaining site lies directly above Coomasaharn lake. This description gives the misleading impression of tight clustering. Unlike the Kealduff complex, beyond their loose association with the spur these sites do not centre on any specific topographical feature. The distribution of rock art around and over the spur does, however, present the 'viewer' with performative opportunities to evoke the tergiversation of the setting. This requires extended time and effort, and as such lacks the immediacy of Kealduff. The focus of connoted paradox, therefore, is physically more diffuse. Moreover, it is over the mountain associated with this spur that the highly changeable weather, characteristic of this area - with its own connotations of transgression and fluidity, enters the valley.

Figure 2.18: Kealduff Cliff (background).

Within this distribution, the group of four engravings identified by O'Sullivan and Sheehan along the crest of the spur presents something of an anomaly. Coomasaharn 1, for example, is located on a pronounced hogsback rock with strong inferences of verticality. The same directionality is evident in the earthfast of Coomasaharn 3, and placement of Coomasaharn 2 amongst a cluster of large 'upstanding' rocks. In all three instances, atypical materiality in the vertical plane is juxtaposed against the similarly atypical 'flat' micro-topography of the spur crest, and the creation of difference appears to override concerns with alleviation. To the west, Kealduff cliff rises above the rock art, suggesting explanation for the 'anomalous' materiality of these carved outcrops. All of these sites 'extend' the alignment of

Kealduff cliff to the east. This is not a precise relationship but one which implies a continuation of connoted verticality along the crest of the spur: an impression enhanced by the predominance of linear motifs and meandering radials which 'follow' the rocks' vertical axis (figure 2.19).

Figure 2.19: the 'vertical' radials of Coomasaharn 1.

Direction of viewing reinforces these connotations of verticality. The imagery of Coomasaharn 1 and Coomasaharn 2 is concentrated on the southern slope of the rock. To view these motifs one must look towards the north, over the concentration of imagery deployed along Kealduff ridge and to the mountains beyond. Significantly, although tree cover may have once obscured the ridge it would also have concealed plain and plateau. As such, direct allusion is made to the mountain top, an allusion which hides the reality of the landscape. Landscape - and image - concealment, and allusion to elevated topography are recurrent features of a number of case study sites. Like the engravings located along the spur crest of Teermoyle mountain, where this occurs it is almost invariably accompanied by a sense of imbalance in the central construct of tergiversation. The placement of art on the upper and north-facing surfaces of Coomasaharn 3, however, appears to argue against a recurrent correlation between spur crest and northern mountains at this particular site. The direction of viewing this imagery, however, retains allusion to the dominating presence of Kealduff cliff, the mountains beyond and prevailing weather patterns.

2.8ii   Glen Lochay, Perthshire

Glen Lochay is one of three Scottish case study sites located in relatively close proximity to each other (figure 2.20). The rock art of this study area is distributed along the narrow valley of the river Lochay, which flows from west to east into the western end of Loch Tay. A number of tributaries run north-south and south-north from the mountains into the river. The topography of the valley ranges from a flat central plain, through a narrow band of gently rising foothills before abruptly ascending into steep mountains. Rock carving is found on the farm lands of Tullich (Glen Lochay 1), Corrycharmaig (Glen Lochay 2) and Duncroisk (Glen Lochay 3-6), as one proceeds from west to east, occupying the first two topographical zones described above (figure 2.21).

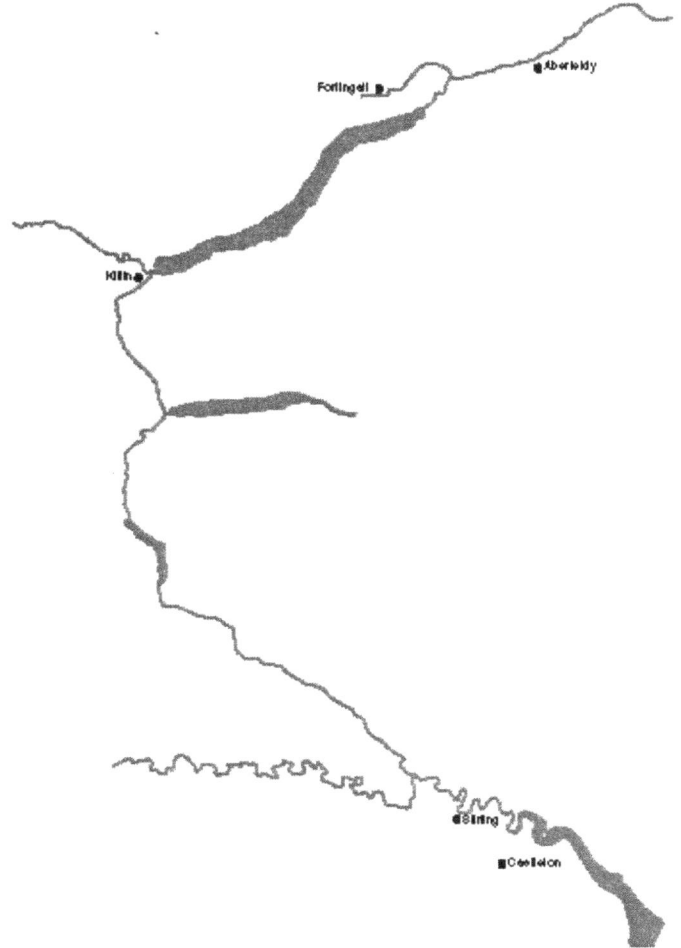

Figure 2.20: The distribution of Scottish Case study sites.

Figure 2.21: The distribution of rock art in the Lochay Valley.

Glen Lochay 2, situated to the south of the river, is the first site of notable interest. This site is located immediately behind the crest of the uppermost incline in a series of foothills which lead up from the river before the steep ascent to the mountains begins. Walking from the valley floor towards the higher ground, the intervening hillocks obscure that on which the engravings are located until the preceding one is crested (figure 2.22).

Figure 2.22: The approach to Glen Lochay 2.

In effect, the hill on which the rock art is located is camouflaged by the prevailing topography in a manner that recalls the intermixing of carved and uncarved surfaces at many sites. Within this setting the imagery is difficult to locate, not only is it set back from the hill crest but it is positioned on three flat outcrops barely discernible from the surface of the foothill (figure 2.23). The tension between concealment and revelation is enhanced by close association between these panels and the prominent outcrop discussed above.

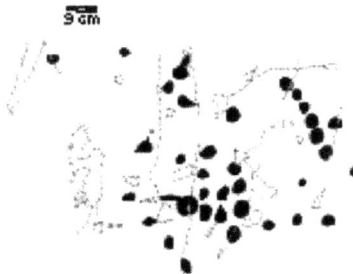

Figure 2.23: Glen Lochay 2.

In the elevated location of this site one can detect the same concern with mountain 'top' topography evident at Coomasaharn: a connotative value further enhanced by a direction of viewing which immediately takes in the mountains above. [The preferred direction of viewing is contrived by the relationship between rock art and local topography. That is, each site is most effectively visually consumed when stood in a particular topographical position relative to the art. It most be remembered, however, that there are many ways of consuming the imagery beyond the limitations of the static eye (see below, chapter 6)]. An elevated view is particularly significant in Glen Lochay as it makes allusion to the topographical zone in which the axe factory of Creg na Caillich is located (see chapters 4, 5 and 6 for an interpretative account of the recurrent association between rock carving and stone extraction sites).

Further east, Glen Lochay 3 is located. This outcrop is situated in the middle zone of lower foothills to the north of the river.

The landscape below the carving gently descends to the river plain whilst that above rises gently until the rapid ascent to the mountains begins. Located 50 metres east of Duncroisk Burn, a small tributary runs over the western edge of the outcrop: an unusually direct association with water, but one which in many ways is comparable to Glen Lochay 5. At one time the imagery of this site appears to have been quite spectacular and significantly out of character with the rest of the valley. Unfortunately erosion has taken its toll. Cormack (1949-50:171) noted four cross rings amongst other more 'typical' motifs during the 1940s. In 1981 Morris (p.58) found only three, but also noted a further seven rings, some of which may have contained crosses, and a series of grooves forming what he describes as an "arrowhead". By the summer of 2000 the surface was highly abraded: only one cross-ring and a single cup with ring were found, and then only visible in the oblique sunlight of late evening (2.24).

Figure 2.24: The surviving imagery at Glen Lochay 3.

The local idiosyncrasies of this site may be accounted for by its unusually direct relationship with water. This would also explain the semi-elaborate imagery of Glen Lochay 5 (see below). [The same line of reasoning can be applied to the occasional carving of vertical surfaces encountered throughout national distribution. These surfaces should be distinguished from those discussed above in that they constitute actual cliff faces which are often directly associated with the watercourse. The art applied to these cliffs is commonly highly elaborate and idiosyncratic.] Returning to the current case study, the micro-topographical characteristics of site 3 suggest a comparable direction of viewing to Glen Lochay 2, only on this occasion it is the northern skyline to which attention is directed (figure 2.25). In so doing the site inferentially conjoins the connotative values of river and mountain top, whilst location in a wooded environment would again conceal significant portions of the landscape and enhance the power of allusion.

East again, Glen Lochay 5 occupies the centre of the flat valley plain where the river meanders south before returning to its easterly course. The art is deployed along a schist and turf ridge that runs for 130 metres along a east-north-east west-south-west axis (figure 2.26), the north-eastern terminal abruptly halting at the river. The northern side of the ridge fades into an earthen bank which in turn gently moulds into the flat plain behind. The south face, however, forms a 'cliff' of exposed rock, reaching a height of up to three metres. Again the imagery is set a little way back from this cliff edge. Although regrowth may account for the absence of art at the eastern end of the ridge - indeed, the ridge itself appears to be separated into a series of rock panels, divided by patches of earth and grass - it is significant that the further east one moves along the ridge - and its elevation decreases towards the river - the closer the imagery is deployed to the cliff edge: striking a tenuous balance between image placement, topographical gradient and water (figure 2.27).

Figure 2.25: Views to the mountains from Glen Lochay 3.

Figure 2.26: The carved ridge of Glen Lochay 5.

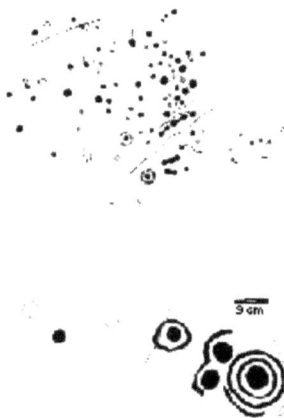

Figure 2.27: Image 'panels' from Glen Lochay 5.

2.8iii   Loch Tay, Perthshire

Loch Tay is a vast expanse of water orientated along a south-west north-east axis. The river Lochay enters to the west and the Tay exits to the east. The southern shoreline is composed by a narrow level terrace behind which the rapid ascent to the mountains immediately begins. Little in the way of rock art is found in this area. North of the loch, the land rises gently towards a road which occupies a narrow shelf approximately half a mile from the shore. Above this a band of steep sided foothills dominates the landscape, from which mountains abruptly ascend to the skyline (figure 2.28). Rock carving is plentiful both sides of the road.

Below the road, rock art is largely confined to a series of massive rocky outcrops which typify the landscape immediately adjacent to the shore. The carvings north of the road appear as a number of discrete clusters. Proceeding from west to east, image concentrations are found on the farmlands of Edramucky, Tombreck, Craggantoul, Cragganester and Shenlarich, between which a consistent spread of 'isolated' petroglyphs, usually composed of between one and three cup-marks, are found amongst a great many uncarved surfaces. These sites are located on Milton Morenish, Machuim and Ben Lawers farmlands. The higher one proceeds into the foothills the less dense the concentrations of imagery become, although both the exclusively cup-marked rocks which dominate the local repertoire and more ornate deployments extend distribution to extraordinarily high altitudes on the lower slopes of the mountains.

The foothills north of the Loch contain a number of false peaks which, by obscuring the high ground further north, create the false impression that, like the southern shore, the rise to the mountains begins immediately from the river terrace. Many engravings hold some form of relationship with these false crests, creating an 'optical illusion' which may account for the anomalous distribution of rock imagery into the highlands (e.g. Shenlarich and Ben Lawers); that is, the unusual location of these panels is naturalised by the encroachment of 'mountains' into the foothills (see figure 2.29 below). The Ordinance Survey indicates a continuation of carving east beyond where the recent RCHMAS (2001) survey, and this case study, terminate at Shenlarich. The eastern end of the Loch (Kenmore) is marked by two impressive hills, Drummond to the north and Creag an Fhudair to the south, landscape features which again bring the mountains and their associated imagery close to the water's edge. Beyond this, Bradley's (1997a) case study of Strath Tay begins.

The concentration of six engravings on the farmland of Tombreck replicates many of the topographical associations discussed above. These carvings are located in the lowest extremities of the foothills, immediately situating them in an

23

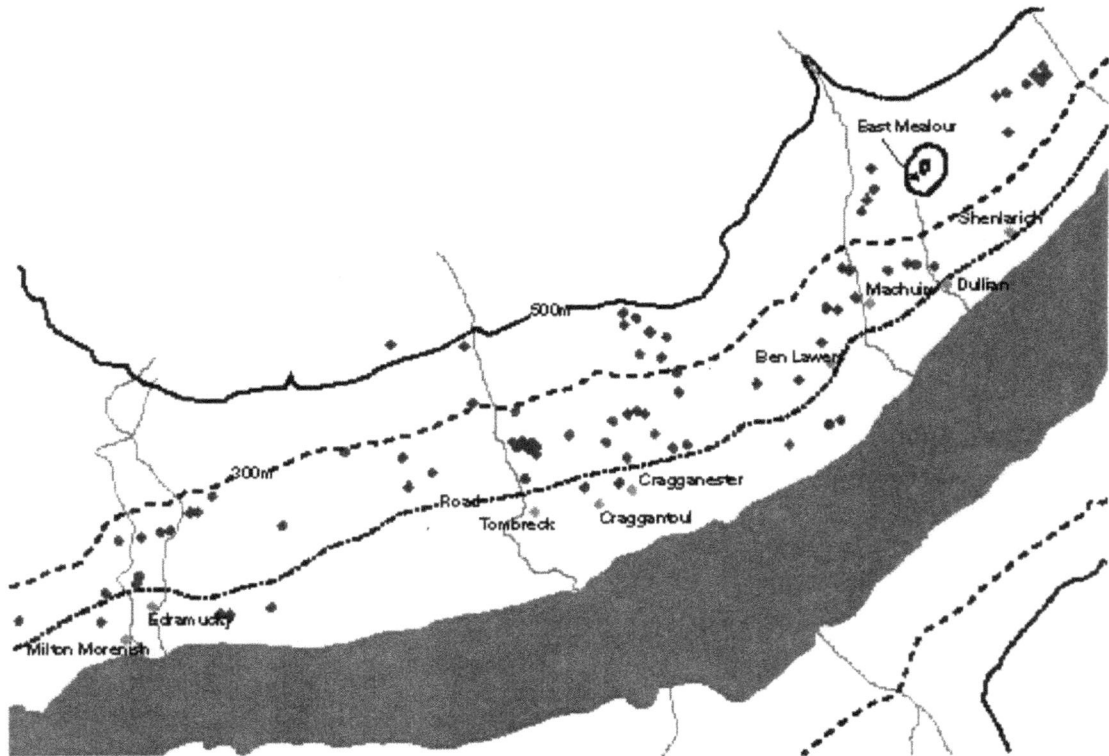

Figure 2.28: The distribution of rock art along the northern shore of Loch Tay.

intermediate zone at the junction of hill and shelf. Within this they are directly, and very specifically, associated with more minor undulations in topography. Surfaces 1 - 3 form an almost straight line southwest to northeast over a low knoll located on the southern face of the first bank of foothills. This arrangement connotes a very specific transgression of topography within the wider context of the particular hill and the broader connotations of the valley system. The same pattern is repeated a few metres to the southeast, where sites 4 and 5 demonstrate the same southwest-northeast alignment over a second low knoll. In both instances, the range of imagery is restricted to the cup-marking which dominates the local repertoire.

The single carved rock at Duallin exhibits a series of very specific connotative relationships. Today this 15 cup-marked rock forms part of a clearance cairn, but appears to be a 'genuine' earthfast around which the rest of the cairn has been constructed. Indeed, the specificity inherent in its topographical relationships supports the identification of original location. This engraving is found at the junction of the valley floor and East Mealour, the most prominent 'false' mountain of the valley (figure 2.29).

When viewed from the position of the rock art this false crest obscures the 'true' mountains to the north, but a few metres to either side the mountains return to view. As such, as one walks towards the imagery an 'optical illusion' occurs in which landscape appears to be transformed. Analogous to the performative engagements of Kealduff and Glen Lochay 5,

physical movement is again integral to effect. On this occasion, however, 'movement' is exercised by both viewer and landscape. Standing with one's back to East Mealour and looking south over the imagery brings further topographical juxtapositions into the engravings connotative matrix. Not only does the view take in the vast watery expanse of the Loch but also the mouth of a valley located on the southern shore (figure 2.30).

Figure 2.29: Duallin (foreground), East Mealour (background)

Indeed, a perfectly straight line connects all three features, recalling the transgressive alignments of Tombreck. One must also consider the issue of tree cover and the obscuration of landscape. In this context, the valley would appear as a 'disembodied' gap in the southern horizon, the fluidity of effect enhanced by the presence/absence of the connotative power of

24

water. Unsurprisingly, solution hollows and natural cracks feature prominently in this panels imagery.

Figure 2.30: The valley south of Duallin.

The rock art at Edramucky is distributed over a series of increasingly elevated shelves with intervening steep inclines. These shelves stand in marked contrast to the band of foothills which characterise the rest of the northern shore. Side 'boundaries' are imposed on this area by the presence of broad fast-flowing rivers frequently manifest as waterfalls. This topography suggests that these sites would be approached from south to north, climbing from the valley floor towards the mountains, access to east and west curtailed by rivers and their deep ravines, and by mountains to the north. Access to these sites is, therefore difficult, requiring the incline between each shelf to be traversed. As such, the thinning of vegetation occasioned by these outcrops would not only evoke the connotative values of the clearing but also recall 'viewers' ascent of the intervening inclines: again uniting the physical, connotative and performative.

Edramucky 1 is located on a prominent boulder, set back from the crest of the first shelf above the road. Despite its large flat top surface, the cup-marks which make up its decoration are deployed on a narrow shelf halfway up the south-facing vertical surface, locating them in a position which and immediately recalls the local character of the local landscape. The low rectangular outcrop of Edramucky 2, approximately one metre wide with a long axis of over three metres, connotes affinity with the landscape through the orientation of its horizontal plane, an impression reinforced by the imagery itself (see figure 2.31).

Northwards from Edramucky 2 the landscape appears to rise steadily into the mountains. This impression, however, is produced by the presence of a false crest created by the southern edge of the terrace above. Behind this crest a deep basin is concealed. Edramucky 3 is located in the area between terrace edge and the basin. While the 'optical illusion' provided by the crest recalls the observations made for East Mealour, on this occasion the basin provides a further level of significance, echoing the southerly descent to the loch below: a reference

which would be enhanced by periodic flooding. The orientation of the outcrop and linear deployment of imagery appear to repeat the landscape relationships of site 2. Image composition, however, is very different, consisting of a series of cup-marks located along the pointed top of this hogsback outcrop. When viewed from a height adjacent to its crest, this rock takes on an almost crenellated appearance, 'mimicking' the southern skyline at a comparable 'scale'. The impact of a wooded landscape and restricted view are not as applicable to this site as others, given that this engraving is located in the fringes of the contemporary tree line whilst the abrupt descent of the incline to the south raises the shelf edge above the canopy below. At this site allusion is again made to the mountain tops, and the foreground concealed through the interaction of rock art and deceptive landscape.

Figure 2.31: The east-west alignment of imagery at Edramucky 2.

Below the road, the engravings of Cragganester and Craggantoul are found. Analogous to the hillocks of Glen Lochay 2, these sites are composed of, and camouflaged by, the massive outcrops typical of this location. More specific connotative values, however, are evoked by their vast size. When viewed from North to south Cragganester appears as a vast rock and turf ridge measuring some 200 metres from west to east, 30 metres in width and five to eight metres in height. The southern face of this outcrop is comprised of a vast imposing cliff which plummets over 15 metres to the flood plain below (figure 2.32).

Figure 2.32: The massive ridge system at Cragganester seen north-to-south.

Craggantoul, although significantly smaller in size (100 metres long and three metres high) shares much with the former site (figure 2.33). Both these outcrops provide an expansive field of view analogous to that obtained from the mountains. This, accompanied by the impression of great height, suggests a deliberate allusion linking the rocky masses of these huge outcrops to the surrounding mountain tops.

Figure 2.33: The large outcrop of Craggantoul.

Placement of the imagery in a wooded environment would curtail the connotations of view afforded by Craggantoul, but in such circumstances this outcrop would create a massive interruption in the forest canopy. The connotations of this clearing would remain comparable to those encountered elsewhere but, because of the impression of height, are more suggestive of the upper tree line than lowland openings in the canopy. Over 100 cup-marks cluster around the summit of this outcrop, again allowing for performative enactments of tergiversation whilst extenuating the allusion of height (figure 2.34).

Figure 2.34: The cup-marked summit of Craggantoul.

Tree cover effects subtlety different associational connotations at Cragganester. To the rear (north), visual reference to the mountains would have been obscured, suggesting some degree of affinity with the foothills 'behind' and their extensive

deployments of rock art. The height of the south-facing cliff, however, raises the ridge crest above the southern tree line, maintaining an open aspect in this direction. From the position of the imagery, however, these southerly views are obscured by the rising outcrop. Consequently, the top of this rocky protrusion is directly juxtaposed against the conjoining of mountain top and skyline along the southern shore of Loch Tay (figure 2.35), once again evoking familiar connotations of landscape presence / absence.

Figure 2.35: Views south over Loch Tay.

2.8iv   Castleton, Larnarkshire

Castleton Farm is located seven miles southeast of Stirling, between the villages of Cowie, Throsk and Plean. Situated in the centre of a low gently undulating plain, this site contrasts markedly with the other case studies. Micro-topographic characteristics and the connotative interactions of these apparently anomalous landscape features, however, demonstrate a clear resonance with many of the patterns discussed above. All but one of the sites identified by Morris (1981:44-50) (Castleton 1, 3-6) are deployed on long turf and rock ridges which rise abruptly, up to seven metres in height, from the crest of plateau undulations: a marked extenuation of the prevailing topography. Recalling the relationship between imagery and geology north of the Tay, amelioration and contradistinction are evident in the local concentration of these ridges. They stand apart from the landscape but are also camouflaged by their local commonality. Moreover, each carving is set back from the crest of its appropriate cliff face so that, although the location of each is clearly signposted by the imposing topography of intra-ridge outcropping (figure 2.36), when looking towards the cliff face the imagery remains invisible. To view the art itself it is necessary to climb the outcrop. With the exception of Castleton 3, whose outcrop is 'stepped', this is impossible from the cliff side. Again, however, it is a simple matter to walk around the ridge and approach from the direction in which the earth bank fades into the plain. When accessed from this direction, however, it is difficult to distinguish the outcrop on which the motifs are carved, reiterating the subtle interplay of advertisement and concealment which has a direct bearing on image consumption and rite (see chapter 6).

26

Figure 2.35: *The intra-ridge outcropping at Castleton.*

2.9 A polysemous context?

The rock art of the British Isles and Ireland has be shown to constitute a coherent unit of analysis; not only in its separation from the other rock carving traditions of early agricultural Europe, but also in its salient manifestation of a particular connotative effect. The 'effect' of each site is centred around the paradoxical concept of tergiversation: a construct evoked through the vacillatory balancing of a common range of connotative devices, including:

- The interaction of rock art materiality and a range of topographical - and micro-topographical - associations.
- A dynamic, ever-shifting interaction with the forest.
- A paradoxical convergence of advertisement and concealment manifest in: the intermixing of carved and uncarved surfaces, the placement of imagery behind the crest of rocky ridges, the juxtaposition of inconspicuous carvings against prominent outcrops, the camouflaging effects of neighbouring micro-topography and so on.
- A 'preferred' direction of viewing which juxtaposes rock art against mountain top, effecting significant landscape obscuration and presence / absence relationships.
- A range of performative movements which encourage a shift in the immediate effect of, and means of engagement with, the imagery.
- The juxtaposition of art and natural surface markings, and the linking role played by the latter.

As well as effecting particular forms of material engagement, there is evidence to suggest that the manner in which these values are balanced influences image content. For example, distinctive ridge systems frequently demonstrate locally elaborate / idiosyncratic imagery, whereas imagery applied to surfaces which are camouflaged by the prevailing topography exhibit an image range which is consistent with the locally dominant repertoire. As demonstrated above and in chapter 6, however, micro-topographical relationships and performative engagements suggest that the combination of distinctive topography and relative image 'complexity' serves to imbue ridge imagery with the same degree of ambiguity inherent in the comparatively 'simple' marking of more typical surfaces. Consequently, the cup-marking of Craggantoul can - in many ways - be considered as idiosyncratic as the cruciforms of Kealduff, and the cruciforms of Kealduff as typical as the cup-marking of Craggantoul. Moreover, this differential balance not only allows specific sites to connote their own particular meanings and become the focus of peculiarly local rites, but also allows for meaning - and associated rites - to change over time. If the spectrum of effect is as pervasive and as flexible as analysis of the rock art suggests then it appears likely that it should, in someway, also be manifest in the monuments of the Neolithic. It is these monuments that constitute the focus of analysis in chapter 3.

CHAPTER THREE

Spectrum saliency
Connoted effect and the monuments of the British and Irish Neolithic

Exploration of the effect connoted by a range of Neolithic monuments demonstrates the widespread saliency of the polysemous spectrum identified in the preceding chapter. This saliency is connoted through a series of strategies which 'redeploy' the primary material devices of the rock art through architecture. Investigation of successive levels of focus and resolution, reveals a widely held world-view, the construction of monument 'classes' and the 'meaning' of specific sites.

3.1   Introduction

There is no absolute sense in which any given work can be seen, either as a recapitulation of a previous work, or as a precursor of a future one; the ensemble of an artist's works, strung out in time, constitutes a dynamic, unstable entity; not the mere accumulation of datable artefacts (Gell 1998:242).

Analysis of the material characteristics of the rock art of the British Isles and Ireland, and the landscapes associated with it demonstrates the existence of a highly pervasive connotative spectrum of effect. In the preceding two chapters, it has been suggested that the recurrent manifestation of this spectrum, through a range of specifically local devices, hints at a world-view which, given its apparent pervasiveness, should be detected throughout the architecture of the Neolithic. This chapter is specifically concerned with the morphological forms and topographical associations of monuments which lack an immediate relationship with the decorative strategies of the Neolithic. Once again, the concern is with the materiality of connoted effect and the construction of penumbral understandings, through which to assess specific routes to focus. Inevitably, this involves a re-evaluation of traditional morphological classifications and established interpretations of the use-life and inter-relationships of Neolithic monuments.

The chronological range of this enquiry, from the first Neolithic to the early Bronze Age, may appear to over-reach the accepted chronology for this body of art (but see Evans 1998; Waddington 1998). There is, however, in the deposition of carved items and strategies of image redeployment, a significant amount of circumstantial evidence to support this range of enquiry (see figure 3.1). Indeed, the compatibility of spectrum connotation with monuments of this time-frame suggests that this is an appropriate temporal context, whilst demonstrable shifts in monumental focus over time bring about greater chronological resolution (see also chapter 5). Consequently, concerns over chronology do not replicate the interpretative impasse identified in chapter 1, but constitute a further avenue of constraining 'context'.

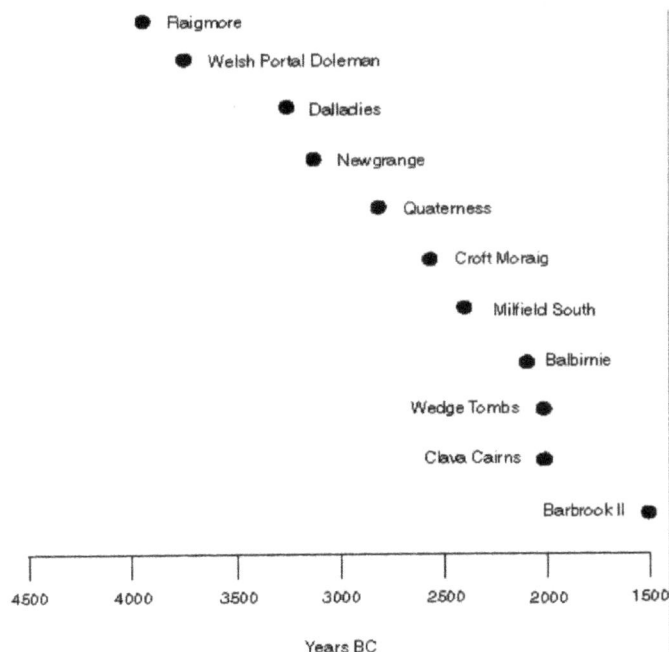

Figure 3.1: The chronology of redeployed rock art in the British Isles and Ireland.

3.2   The *power-full* allure of procession

In recent years, interpretations that seek to explore how Neolithic monuments were experienced have done so through emphasising the significance of formalised movement, choreographed procession, and the sectional organisation of space, people and knowledge (see, for example, Tilley 1994; Edmonds 1995:125; Thomas 1992, 1999a:52; Harding 1997). The pervasiveness of these interpretations, is attributable to a sophisticated theoretical underpinning, developed from the phenomenological philosophers, which provides the archaeologist with a method of recounting worldly experience (Fleming 1999:119; Brophy 2000:45). Moreover, monuments do, by their very nature, influence the ways in which space can be experienced.

The 'first' monuments of the Neolithic - causewayed enclosures and long mounds - are widely believed to occupy the margins of the prehistoric landscape, located in clearings at the beginnings and ends of paths (Barrett 1994:93; Tilley

28

1994:159; Woodward 2000:50). Within this interpretative scheme, the concentric structure of the causewayed enclosures is thought to emphasise depth of passage and the manipulation of sectional interests (Bradley 1998a:72; Thomas 1999:58). The emphasis on processional movement is retained in the 'second' generation of monuments; only now, this is accompanied by suggestions of a greater proscription and more overt power relations. Last (1999:90), for example, speaking of the Eynesbury cursus, contends that this monument channelled people towards the facade of a pre-existing barrow (see especially Tilley 1994). Timber avenues at Durrington Walls and Ogden Down (Gibson 1998:84), amongst others, and multiple entrances at a number of other monuments (Waddington 1999:161), draw the henges into this interpretative framework (figure 3.2).

Figure 3.2: Henges as pathways (after Waddington 1999 with modifications).

Rock art was first introduced to this processional scheme through the passage tombs of Ireland. Fraser (cited in Woodward 2000), for example, suggests that the open spaces between the tombs at Loughcrew provided an arena for public gathering, for which ascent from the encircling plain was necessary. Speaking of the same collection of monuments, Thomas (1992) ascribes movement between tombs to the distribution of imagery within them, arguing that it was only a few individuals, with access to the deepest parts of all structures, who were fully able to engage with and interpret the art. It is not surprising, therefore, that the most influential interpretation of the rock art in recent times also adopts the themes of paths, procession and movement. Bradley (1997a:120-4), borrowing heavily from the themes of inter-visibility and the proscription of movement prevalent in archaeological phenomenology, contends that rock art distribution corresponds to well-established route-ways, directing a dispersed population towards major ceremonial

complexes where rituals of exclusion were performed. This interpretative scheme brings a distinct linearity to these proposed processional movements (figure 3.3), at the expense of less proscribed motion patterns and fields of view (but see Waddington 1996:157, for example), and perpetuates implicit social-evolutionary arguments of increasing levels of social sanction and sectionalism over time. Monumentality, in this context, becomes a technology of control (McMann 1994:533; Scarre 1998:181), and power is restricted to the possession of a few: the rest rendered mindless and bereft of choice (Bruck 1998:32-4). As such, power becomes an objectivist discourse, applied from the top down, the complex interplay of manipulation and emancipation is ignored (Gosden 1994:143-6).

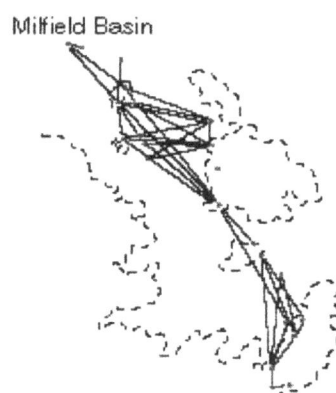

Milfield Basin

Figure 3.3: Patterns of rock art intervisibility approaching the Milfield Basin (after Bradley 1997a with modifications).

It is not just theoretical critique, but archaeological evidence, which suggests formalised procession is often interpretatively restrictive. For example, it is not necessary to see the location of causewayed enclosures as marginal. In conception, at least, the clearings in which they are located have been shown to be fundamental to the daily existence of Neolithic communities: a concept removing the impetus to interpret these places as the end/start points of route-ways traversed only in exceptional circumstances. Similarly, many linear monuments were constructed as a series of "stuttering addition[s] to a monumental statement", suggesting the repetition of small-scale effort (Barclay et al 1998:111-2). Within this segmented structure, each section was often neatly finished, which, in addition to fluctuations in scale and alignment, suggests an attempt to emphasise the separation of constructional events. Although this does not preclude future re-use as such, this construction technique argues against a primary use-life as a processional route-way.

Procession may well have played a part in the use-life of these monuments. This, however, is likely to have been only one particular manifestation of practice, not an interpretation of meaning and significance in its own right. Consideration of the structural embodiment of the connotative spectrum identified for the petroglyphs suggests alternative interpretations of the evidence for a number of different monument types.

3.3 The causewayed enclosures

The relationship between the causewayed enclosures and the landscape is as diverse as that noted for the rock art. Unlike the rock art - and although the majority of these monuments occupy a lowland position (Pryor 2001:112) - these enclosures are found throughout all landscape zones: the consistent relationship between rock carving and 'intermediate zone' is absent with regard to any recurrent topographical correlate. Alongside this apparent diversity, however, these monuments connote a range of salient relationships which not only allow for their analysis as a 'class', but also demonstrate a pronounced affinity with the spectrum of effect engendered by the rock art.

Located in the expansive chalk downlands of Wiltshire, the Windmill Hill causewayed enclosure forms an integral component of the Avebury landscape. Like many upland enclosures this monument is offset from the hill summit (Pryor 2001:138), causing it to sit "uncomfortably" in its topographical setting (Oswald et al 2001:61). Although the offsetting of this monument in someways recalls the relationship between imagery and ridge crest, to describe this relationship as uncomfortable immediately appears to run contrary to the topographical 'blending' characteristic of many rock art sites. When one considers how this relationship is materially played out, however, many of these upland enclosures take on a very different appearance. At Windmill Hill - and Trundle, for example - the outer circuit of the monument dramatically plunges down the hillside (Oswald et al 2001:64 & 103), evoking a simultaneous overcoming and evoking of topographical contrast. As such, rather than the subtle inference of tergiversation evoked by the rock art, a more pronounced expression, reminiscent of the source-to-sea movements of the river (see chapter 2), is encountered at these sites.

Other upland sites, such as the triangular enclosures of Knap Hill and Dronegore Hill (Oswald et al 2001:61-4; Sheridan 2001:174), or the irregular promontory of Bryn Celli Wen (Thomas 2001:133), respect the counters of the local landscape: suggesting a paradoxical balance of extenuation and alleviation familiar from the material blending of the rock carvings. Although there is some debate as to the exact nature of their classification, upland enclosures constructed of stone connote comparable effect.

The enclosure at Gardom's Edge (Derbyshire), for example, is positioned on a gritstone scarp located on the eastern side Derwent valley. Situated on highest part of shelf, between the scarps two principal water courses (Ainsworth & Barnatt 1998:

7; Barnatt et al 2001:111 - 122), the enclosure is defined by a discontinuous rubble bank which ranges from between 5 - 10 m in width and up to 1.5 m in height. The enclosure exhibits regular changes in form in response to the immediate topography: a low bank where the slope provides elevation, and a heighten bank where the land outside is flat (Ainsworth & Barnatt 1998: 9-15; Barnatt et al 2001:112-9). As such, the morphology of this monument suggests that the variation of form was deliberately entertained to 'ameliorate' inconsistency in the relationship between monument and topography and retain the paradoxical balance of tergiversation. Within this sense of balance, the incorporation of earthfast blocks in the perimeter of this monument - particularly at the southern and northern terminals - suggests a more immediate symbiosis with local topography. In this context, it may be more than coincidence that this monument is closely associated with four instances of rock carving (see Ainsworth & Barnatt 1998:16-7).

Returning to the more common earthen enclosures, it is often suggested that the clearing location and the monument would have stood in dramatic contrasted to the surrounding landscape (e.g. Edmonds 1993:102, 1995:68, 1997:108). This interpretation of the clearing has already critiqued and, instead, posited as paradoxical convergence of the physically liminal and the conceptually familiar. It is also possible to re-evaluate the appearance of the monument within this setting. Although these earthworks may have appeared 'at odds' with their landscape immediately after digging, this effect is likely to have been short lived (Brophy 2000:52). This is of particular significance for monuments that exhibit more than one circuit. Approximately two-thirds of all causewayed enclosures are comprised by more than one circuit. Windmill Hill, for example, exhibits three concentric circuits; the outer circuit - enclosing 8.5 ha - takes the form of a segmented bank and ditch, the middle circuit pit and ditch segments, and the innermost an oval ditch (Pollard & Reynolds 2002:46). Oswald (et al 2001:67) suggests that it is unlikely that each circuit was contemporaneous, whilst Pryor (2001:151) positions a number a generations between episodes of excavation: a much greater length of time than the 10 or so years which separate the road protests of Tywford and the now grass-covered scar through the South Downs which contains the M3 (figure 3.4). Consequently, the digging of secondary circuits may have been undertaken as the addition of supplements to artificial features of 'natural' appearance. At one level, this practice can be interpreted as an attempt to re-evoke the structural ambiguity and paradox inherent in the monument. At another more specific scale, it suggests that the fluidity espoused by this paradox was also manifest in the reclaiming of these structures by the processes of nature, recalling the accumulation of detritus in the horizontal carvings of the rock art. Amongst these monuments, however, rather than reiterating the fluidity of balance through the removal of these accumulations, the digging of additional ditches was adopted.

Figure 3.4: The M3 through Twyford, Hampshire.

The nature of the relationship between the successive circuits of these monuments is most succinctly clarified through reference to the Loughcrew passage tombs and the megaliths of Bodmin Moor. McMann (1994) notes a contrast between the proud hilltops which house the Loughcrew cemetery and the geomorphological conformity of the cairns themselves. These 'artificial' mounds are positioned on the knolls and subtle rises which surmount the hilltop: in effect, continuing and extending the volume of these natural landforms. This is an arrangement which ameliorates and softens cultural intrusions, promoting a fluid interrelationship that echoes as much as alters the landscape (figure 3.5).

Figure 3.5: The Loughcrew cairns in their hilltop location.

Similar interrelationships are at work on Bodmin Moor, an example selected because of the attention given to this area by two prominent scholars. Both Tilley (1996) and Bradley (1998c) explore the intimate relationship between the moor's megalithic tombs and its granite tors. Citing comparable form and an alignment of monuments towards major tors, Tilley suggests a relationship between cultural monuments and natural outcrops which "indicates a new ideological concern - to

stabilize a cultural relationship with significant features of the topography by freezing them in time - [a] cultural triumph over the sleeping powers of the rocks" (Tilley 1996:175). Although the emphasis placed upon an active enculturation of a passive nature is reminiscent of his wider rather evolutionary scheme - which progresses from the veneration of natural features to purely cultural monuments, as power is accumulated through the appropriation of topography during the early Neolithic (see Tilley 1994) - Tilley's account does suggest that these monuments are again 'camouflaged' by the landscape, evoking a sense of 'landscape harmony' (see also Field 1998; Tilley 1994; Richards 1996b; Nash 1997a; Cooney & Grogan 1998; Waddington 1999; Vyner 2000). As such, both tombs and tors connote comparable effect, yet each shifts the focus of the penumbra, and, although each monument appears 'incognito', it is at the same time incongruous in its landscape. In one sense, the tors and the monuments are one and the same. This marks the tombs of this area as different from any other. In another sense, the monuments hold wider affinities with other architectural manifestations, distancing them from the tors.

Developing his argument, Tilley suggests a recurrent juxtaposition of tors and cairns alongside natural boundaries comprised by streams and bogs. This is consistent with his wider observation that "[n]atural boundaries in the landscape ... always seem to have been important in defining the margins of sacred spaces" (Tilley 1996:174). The postulation of margins and isolated sacred spaces may be problematic, but the contradictory connotative properties of the boundary itself suggest that this was a place of significant transgression, where landscape could become monument, and vice versa. In this context, the material values of the boundary suggest that division - be it topographical, monumental or conceptual - could be overcome and manipulated whilst remaining evident.

A large number of causewayed enclosures exhibit intimate relationships with 'boundaries' of comparable effect to those found on Bodmin Moor. The enclosure at Windmill Hill, for example, lies in close proximity to the source of River Kennet and numerous scarp edge springs (Pollard & Reynolds 2002:46). More consistent, and revealing, evidence, however, comes from the monument at Etton (Cambridgeshire). Etton is one of three definite - alongside Uffington and Barholm - and two probable - Etton II and Northbourgh - causewayed enclosures found within a five kilometre radius of the village of Maxey. With the exception of Uffington, which lies on the side of a valley, all these enclosures are associated with slight rises in the river Welland's flood plain (Oswald et al 2001:60, 109-10).

The enclosure at Etton is positioned at the edge of low rise which abuts a stream channel located in a meander of river Welland: adjacent to higher, dry land of Maxey Island (Pryor 2001:134). By virtue of this position, Pryor (2001:138) suggests that to enter the monument it was necessary to ford the stream:

31

to physically, and performatively, cross the conceptual fluidity of the watercourse. [Similarly, the enclosures at Mavesyn Ridware and Fornham Allsaints, for example, lie adjacent to major rivers, whilst those at Sawbridgeworth (Hertfordshire), Buckland and Broadwell (Oxfordshire), and Dorney (Buckinghamshire), incorporate rivers into their structure (Oswald et al 2001:67)]. Eighty metres northwest of the primary monument, two crescent-shaped bank and ditch arrangements are located either side of a further stream (Oswald et al 2001:130). This arrangement acts to enhance the concentricity of this monument through the provision of 'extra' circuits, which, although of different physical appearance, convey the 'same' conceptual connotations of tergiversation inherent in the morphology of the monument (see below).

Throughout much of its use-life the ditches at Etton periodically held water and the interior was subject to regular flooding (Oswald et al 2001:94). Indeed, by the time the enclosure was 'abandoned' (3500 BC) much of the monument was permanently water logged (Pryor 1998:20, 2001:153). This accumulation of water finds analogy in the retention of rainfall and detritus in the horizontal carvings of the rock art. Darvill and Thomas (2001:16) suggest that such flooding served to tie the enclosures to the elemental forces and seasonal cycles of the cosmos. The postulation of elemental forces may be somewhat problematic (see chapter 1), but it is easier to accept that periodic flooding *did* connect these places to understandings of the wider world: to at times conjoin, and at other times separate, the monument from the myriad of associations conveyed by the river. Moreover, evaporation and drainage would 'soon' return the enclosures to their 'dry' state, evoking a transience which again enhances connotations of fluidity, ambiguity and transgression.

In chapter 2 it was suggested that in progressing from source to sea, rivers simultaneously overcome and evoke topographical contrast. Nowhere is this more apparent than at the source itself, where the very surface of the earth is transgressed by this contradictory medium. Consequently, it is not surprising to find a number of enclosures, such as Blackshouse Burn in Lancashire (Barclay 2001:146), encircling important springs. The rivers, which arose from the transgressive effects of the source, pass through the circuits of the enclosure, producing specifically local evocations of effect.

The enhancement of entrances through earthworks or material deposits, coupled to the provision of multiple causeways, at many enclosure sites suggests that these monuments were imbued with multiple connotations of permeability. The offset alignment of banks and ditches, and the provision of timber palisades (see Kinnes 1985:29; Cooney & Grogan 1994:50), however, simultaneously enhances the solidity of the monuments' circumference, supporting Thomas' (1996b:3) suggestion that the principal effect of architecture was to

introduce discontinuity into social space. The dual nature of the enclosures - as both boundary and threshold - creates an ambiguous functionality which allows Pryor (quoted in Oswald et al 2001:41) to conclude that they "enclose, yet at the same time do so with manifest and calculated inefficiency". This suggests that the causewayed enclosures created a permeable and flexible 'barrier' within the pre-existing, fluctuating and accessible edge of the clearing (figure 3.6), through which performative displays of desirable 'inefficiency' could be enacted.

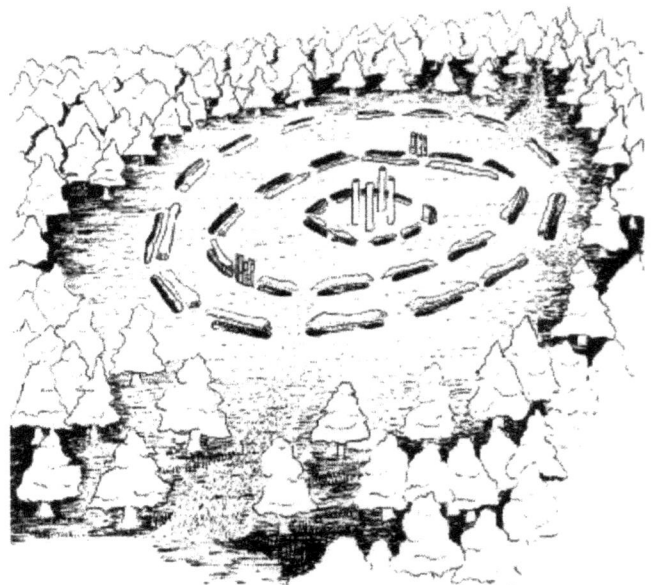

Figure 3.6: The causewayed enclosure in its clearing location (drawn by Netty Galvin).

As well as providing an obstacle to movement, the erection of timber palisades evokes the materiality of forest edge. Significantly, these structures find further analogy in the incorporation of uncleared patches of woodland, or hedging, within the circuits of a number of enclosures (see Oswald et al 2001:61). At Etton, for example, hedging took the form of coppice stools; 5000 pieces of coppiced wood were recovered from the western ditch alongside evidence for woodworking - a broken axe haft, for example - and worked antler (Pryor 1998: xix, 21, 66). As such, it was not only the connotations of the forest that were brought to bear in the materiality of this monument, but also those of the human activities undertaken there. Moreover, the recovery of bones from several thousand animals, 20,000 pottery sherds, 1000 flints, knapping debris, worked chalk and antler, disarticulated human remains and so on at Windmill Hill (see Pollard & Reynolds 2002) suggests comparable practices. The presence of these artefacts, coupled to their former functionality and biography (see Edmonds 1993; Bradley 1998a; Thomas 1999a; Pryor 2001), suggests that the whole spectrum of Neolithic life - from economy to cosmology

- was brought together at these sites in a 'tergiversation' of practice. In this context, it is significant that a number of enclosures, including Crofton in Wiltshire (Oswald et al 2001:97), 'enclose' the confluence of rivers. As such, monument construction marks these areas as places where the connotative values of spatially disparate - but probably named and well known - places were combined and manipulated through architecture (see sections 3.4, 3.5; chapter 4).

3.4   The Cursus Monuments

Many of the connotative associations discussed in relation to the causewayed enclosures, also appear amongst the cursus monuments. These monuments, for example, continue to be deployed in a landscape of shifting clearings and fluid vegetation. They are also composed of causewayed banks and ditches, and demonstrate a particular relationship with natural landscape forms (see Bradley & Chambers 1988:274; Barclay & Hey 1999:31; Brophy 1999:6; Harding 1999:31). In their pronounced linearity, however, these monuments are markedly different to the causewayed enclosures. Commonly, cursus monuments occupy areas relatively flat topography (Barclay & Hey 1999:72). They are also, however, found in areas of more variable relief. It is in these latter monuments that the first clues to the connotative focus of these constructions is found.

The Dorset cursus runs for almost 10 km across the prevailing ridge and valley system of Cranbourne Chase, following, throughout much of its length, the spring line (Barrett et al 1991:10). The chase itself is roughly rectangular, stretching for some 30 km along a southwest-northeast access, and cross-cut by a series of deep coombes. To the south, the chalk is broken by a number of small streams and the headwaters of the rivers Allen and Crane (Tilley 1994:143; figure 3.7). This area of undulating downland is 'bordered' by the rivers Stour, Nadder and Avon, which inturn are juxtaposed against the broken chalk plateau, with its precipitous scarp edges and more gentle dip-slopes (Tilley 1994:143-9; Johnston 1999:42; figure 3.8). The cursus consists of two parallel banks with external ditches, linked at the two terminals by cross banks and external ditches. In fact, this monument is comprised by two self-contained structures; the first running from Thickthorn Down to Bottlebush Down, and the second from Bottlebush to Martin Down (Barrett et al 1991: 36; Tilley 1994:170).

The Dorset cursus was constructed in a predominantly wooded environment with restricted open areas; indeed, mollusc analysis suggest that, within a few hundred metres, the monument passed from open down land into forest (Barrett et al 1991:18; Tilley 1994:149), crossing and re-crossing the fluid boundary of woodland edge. A similar picture emerges from the concentration of cursus monuments at Rudston (Yorkshire). Three of the four monuments found at Rudston cut across the side and floor of their valley location, whilst the fourth re-

ascends the high ground opposite (figure 3.8). Each of these monuments in turn bisects, or 'terminates' at, Gypsey Race in close proximity to a prominent easterly meander (Woodward 2000: 96-7).

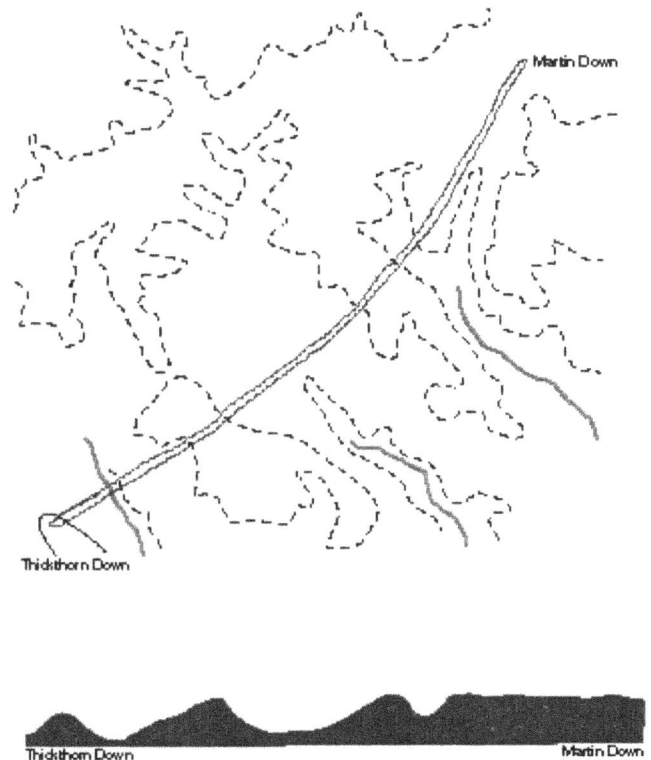

Figure 3.7: *The Dorset Cursus (after Tilley 1994 with modifications).*

The relationship between these monuments and their immediate topography suggest that rather than seeing the cursus as creating a division in a flat landscape - operating as an obstacle to free movement - it may be more profitable to consider it as integrating perceptually different topographical zones (Harding & Barclay 1999:5-8). The manner in which many monuments cross-cut the prevailing topography, however, immediate recalls the connotative associations of the river as it moves from source to sea. In this context, despite its location in an area of relatively flat relief, the monument at Dorchester on Thames takes on many of the connotations evoked by both the Dorset and Rudston cursuses. This monument aligns itself with the west-to-east flow of the Thames (Bradley & Chambers 1988:274; Barclay & Hey 1999:73), not only locating it in an area of topographical contradistinction, but also suggesting that monuments whose long axis follows the direction of water flow may be understood as direct emulations of the watercourse. Indeed, Brophy (1999b) suggests that the cursus monuments as a class can be understood as symbolic rivers: an interpretation that periodic flooding and water retention - as seen at Astonupon-Trent, Drayton and North Stoke (Brophy 2000:52), for example - supports.

Figure 3.8: The Rudston Cursus monuments (after Woodward 2000 with modifications).

The monument / landscape relationships evident at Dorchester on Thames, however, suggest that more specific interpretations of the relationship between cursus and water can be constructed. The northwestern terminal of this monument once abutted a significant tributary of the Thames, whilst its opposing end was located inland. This not only enhances the topographical contrasts embraced by the monument, but also perpendicularly conjoins architecture and watercourse. The orientation of the Drybridge cursus, Ayrshire (Brophy 2000:50) and the four monuments at Rudston, suggests that this perpendicular juxtaposition held a widespread currency amongst this monument type (see also Last 1999:92). As such, rather than simply being a symbolic river, the conjoining of monument and water effects connotations of confluence (see 3.3). The same affectation is encountered at the Dorset cursus where the monument crosses the river Allen. Significantly, in this instance the cursus bisects the river in close proximity to its spring head (Green 2000:58), evoking not only connotations of confluence, but also those of source. The commonality of

connoted confluence suggests that it is the linking role of the cursus that is most significant, its ability to conjoin and manipulate the meanings of geographically diverse places at a single location: an interpretation enhanced by the conjoining of two such linking monuments on Cranborne Chase.

The cursus, however, is more than a symbolic river, more than an affectation of confluence. The ways in which it is more than a river, however, lie beyond the realms of topographical connotation. The cursus does not appear in a virgin landscape (Barclay & Hey 1999:70; Johnston 1999:43), and many preexisting monuments are physically incorporated in its structure (Harding & Barclay 1999:5). Harding (1999:36-7) suggests that in forming an interlinking "chain complex" the cursus operated as a means to disguise fundamental disharmonies in social structure through the creation of symbolic integration. Although this interpretation may smack of the "all roads lead to social solidarity" (Lewis-Willams 1982:430-1) stance of the functionalists, it is far more than this: but, at the same time, not enough. Rather, "the curious layout [of the cursus monuments] is best understood as an attempt to link existing features together in a single design" (Bradley & Chambers 1988:285; see also Last 1999:90), establishing direct, and specific, links which "pull together individual monuments to form an integrated landscape" (Gosden 1994:160). At Dorset, for example, at least nine long barrows are drawn into close association with the cursus (Tilley 1994:172). Similarly, Pryor (2001:153-66) suggests that the course followed by the Maxey cursus - from the causewayed enclosure at Etton, across the stream belt and on to Maxey 'Island' (see 3.3) - served to conduct the power of Etton to the later monumental complex located on the higher ground of the 'island', following the 'abandonment' of the enclosure around 3500 BC. The juxtaposition of the connotative values of confluence against the integration of monuments of disparate temporal origin, suggests that the cursus effected a temporal transgression in which geography was deployed as an allegory for time. As such, rather than simply being a symbolic river, the cursus can perhaps be better understood as a river of time. Greater resolution is brought to this interpretation through consideration of the henge monuments.

3.5   The Henge Monuments

As a generic - and highly simplified - class (see Clare 1987; Barclay 1989) the henges can be considered roughly circular monuments defined by an internal ditch and external bank, broken by one to four entrances. Frequently, these monuments contain a range of internal wooden or stone settings: the latter commonly seen as superceding the former as part of a process of 'lithicisation' (see Pollard & Reynolds 2002: 88). Rather than concentrating on formal morphology, this discussion of the henges takes its point of departure from one of the most imaginative interpretations of these monuments produced in recent years: Colin Richards' 1996 *Henges and Water*. In this paper Richards (1996a) explores the significance the actual image and outward appearance of the henge monuments as cultural representations of the perceived world, investigating the importance of materiality and substance as part of the social construction of landscape (Richards 1996a: 314).

As the title of his paper suggests, Richards is primarily concerned with the relationship between henge monuments and water. Selecting from a range of case studies - including, the Orcadian henges of Brodgar and Stenness, the henge complex of the Milfield Basin and the six Thornborough henges - he explores the multifaceted ways in which these phenomenon are conjoined.

The location of the Orcadian henges - on two opposed narrow promontories that separate the lochs of Harray and Stenness - typify the topographical placement identified by Richards as characteristic of the henge monuments: a recurrent positioning in lowland locales in close proximity to water. Within such a location, a number of henges exhibit stone avenues which link the monument to watercourse (see Harding & Lee 1987:34; Richards 1996a; Darvill 1997a:195).

Extending his argument, Richards points to the disproportionately large size of the Thronborough ditches - measuring some 16 m wide and 2 m deep - and a lowland location susceptible to flooding, to suggest that these monuments were prone to waterlogging during the winter and spring months (Richards 1996: 331). The same line of reasoning is applied to both Brodgar and Stenness, whilst the clay ditch linings of Cairnpapple Hill and the Bull Ring, for example (Richards 1996a: 332; Cooney 2000:165), are interpreted as intentional architectural devices to aid water retention. As such, each of these monuments is encircled - for at least certain parts of the year - by standing water. There are also a number of instances where water is more 'immediately' applied as natural architecture. One side of the Marden henge, for example, is delimited by the river (Harding & Lee 1987:34).

In this context, although it is relatively common to suggest that the provision of more than one entrance suggests processional passage through the monument (Waddington 1999) (figure 3.2), it is significant that many henges with double causeways mimic the axis of river flow (Loveday 1997:18). This suggests a connection between the direction of water flow and the movement of people into the monuments: performative enactments of a potent symbolic agent (see also Richards 1996a: 313-23).

It is not just water, however, which plays a significant role in Richards account. Looking beyond the lochs of Harray and Stenness, Richards draws attention to the surrounding headlands to suggest that if the flooded ditches correspond to the surrounding lochs, then the external banks find allegory in the higher ground that encircles the water. As such, each monument is seen as manifesting a particular physical representation of local topography. This argument is brought to greater resolution by his interpretation of the six henges at Thornborough. In these monuments, Richards posits a direct correspondence between architecture and the natural world: an alignment which mimics the orientation of the valley, internal water-filled ditches - comparable to the rivers located northwest and southeast of these monuments - and external banks, which correspond to the range of hills beyond. In this context, the Orcadian henges, for example, are interpreted as embodying the sense of living in an island world (Richards 1996a:324).

Richards' account stands at the forefront of a series of recent interpretations which suggest that the henges should be understood as "a metaphor for the wider landscape" (Bradley 1998a:123; see also Darvill 1997a; Watson 2001, amongst others). It is to Watson's (2001:301) interpretation of the henge monument at Avebury that discussion now turns.

The great henge monument at Avebury is situated at the foot of Waden Hill on a slight saddle of Middle Chalk, adjacent to the river Winterbourne. The monument is roughly circular in shape and measures 420 m in diameter. The four entrances - located to the south-south-east, west-south-west, north-north-east and east-north-east - cut the monument into four unequal arcs. Even today the scale of the henge is imposing, the bank rising to a height of 4-6 m and the ditch measuring some 4-5 m deep. Excavation suggests, however, that these dimensions do not convey the full magnitude of this setting: the original depth of the ditch, for example, is thought to have measured some 10-14 m. Contained within this earthwork a ring of massive sarsen stones follow the inner perimeter of the ditch, encircling two inner circles located in the northern and southern quadrants. Each of these inner circles contains its own internal settings: the southern circle the now destroyed Obelisk and associated stone row, whilst the famous cove occupies the centre of the northern circle (Pollard & Reynolds 2002: 83-4).

Like many other interpretations (e.g. Pollard & Reynolds 2002: 81) Watson (2001) considers Avebury to be a circular monument occupying a circular landscape. For Watson, this is to evoke a complex interplay between monument and topography, in which the surrounding hills fulfilled the role of the bank in areas of the henge's interior where the latter is obscured from view by the internal topography of the monument. In so doing, this monument is said to embody "one of the most fundamental aesthetic qualities of the henge; a sense of enclosure" (Watson 2001:301). This sense of enclosure engenders interpretations which present the henge as space set apart: a world in itself, "remote from the landscape outside" (Bradley 1998a:127).

The interpretation of henge monuments as embodiments of the landscape presents a convincing collection of arguments, each of which is strengthened by demonstrating the flexibility of the central concept in response to specifically local conditions. There is one particular element of Richards' analysis, however, which suggests that interpretation should look beyond the enclosure of 'remote' areas of the landscape. In the concluding paragraphs of his paper, Richards' (1996: 333) draws parallels between the deposition of artefacts in the water-filled ditches of the henges and the more widespread Neolithic practice of placing artefacts in rivers and streams. This suggests that rather than seeing the henge as space set apart, the activities undertaken at these monuments deliberately reference the wider world in a manner analogous to the interpretation of the causewayed enclosures offer above. Exploration of the connotative effect of these monuments provides one means to follow up the implications of Richards' proposed parallel and rethink the interpretative schemes produced by landscape orientated studies.

Many of the features of the henge monuments discussed above offer a range of connotative devices through which to develop interpretation. It could be argued, for example, that the two causeways of the Ring of Broggar assume the same orientation as the neck of land on which the monument is situated (Richards 1996a: 325, 1996b: 325), evoking the familiar connotations of the intermediate zone and its juxtaposition against water. Similarly, the chalk ditches of Wessex henges would only effect a temporary retention of water (Richards 1996: 332), recalling the connotative transience of the causewayed enclosures and rock engravings. That it is structural tergiversation - rather than a straightforward relationship with water - which is significant, is further suggested by the successive setting of fires - a medium which echoes many of the transformative properties of water - in the ditch terminals of the Devils Quoits and Stanton Harcourt (see Loveday 1997), for example. Rather than simply listing all such features, the remainder of this chapter concentrates on developing a connotative interpretation for perhaps the two most famous henges of all: Avebury and Stonehenge.

Watson's (2001) interpretation of Avebury rests heavily on his proposed relationship between monumental bank and surrounding uplands. He suggests that movement between southern and eastern entrances effects a transformation in the visual appearance of the monument, in which the observer becomes unclear as to whether it is the monument or the landscape beyond they are looking at (see Watson 2001:301; figure 3.9). This serves to create an 'illusion' which exercises movement on behalf of both landscape and viewer, echoing the relationship between the rock art of Duallin and the false peak of East Mealour. Importantly, this movement also serves to connect the inner circles of the monument to the ring of sarsen stones which follow the internal perimeter of the ditch: two

different but materially analogous areas. Indeed, consideration of these sarsen settings suggests that it is possible to interpret the bank / upland relationship at Avebury in ways which overcome the evocation of enclosure.

Figure 3.9: *The bank / landscape relationship at Avebury.*

Sarsen stones are found across the downland and valleys of the Avebury area (Pollard & Reynolds 2002:14). These stones form an integral part of the landscape, attaining an ubiquity that makes their significance easy to ignore. Yet, it is this ubiquity - and the unworked appearance of the internal settings - that serves to 'integrate' the megaliths of the monument to the sarsen spreads of the wider landscape. As large blocks, the sarsens would appear as prominent, even named, features of clearings and woodland paths. Some of these stones, such as the cup-marked block from Totterdown, were deliberately marked. Others exhibit the deeply worn grooves of the polissoir: such stones are found amongst the megaliths of the henge and at the West Kennet long barrow (Pollard & Reynolds 2002:72). This suggests further analogy to both rock art and the monuments discussed above, in that, these monumental settings may be seen as a reworking of the 'natural' sarsen spreads of the landscape (see also Pollard & Reynolds 2002:96).

In this context it is significant that the positioning of the innermost circles on a slight internal ridge, affords the most far reaching views out of the henge from the greatest depths of the monument (see Watson 2001:306; Pollard & Reynolds 2002: 94). As noted above, however, to look out from this monument is not a passive exercise but one that involves an altered conception of landscape. Watson's interpretation of the bank / landscape relationship at Avebury finds clear resonance in Bradley's (1998a:116) suggestion that the large banks of many henges served to mask much of the surrounding landscape. In so doing, these monuments, and Avebury in particular, strongly connote verticality (see also Pollard & Reynolds 2002: 95). Taking this context of viewing into consideration, it is significant that it is not the sarsen spreads of the valley or the immediate hinterland with which the internal settings of the monument connote affinity, but those of the Marlborough Downs. As such, through the juxtaposition of bank and landscape, and the material analogies of the stone settings, this monument creates a 'foreshortened' field of view in that what is visible is set some distance away: linking the greatest depths of the monument to the visually distant and obscuring the immediate reality of the landscape.

This relationship is echoed in the megalithic avenues which served to connect the henge to other monuments in the Neolithic landscape. The West Kennet Avenue, for example, links the henge at Avebury to the timber and stone monument of the Sanctuary on Overton Hill. This second monument occupies the 'same' elevated and distant location evoked by the contrived views of the inner circles, reaffirming the significance inherent in the obscuration of the immediate hinterland. Unfortunately, the terminal of the Beckhampton Avenue remains unknown. To look out from the monument, however, it is first necessary to enter it. In this context, approach to the monument, along an avenue of 'foreign' sarsens would ensure that the vagaries of the immediate landscape would remain present, at the very least conspicuous in their 'absence': evoking the presence / absence connotations of many rock art sites.

Taken as a totality this analysis suggests that rather than implying enclosure, the recurrent 'integration' of these spatially distant zones suggests deliberate attempts to create a very particular kind of ambiguity in the relationship between henge and landscape: a lack of distinction which prompts consideration of the monument as belonging to the distant landscape. As such, Avebury cannot be considered an enclosed place set apart, but a monument that evokes connotations of far reaching penetration.

This discussion of Avebury has presented a rather broad brushed interpretation of the monument. A range of as yet unexcavated internal features - such as the possible existence of multiple timber circles suggested by geophysical survey or the crop-marked enclosure in the northwestern quadrant - suggest that many other factors were at work in creating the specific effect of this monument, whilst the pre-existence of an earlier enclosure suggests a reworking of significance over time (see Pollard & Reynolds 2002:88). Unfortunately, without further excavation, analysis of these features is problematic. Consideration of the more clearly defined temporal sequence at Stonehenge, however, allows greater resolution to be brought to this interpretation of the henges.

The earliest phase of construction at Stonehenge (3000-2900 BC) consisted of a causewayed enclosure with an external ditch, of approximately 60 segments, and internal bank. This impression of segmentation, however, obscures a perimeter of more 'continuous' form, containing only three formal entrances. A concentric palisade of large posts was erected along the

internal edge of the bank at this time. The second phase of activity (2900-2400 BC) witnessed substantial remodelling of the monument. Much of the ditch was in-filled, and the bank reduced in scale. To the north, a setting of 10 parallel rows of posts was erected across the causewayed ditch whilst, in the southern quadrant, two parallel lines of wooden uprights, interrupted by a substantial wooden 'screen', lead from a second entrance towards the centre of the monument. This central area was occupied by a considerable concentration of post holes, suggestive of a substantial timber circle (Bradley 1998a:92-96).

Darvill (1997a:181) interprets the post deployments of phase one as a particular embodiment of the wider landscape: the monumentalised equivalent of woodland (see also Woodward 2000:25). Support for this interpretation comes from Gibson's (1998:106) reconstruction of the timber circle at Sarn-y-Bryn-Caled. Without lintels, this monument loses much of its circularity. Consequently, although both the 'monumental' - the circle - and 'natural' - the forest - are apparent, the former is camouflaged through the 'embodiment' of the distant latter. Rather than seeing these posts as the monumentalising of woodland, it is more profitable to consider them as manifestations of the connotative values of the forest. In the first phase of Stonehenge, these levels of connotative significance are enhanced through the juxtaposition of the posts against the topographical tergiversations of the foothills: themselves manifest in the earthen bank of the monument (see also Darvill 1996a). This juxtaposition suggests that it is the distant upper tree-line which connotes effect within this monumental setting. As such, although the immediate environs of the landscape remain visible, as at Avebury, their presence is overcome by the creation of a connotative balance which moves the practices of this setting out into the distant landscape.

Something similar may have been at work in the second phase of this monument. The cluster of post-holes at the centre of Stonehenge, and the internal avenue with its associated screen, are parallelled at Durrington Walls, located some three kilometres to the north. In this convergence, Bradley (1998a:95) detects a concern to make Stonehenge more like these "new constructions", the 'true' henges, at the same time as the perimeter was being remodelled to create a similar effect. In the internal settings of many 'true' henges, paradox is again effected, in that, whereas plan and location emphasis accessibility and movement, the architecture connotes exclusion (see Loveday 1997:26). More consistent with the argument formulated above, however, the creation of facades and substantial concentrations of central posts effectively act as visual screens, obscuring views of the immediate hinterland from inside the monument (see Loveday 1997:15). As such, as the monument changed from 'causewayed enclosure' to henge, connotations of distant places were more strongly effected through visual mechanics than by material juxtaposition, at a

37

time when deforestation was rapidly extending the vista available from inside the monument.

For the nine hundred years which followed phase two, the stone deployments for which this monument is famous were erected and remodelled on at least five separate occasions (Bradley 1998a:96-7; figure 3.10). The first stone settings were comprised by Preseli bluestones (Bradley 2000a:94), imported from the spectacular landmarks and topographical tergiversations of southwestern Wales. The characteristics of this place of procurement were retained in the architecture of Stonehenge, through the exclusive deployment of different stone types. The most central setting, for example, was composed of spotted dolerite, a stone type which occupied a similarly central position in the Preseli Hills. Around this setting, other bluestone geologies were deployed, their positioning again corresponding with their distant topographical correlates. Moreover, the patterns of natural cleavage evident at the place of procurement were replicated in the 'vertical' architecture of the monument (Pryor 2001:96).

Figure 3.10: *Stonehenge as it appears today.*

Bradley (2000a:95-6) interprets this as the reconstruction of an entirely artificial world: a form of transported landscape. To transport a distant locale to a monumental setting is to recreate this landscape: a significant reversal of the outward directionality evident in phases one and two, and at Avebury. It is possible, however, to rework Bradley's transported landscape, to one transformed and inverted by its monumental conceptualisation. It is in this inversion that movement 'outwards' from these later phases at Stonehenge is again apparent.

In his interpretation of the henges, Richards (1996a: 315) likens the natural architecture of these monuments to the constitution of ritual practice, suggesting that this architecture brought together, and engendered the participation of, material elements within the physical context of ritual practice to symbolise destruction, transformation, rebirth and transcendency.

Moreover, in many small scale societies, the spirit world is believed to be "immanent, interdigitating with the real world" (Lewis-Williams 1997:327-8). This alternative realm runs parallel to experienced reality (Ouzman 1998:34), sustained by ideas of laterality and movement through a cosmos which was far from coherent (see Humphrey 1995). With specific regard to Stonehenge, the central arrangement of bluestones was eventually dwarfed and enveloped by massive sarsen settings. These sarsens were of more local origin: striking features of the upland Wessex landscape. These different stone types were never intermingled. Bradley (2000:92-5) interprets this exclusivity as the creation of a precarious balance between alien and local. Significantly, the sarsens remained 'outside' the bluestones, suggesting an inversion of their spatial reality and conceptual understandings of the real world. In so doing, they created a parallel realm which was both recognisable as, and yet distinctly different from, reality. That this balance was precarious suggests that this was not an absolute division, but rather something that could be overcome and transgressed. In this way, it became possible, physically and conceptually, to move between two very different worlds: from the everyday to the esoteric, and back again. In this context it is significant that it was the internal arrangements of bluestone which were repetitively taken down and remodelled, leaving the local stone in place (Bradley 2000a:94). This suggests that it was the world of the geographically alien, the spiritual, that was controlled, manipulated and accessed. As such, the henges can be understood as tools for entering alternative realms: movement facilitated through large-scale landscape illusions and performative devices, which incorporated a plethora of transgressive material correlates.

In this context, it is significant that the bluestones at Stonehenge were obtained from a high, windy location (Pryor 2001:96): a place analogous to the juncture between upper worldly tiers. Stonehenge, therefore, can be considered a place where multiple worlds interconnect, and movement between stone settings is understood as the equivalent of crossing the tiers of the universe. This suggests that the henge monuments were not a recreation of the physical landscape, but an embodiment of the spirit world: not space set apart, but a place which was simultaneously of the wider, real and metaphysical, world.

Although articulated through different media, all phases of Stonehenge connote the 'same' basic concern. Significantly, the two earliest wooden phases chronologically correspond to other Neolithic monuments which extend this concern beyond the henge class: most notably the Irish passage tombs (see chapter 4). The localised preoccupations of Stonehenge, however, suggest a longevity which runs counter to the cognitive adjustments evident in the spectrum of effect as the Neolithic became the Bronze Age (see chapter 5): a time corresponding to the stone deployments at this site. Significantly, however,

Pryor (2001:184) chronologically equates the remodelling of Stonehenge to the relocation of economic and political power, away from Salisbury Plain, to the Thames Valley. For Pryor, the stone settings of this monument are a retrograde step, a scheme to restore pride to an area fallen on hard times. The superfluous use of woodworking joints at this monument, and a number of structural convergences with known timber circles, suggests a similar backward reference, in that "Stonehenge has no parallels ... amongst the stone circle class, but in timber circles the architectural similarities are too close to ignore" (Gibson 1998:121; see also Whittle 1997; Parker-Pearson & Ramilisonina 1998). Without endorsing the existence of a Bronze Age public works scheme, it is perhaps this reference back to the past which accounts for the anomalous longevity and 'stability' of connoted effect at this monument. Consequently, these stone settings constitute a monumental manifestation of an earlier world view, presented in a more dramatic manner, with more powerful allusions to the obviously alien. Perhaps similar concerns with temporality are evident in the retention of views over Windmill Hill at Avebury (see Watson 2001).

The interpretation of the henges, in terms of optical illusion and allusion to the crossing of spiritual realms, finds resonance in a number of cursus monuments. Barclay and Hey (1999:72) suggest that the concern to incorporate areas of dramatic topographical change ensured that it was not possible to see the entire length of a number of cursus monuments, including Drayton and Dorset, from a single position of viewing. The same is true for the Stonehenge cursus where, although both terminals are inter-visible, the middle is 'lost'. In these 'missing' areas, monumental and temporal integration is absent until one changes position. Consequently, the missing sections of the monument become prominent: an obvious absence, which is resolved by passage into a different 'realm'. Given that the cursus monuments have been identified as a river of time, it is history which is lost, transgressed and altered amongst this monument type: a connotative effect which is supported through the consistent incorporation of monuments to the dead in their structure (see Pryor 2001:166).

3.6   The monumental spectrum

The recurrent manifestation of a readily identifiable polysemous spectrum throughout the monuments of the Neolithic suggests that there was a fundamental concern to connote the ambiguities and tergiversations of material paradox through architecture. The causewayed enclosures, for example, manifest these values in a fluid interrelationship between monument and clearing, and the tergiversation of practice; the cursus as a river of time, linking monuments of disparate temporal origin and the henges - through their relationships of illusion and allusion - as devices to facilitate entrance to, and the manipulation of, the spirit world. The ambiguity produced by this paradoxical construct, however, is in many ways misleading. Certainly, a shared penumbra brings a generalised 'unity', whilst a commonality of resolution allows for the identification of particular monument types. Within this, however, each monument exhibits its own peculiar balance of focus and penumbral associations, which gives individual sites their own specific effect. Retaining the interpretative focus of this section, subsequent chapters posit interpretations of the various decorated monuments of the Neolithic and early Bronze Age, through their particular manifestations of this spectrum and specific deployments of imagery: deployments which both extend the range of connotative effect and constrain the meaning of the rock art.

CHAPTER FOUR
Watery graves and high spirits
Rock art and the passage tombs of Ireland

Eion MacWhite's (1946) study of Irish rock art made popular the idea that strategies of carving landscape art and the deployment of imagery in the passage tombs of Ireland were distinctive phenomenon. More recently, and pointing back to studies completed before MacWhite's work, there is an established trajectory of research in which precedent for the open-air rock art is found in these same monuments. This research, however, has often been carried out in an uncritical manner which has lead to the erroneous transfer of an interpretative schemes developed for the passage tombs to landscape art. The presence of a common Neolithic spectrum of effect suggests that exploring the relationship between open-air rock art and that of the passage tombs is a profitable enterprise. This chapter examines the grounds on which comparisons can be made and how interpretation of the passage tombs can critically inform understandings of the open-air art.

4.1   Introduction

Though much of what is to be said ... is very uncertain ... [it] deserves as much credence as the early histories and stories of other nations Callary (1926:4) on the legend of Taillten and the Loughcrew cemetery.

only by contrasting the evidence for the different stages in the life history of a particular artefact ... can [we] begin to identify the thresholds across which they might have been engaged in quite different roles (Edmonds et al 1992:78).

Many archaeologists today accept that the conception of place embodies connotations of past, present and future, whilst artefacts are recognised as exhibiting biography. Unfortunately, the powerful image of absent origins remains subconsciously strong (Barrett 1999:21). Often, at most, the "birth and early childhood" of a monument are considered (Holtorf 1998:24). Rock art research displays a similar fixation with origin, abandonment and closure (see chapter 1; Helskog 1987:23; Sognnes 1996:16). These ideas are part of an archaeological tradition which continues to "privilege the date of creation over a chronology of appreciation" (Barrett 1999:22). The past is never dead and buried, never irrevocably over. Even when it comes to human life, Neolithic post-mortem treatment of the dead demonstrates that death and 'burial' did not mark the end of social interaction between the deceased and the living (see below; also Haley 1996; Thomas 1999b). The materiality of the rock art gives it great longevity, the durability of stone making them an integral component in the constitution of landscape for a considerable period of time. It makes little sense, therefore, to consider the art as only active at a single date. As a locale is "rethought and remodelled, so the possibilities of human involvement ... [are] ... transformed" (Kirk 1997:60). The same is true for rock art, where each deployment is contingent upon

previous deployments and their accumulated histories. Given the looseness of the chronology, analysis of such change appears to be beyond the reach of British and Irish rock art research. Dowson (1998a:85 cf his 1994 paper), however, demonstrates how it is possible "to write a new kind of history" for imagery "for which we have no reliable dates". Consequently, it is not only possible to explore how the past was deployed in a changing present (Bradley 1998a:91) but also how the present was deployed in relation to a changing past.

The clearest evidence of historical change in the trajectory of British and Irish rock carving is found in the redeployment[4] of imagery, in monuments of a Neolithic or early Bronze Age date. The valley system immediately north of Loch Tay, for example, contains a significant concentration of monuments centred around the village of Fortingall (see also chapter 5). Amongst these, is what appears to be a long cairn with an eastward projecting turf and stone segmented bank: a structure Henshall (1970:31) interprets as "comparable with the very much larger bank barrows of Wessex". A short distance east of the cairn, a single domed boulder, with a row of cup-marks along its 'spine', is located (figure 4.1). This boulder occupies the top of a low mound, which, at some point in the past, had a continuous circular enclosure constructed around its summit. The 'tail' of the cairn halts at the enclosure edge (see also Walker & Ritchie 1987:175). Coles' (1909-10) account of this barrow notes the presence of a cup-marked monolith in a trench to the east of the cairn: a monolith which local knowledge suggested once stood on the summit of the cairn itself. This

---

4

Redeployment refers to the subsequent inclusion of quarried rock art in monumental structures, and presupposes a primary use life in the carving of living rock. It is favoured over reuse because of attendant social connotations (see Evans & Dowson 2003).

monolith could not be located during field investigation. Whether it is the stone currently positioned on the mound to the east is unclear, as Coles' account presents neither detailed description nor diagram. Regardless of the specifics of this association, there appears to be some kind of relationship between this monolith and the nearby cairn: a relationship more intimately expressed in another Scottish long mound.

Figure 4.1: The 'long barrow' at Fortingall (in mid-ground, seen from tail to 'facade').

Figure 4.2: The cup-marked boulder associated with the Fortingall barrow.

For a number of years, Dalladies has held fame within British rock art research for containing the oldest dated petroglyph. Although the discovery of the Raigmore pit slab has pushed the dating of this rock art back from 3390 BC (Henshall 1970:32; Piggott 1971-2:44, 1973; Ritchie & Ritchie 1981:72) to 4000-3750 BC (Ashmore 1996:31), Dalladies is still perceived as little more than a chronological indicator. Evidence from Fortingall, and the recurrent cup-marking of the Welsh portal dolmen, however, suggests that associations between earlier Neolithic funerary monuments and the most standardised expressions of the rock art repertoire may be more widespread

than hitherto recognised. The redeployment of carved imagery amongst these monument 'types' remains rare, however. For example, although contemporary with, and morphologically comparable to, Dalladies, the barrow at Lochhill revealed no carved rock on excavation (see Masters 1973; Piggott 1973:34; Ritchie & Ritchie 1981:32), whilst the double spiral and concentric rings recovered from the long barrow site at Lilburn (Northumberland) (Burgess 1990:167; Beckensall 1999:130), and the idiosyncratic imagery of Old Parks (Cumbria) (Frodsham 1989:15; Beckensall 1999:15), suggest that too great an emphasis should not be placed on the standardised repertoire range. These latter two sites, however, are part of specifically local redeployment strategies, and more anomalous to the national picture than they appear here (see chapter 5). In contrast to the rather ambiguous evidence from these long barrows and portal dolmans, the passage tombs of Ireland provide a wider range of evidence for the interpretation of Neolithic image redeployment. In turn, analysis of these patterns opens up the possibility of exploring the relationship between landscape and passage tomb art in a critical manner.

4.2   Landscape art and the passage tomb: A single tradition or separate strategies?

The presence of decorated stones in both an open-air context and in association with the architecture of the passage tombs has led to the production of numerous interpretations which attempt to conjoin these two phenomena. Anati (1963:14), for example, contends that a convergence between these decorative repertoires is "undoubted". More sophisticated in his analysis, Bradley (1995c:109) suggests that the common ground held between these artistic trajectories is "not in any dispute", elsewhere elaborating that "rock art is almost the only medium that links the archaeology of the monuments to the study of the prehistoric landscape" (Bradley 1995d:9). These schemes are often accompanied by a chronological assumption that the art of the passage tombs predates that of the open air, the former providing inspiration for the latter (Fett & Fett 1979:77; Shee-Twohig 1981:11; Bradley 1997a; but see chapter 1). Support for this chronological trajectory is often sought in the petroglyphs of Achnabreck. The motifs of this vast outcrop sheet are deployed in two distinct zones: a series of double spirals clustered at the 'top' of the panel, with the more 'typical' cup-and-ring repertoire dispersed below. It is the spiral motifs that show the greatest evidence of weathering, prompting suggestions of two phases of carving with the cup-and-ring motifs applied after those 'inspired' by the passage tombs (Morris 1970-1:43; Frodsham 1996:115; Bradley 1997a:64-5; figure 4.3). Given the propensity for protective regrowth at many open-air rock art sites, however, interpretations derived from differential weathering should be treated with care.

41

Figure 4.3: The double-spirals at Achnabreck.

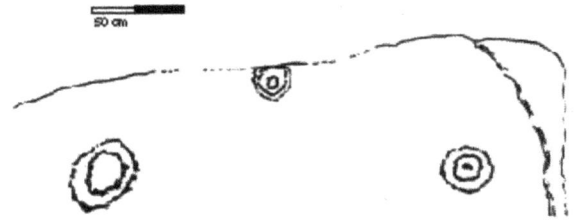

Figure 4.4: Newgrange kerb 17 (after O'Kelly 1982).

Unsurprisingly, the opposing view also circulates through the literature. These interpretations contend that "the ornamental repertoire" of the open-air art is "quite distinct from that of passage grave art" (Davidson 1950:40; see also MacWhite 1946:59-60; Walker 1977:454; Van Hoek 1993:11; Harding 2000:339). Such arguments are often implicitly informed by an evolutionary understanding of the development of artistic skill over time. It is simply assumed that the appeal of passage tomb composition to our own aesthetic sensibilities marks a quantifiable progression in artistic talent over time. Consequently, the chronological placement of passage tomb art later than landscape art becomes a self-fulfilling prophecy.

Whatever approach is favoured, it is clear that the presence of monumental art has coloured the context and interpretation of the open air art. If trajectories of landscape and monumental art are to be conjoined, or indeed separated, then the mechanisms, strategies and reasons for this must be demonstrated, not simply assumed.

4.3 Rock art and passage tombs: A convergence of repertoire?

Although, with the exception of Loughcrew, the distribution of Irish landscape art and passage tomb imagery is spatially disparate, the redeployment of quarried rock imagery has long been recognised as a recurrent feature of these monuments (see Burgess 1990; Beckensall & Laurie 1998; Waddington 1998; Eogan 1999; and Thomas & Tilley 1993 regarding Brittany). Burgess (1990:160), for example, contends that "the peripheral placing of cup-marks on some decorated Boyne slabs, and the fact that they may even have been broken through, allows the possibility that the passage tomb builders cannibalised and added their own decoration to pre-existing cup-marked rocks". The truncated ring motifs of Newgrange kerbs 13 and 17 (Waddington 1998:31; figure 4.4), however, suggests that, although it is again the more standardised range of the rock art repertoire which is redeployed in this context, this practice consumes more than cup-marking alone.

Commonly, images which are the subject of redeployment resemble the early Loughcrew style of tomb decoration (Shee-Twohig 1981:122; O'Sullivan 1993:69). Taken as a whole, the corpus from Loughcrew does bear the closest resemblance to the landscape repertoire (see Shee-Twohig 1981:26; Johnston 1993b:267; O'Sullivan 1989, 1993; Bradley 1997a:63; Brindley 1999a:135). The decorative range of cairn V, for example, is almost entirely composed of cups surrounded by concentric rings. Shee (1972:229) identifies a total of 88 comparable motifs, from 35 of the 120 decorated orthostats in this cemetery (figure 4.5).

Figure 4.5: Cup-and-ring style art at Loughcrew cairn V.

Significantly, Shee's analysis identifies a particularly high concentration within cairn T. Many of the individual images of Cairn T appear as direct 'extracts' from the landscape repertoire. The cups-and-two-rings, three rings and four rings of orthostat L2, and recess orthostats C3 and C11, provide clear examples of this. To extract imagery in this way, however, replicates the intellectual 'snap' inherent in inter-regional comparisons of rock art design elements. More convincingly, this cairn also contains orthostats whose motif characterisation *and* composition recall the landscape repertoire. Notably, this is manifest in the two innermost passage orthostats, L5 and R5 (figure 4.6). Both these stones are heavily covered in isolated cup marks, a feature common amongst the open-air carvings. Similarly, the presence of a number of cup-and-ring marks (numbering one to four rings) on L5, and the cup-and-penannular of R5, suggest further decorative convergence. This patterning continues into the chamber (see below).

Figure 4.6: *A cup-marked orthostat from Loughcrew cairn T.*

Amongst the other Irish passage tombs, visible parallels to landscape art are infrequent. The exception is Sess Kilgreen, where cup-and-ring style imagery predominates. At Newgrange, *visible* imagery which recalls this range does so at the more ornate end of the spectrum: the four-ringed cup-mark of Co.3 and the low-ringed cup-marks and four spirals of K95, for example (figure 4.7). Artistic resemblance to the open air rock art is equally sparse at Knowth I where, beyond occasional inclusion in Eogan's (1986) "chaotic" style, individual motifs comparable to the landscape repertoire are almost entirely absent, whilst composition demonstrates greater divergence.

Panel carvings, such as those of orthostat L1 at Loughcrew T (figure 4.8), once again appear ostensibly distant from

deployments of landscape imagery. Individual motifs, common to the landscape repertoire, are seen, but are grouped into tightly packed clusters which cover substantial areas of the surface: a compositional trait more directly comparable to passage tomb art. Similar deployment conventions are also evident at cairns U and L, Sess Kilgreen and Newgrange. Although these panels imply some form of artistic convergence, this is not to suggest the creation of an intermediate style, but to approach a manipulation of focus which evokes a disparate, but comparable, effect and purpose which is echoed in the relationship between imagery and tomb structure.

Figure 4.7: *Newgrange Kerb 95 (after O'Kelly 1982).*

Figure 4.8: *Orthostat L1 Loughcrew cairn T.*

The distribution of imagery at Loughcrew is unlike that of the Boyne valley tombs, in that it does not occupy a threshold location (Shee-Twohig 1996:79; see also Bradley 1989; Thomas 1992; Lewis-Williams & Dowson 1993). The emphasis on thresholds at the Boyne tombs suggests reference to the placement of landscape art in the topographical contradictions of the intermediate landscape zone. The imagery of these

43

tombs, however, bears little resemblance to the open-air art. By contrast, although demonstrating a greater consistency of image 'convergence', the internal positioning of imagery, and hilltop location of the Loughcrew cairns are anomalous to both the remaining passage tombs and the open air art. Commonalities in the spatial organisation of the Loughcrew and Boyne cemeteries, to which can be added Carrowkeal and Carrowmore (Cooney 1990), suggest that these anomalies cannot be attributed to the spatial interaction of the Loughcrew tombs.

Figure 4.10(a): Rock art site '1' at Carnbane East.

Figure 4.9: The distribution of passage tombs and rock art sites (numbered) at Loughcrew (after McMann 1993 with modifications).

It is not unreasonable to suggest, however, that the idiosyncrasies evident amongst the Loughcrew tombs may be related to the close proximity of the cemetery to a number of open-air rock art sites: sites which occupy their 'typical' topographical location (see Johnston 1989:8). In the townlands immediately north of the hills on which the tombs are located, Shee (1972) identified two such sites. Moreover, this area has been subjected to much agricultural improvement and, consequently, the former existence of additional sites is clearly possible. Although lying towards the more elaborate end of the open-air spectrum, the imagery of both Ballinvally 676 and the Loughcrew Fence site, remains firmly within this repertoire. The only exception to this is the angular imagery of Ballinvally which, according to Shee (1972:227), is the "only example of a lozenge motif ... in Irish rock art", and possibly attributable to this same spatial relationship. In closer proximity to the tombs, a series of carved rocks encircles the lower reaches of Carnbane East. With the exception of the almost angular 'penannulars' of site 4, these rocks all exhibit isolated cup-marks, associated with natural solution holes (figures 4.9 and 4.10a/b). Although it is unclear if these are the remains of denuded cairns, imagery and stone characteristics are more suggestive of open-air sites. Site 4, however, is again different. Not only does this rock table recall the size and shape of the orthostats used in the construction of the hill top cairns, but a number of additional stones are associated with it, suggesting the remains of a structure.

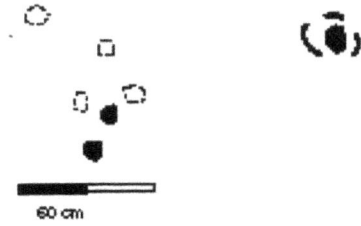

Figure 4.10(b): Rock art site '4' at Carnbane East.

Taken as a totality, the topography-image-architecture interaction of the Loughcrew cemetery suggests the pre-existence of a local tradition of carving living rock, and the existence of a meaningful relationship between these 'two' artistic phenomena. Why such a dramatic alteration in the contexts of production and consumption should occur, and what this says about the dynamic interplay between these decorative strategies - which ultimately led to the depiction of a distinctive image range and the concealment of imagery that was formerly accessible in the landscape - remains to be explained (see below and chapter 6). To address these questions, however, it is first necessary to explore the interpretative possibilities of the passage tombs.

4.4   Image concealment and the altered state

In contrast to much of the imagery from Loughcrew, the visible art of Newgrange and Knowth appears less performative and less spontaneous: planned rather than accumulated (McMann 1994:541). A greater convergence between the open-air and passage tomb repertoires, however, is seen in the so-called 'hidden' art of Newgrange. Although only amounting to only a fraction of the tomb corpus, this imagery is found on the rear of the kerb stones and along the upper surfaces of the passage roof panels: including roof stone X, the rear of kerb 11, obscured corbel Co.1/C7, recess stone C3, and stones R3, K4, K13, and K18 (figure 4.11). At Knowth I, only 30 stones 'exhibit' concealed imagery. This art is again of a restricted range. Cup-marks, for example, although rare in the passage tomb corpus, are confined to the rear of the kerb stones (Eogan 1986:153). Appropriative schemes, in which the imagery of previous generations was first visibly co-opted into the passage tombs to legitimate new ritual practice - as at Loughcrew - and then concealed as this later practice took hold, and new trajectories of image production dominated - the tombs of the Boyne valley - may appear interpretatively appealing, but, as explanation, fail to account for the highly contingent nature of image placement. It is this contingency, however, which suggests interpretative constructs for the passage tombs.

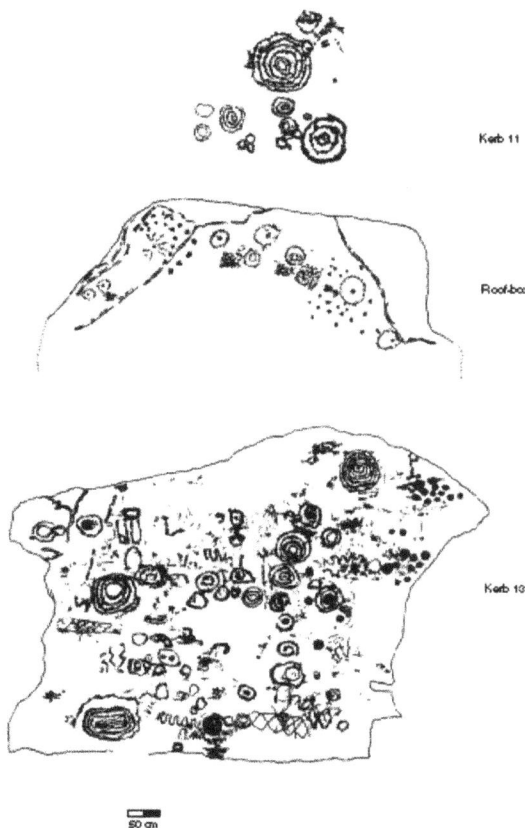

Figure 4.11: Hidden imagery from Newgrange (after O'Kelly 1982).

Wallis (1995:9), for example, accepting the identification of passage tomb imagery as derived from the altered state (Bradley 1989; Lewis-Williams & Dowson 1993; Dronfield 1993, 1994, 1995, 1996), seeks to account for the difference in character between the visible and hidden art of Newgrange in terms of a shamanistic explanation. He suggests that hidden imagery closely corresponds to the mental visions of the altered state and is representative of actual hallucinations. In contrast, the more formalised visible imagery he attributes to secondary deployments of more didactic expression (see below).

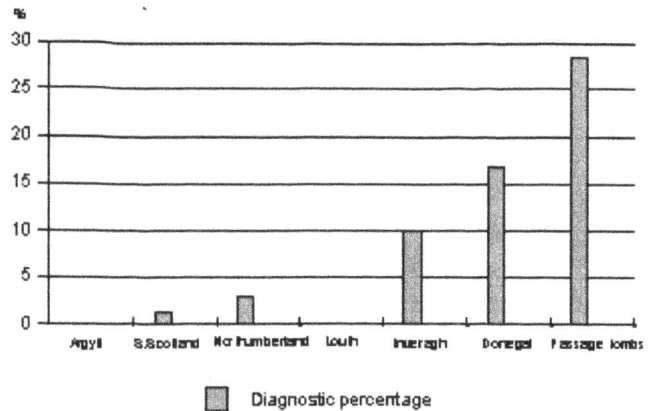

Figure 4.12: The diagnostic content of rock art in the British Isles and Ireland.

Wallis' interpretation of the hidden art of Newgrange and suggestions that the imagery located in these places lies closer to the landscape repertoire than the passage tombs, initially appear fundamentally at odds. Previous work (Evans 1998), indicates that the petroglyphs of the British mainland are substantively non-endogenous in character: not exclusively derived from the altered state. Diagnostic motifs only constitute 2.9% of imagery in Northumberland, 1.3% in southern Scotland and none at all in Argyll. Application of Dronfield's (1996) methodology for the identification of motifs exclusively derived from the altered state to the open-air art of Ireland reveals similar results. Interestingly, the rock art of Loughcrew and Louth, the two areas with a direct relationship to the decorated passage tombs (see below), lacks any indication of diagnostic imagery. A slightly different picture arises from the imagery of Inveragh and Donegal, which exhibit a diagnostic percentage of 10% and 16.7% respectively (figure 4.12). This suggests that the imagery of western Ireland is significantly different in its subjective visual characteristics to that of the eastern coast, or the British mainland (see chapter 6). These values, however, remain substantively lower than the diagnostic percentages of the passage tombs. Throughout all tombs investigated by Dronfield, diagnostic imagery averages 28.37%, allowing him to conclude, with 80% confidence, that the art of the passage tombs is derived from the altered state. If the petroglyphs of Louth and Loughcrew are included, then the corresponding cumulative percentage for the Irish rock art is only 6.68%; if not, the average remains at the relatively low value of 13.35%. Contrary to the immediate conclusions suggested by this, consideration of the distribution of landscape-like and diagnostic imagery within the structure of the passage tombs allows these apparently contradictory identifications to inform each other. To address this, however, it is first necessary to explore the methodology through which these results are obtained.

45

The publication of Lewis-Williams and Dowson's (1988) *Signs of all times* presented a model which was proposed to furnish an explanatory link between the iconic and geometric imagery of the European Palaeolithic (figure 4.13). This model was subsequently adopted in attempts to provide an explanation for the largely abstract arts of the western European Neolithic. Dronfield (1993:183) considers Lewis-Williams and Dowson's (1988, 1993) table of neuropsychological parallels, the central tenet of their model, to be unreliable, presenting both indicators of the altered state and potentially non-subjective art forms. Retaining essentially the same format, Dronfield reworks the table to contain only motifs he considers diagnostic of the altered state. His exhaustive analysis of many traditions of 'abstract' image making resulted in the formulation of a diagnostic methodology, purported to overcome the weaknesses he perceives in the original model (figure 4.14).

Figure 4.14: Dronfield's diagnostic entoptic forms (after Dronfield 1996 with modifications).

The confidence and commonality now seen in the identification of the 'enigmatic' imagery of the European Neolithic, in terms of the altered state, owes much to the intellectual rigour of this neuropsychological research. Lack of revision, and widespread citation, in the years following publication of the diagnostic method suggests that much of this 'certainty' can be directly attributed to Dronfield's contribution and its publication in prestigious journals. Limited criticism has been applied (see O'Sullivan 1998; Jones 1999), but this contrasts markedly with the strong opposition levelled at the original model (see, for example, Bednarik 1990). Although much of the opposition to the original model may be due to the body of art to which it was applied - the highly valued cave imagery of the European Palaeolithic - the statistical quantification of Dronfield's analysis is widely accepted as giving a scientific rational to the inherently subjective analysis of abstract arts. Difficulties with the model's deconstruction of hallucination, however, have resulted in a widespread misunderstanding of subjective visual imagery and its contexts of production and consumption. Indeed, to turn Dronfield's (1993:179; also 1995:539) critique of Lewis-Williams and Dowson's model back on to his own diagnostic approach, it is not unreasonable to suggest that "while ... [his] conclusions are probably substantively correct, the methodology employed is ... unreliable".

Despite the apparent scientific security which many derive from the statistical quantification of his model, a critical approach to Dronfield's diagnostic method reveals a marked subjectivity in the allotment of image type to diagnostic category. By way of experiment, application of Dronfield's method to the same body of passage tomb art used in his original analysis, demonstrates a noticeable divergence in the percentage values obtained for both diagnostic and non-diagnostic categories from the results

Figure 4.13: The Signs of All Times (after Lewis-Williams & Dowson 1988 with modifications).

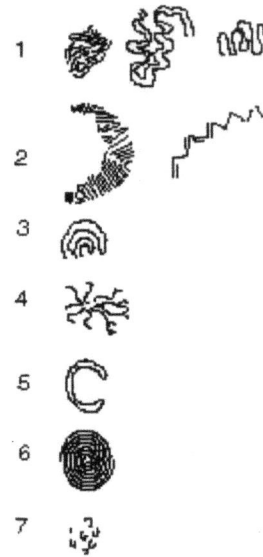

presented by Dronfield (because of the limited publication of the corpus from Knowth this tomb was excluded from analysis). When the process was repeated over a month later, not only were the same patterns of divergence noted, but these values differed from those obtained from the first application of the model. Although not numerically great, the inconsistencies evident in motif allocation and the pigeon-holing effects of tabular methodologies (see chapter 1) give Dronfield's approach a degree of subjectivity that the model seeks to exclude.

These methodological difficulties are compounded by a tendency to under-represent more qualitative areas of analysis. Dronfield's model attempts to eliminate any features of the art which are dependent upon a "motif's edge morphology ... its spatial relation to other motifs, and the effect of aesthetic compositional principles (e.g. symmetry) on frequency of occurrence". This, Dronfield (1993:180) attributes to a desire to avoid modernist aesthetic judgements. Consequently, Dronfield's approach determines that each shape-type would only register one count, regardless of the number of occasions it appeared in a specific composition. As a result, diagnostic analysis limits the scope for interpretation to isolated abstract forms, and all abstract compositions begin to look alike: erroneously positing the neuropsychological model as a monolithic catchall. More damaging still, the deliberate exclusion of qualitative areas of analysis actively misrepresents the characteristics of the art and misinforms subsequent interpretations.

Although embodying greater subjectivity than is often acknowledged, the degree of statistical convergence evident in the experiment cited above suggests that the diagnostic potential of Dronfield's motif categories remains strong, but, is attended by concerns regarding the methodological misrepresentation of style and the 'aesthetic'. Diagnostic forms *can* be identified which confirm the subjective origins of the art. But the passage tombs also contain undiagnostic components and compositional characteristics which, although not exclusively derived from the altered state, can be used to explore the more qualitative dimensions of subjectively derived imagery. Dronfield's (1995:548) own pilot study of non-Irish European megalithic art reveals a lower degree of inter-site consistency than that seen in Ireland, and a recurrent intermixing of subjectively derived images with those potentially from other sources. Such intermixing suggests that these diagnostic / undiagnostic combinations are meaningfully constituted and that the search for statistical regularity is inappropriate, providing only half the picture. Although he suggests that aesthetic values and symbolic significance "could still determine a shapes perceived ... culture-specific importance as a suitable image to represent", Dronfield (1993:190) in no way applies these concerns to his model. Form dependent shapes are also discounted, again more "for the sake

of extracting motifs for analysis" (Dronfield 1993:185, 1995:543) than because of any essential reality in the corpus. By contrast, Lewis-Williams and Dowson (1993:60) suggest that "artists do not automatically produce facsimiles of their visions: they select and modify them meaningfully". This gives the original model a means for exploring the qualitative dimensions of the art which has subsequently been overlooked: the principles of endogenous perception and stages in the development of mental imagery.

The identification of an origin in the altered state for Irish passage tomb art rests on more than the presence of diagnostic components alone. The images are not isolated and static, as diagnostic analysis makes them appear, but fluid. Rather than statistically quantifying the abduction of individual motifs in a manner analogous to Dronfield, the corpus of images, and their internal interaction, are fundamental to understanding hallucinatory art, for, without this, the internal agency of composition is lost (see Gell 1998). Hallucinations in all three stages of trance are fluid, and entoptics constantly subjected to transformation by the principles of replication, integration, fragmentation, polyopia, superposition, juxtaposition and rotation. Lewis-Williams and Dowson (1993:57-9) suggest that polyopia, for example, explains the tightly nested and repetitive characteristics of passage tomb imagery, whilst integration is said to account for the intimate convergence of different motif types: such as dots and zig-zags. At Loughcrew, for instance, the motifs on panel C9, cairn U, are replicated and integrated (figure 4.15). Similarly, 'pick-dressing' is particularly common at Newgrange (figure 4.16).

Figure 4.15: Orthostat C9, Loughcrew cairn U: an example of Integration (after Shee-Twohig 1981).

In terms of the principles of endogenous perception, the juxtaposition of pick-dressing and more formalised motifs challenges Western aesthetic sensibilities which have long suggested that pick-dressing serves to obliterate the spirals of orthostat L19, for example. Rather, this engraving may have been part of a 'single' composition, portraying the fluidity of mental imagery (see Evans & Wallis in prep). Moreover, the focus on polyopia and integration, like the selection of a specific range of entoptic forms - including those which Dronfield identifies as diagnostic - was socially determined (see Lewis-Williams & Dowson 1993). These principles are fundamental to the hallucinatory experience and, consequently, are equally vital in the interpretation of passage tomb art. For the sake of consistency with published data, the statistical qualifications of subsequent analysis comply with Dronfield's criteria. They are, however, presented within the context of the above critique. As such, each approach informs the other in a manner analogous to the methodology espoused by Lewis-Williams and Dowson.

Figure 4.16: An example of pick-dressing: Orthostat L19 at Newgrange (after O'Kelly 1982).

As the earliest manifestation of the decorated passage tombs (McMann 1993:37), accompanied by substantial deployments of landscape-type imagery, one might expect little in the way of diagnostic content at Loughcrew. The very opposite, however, is seen. Cairns F and U stand apart from the other passage tombs of this cemetery, exhibiting a diagnostic content of 46.14% and 38.33% respectively. Similarly, cairn I exhibits a diagnostic percentage above the passage tomb average (29.29), whilst cairn H falls just below (27.78). Conversely, the later Boyne tombs illustrate a slight decline in the percentage value of diagnostic content: Knowth 27.74 % and Newgrange 21.48%. Significantly, the two principal tombs at Loughcrew, cairns L and T, demonstrate diagnostic percentages that fall between these Boyne values: 25.98% and 24.65% respectively. If one follows Thomas' (1992:145) suggestion that these tombs constitute the final additions to this cemetery, a sequence emerges which posits a decision to move from the depiction of non-diagnostic imagery in the landscape to one in which the

same components appear alongside diagnostic motifs: possibly as a result of the tomb acting as some kind of adjunct to trance (see Lewis-Williams & Dowson 1993). Over time, at a moment which corresponds to the contemporary construction of the principal tombs at Loughcrew and the Boyne valley monuments (O'Kelly 1982:122), the diagnostic 'impetus' behind this decorative strategy declines. The imagery becomes more formalised and the immediacy in the relationship between hallucination and depicted image is lost. As such, a changing role for the altered state, and the imagery derived from it, can be traced through a series of distinctive phases. This is not to suggest that the people of the Neolithic classified their imagery according to diagnostic and undiagnostic categories; rather, it is the tools provided by Dronfield which make this an observable factor of difference. What this difference does suggest, however, is that the people of the Neolithic were making some form of visual discrimination between the artistic cues of subjective vision according to the context of deployment (see chapter 6).

Although this sequence appears plausible, and possibly indicative of general tendencies, it embodies monolithic and evolutionary understandings: all tombs are co-opted into a single trajectory which retains the principal Boyne monuments as the peak of Neolithic artistic achievement. Moreover, it does not explain why these things should occur. By contrast, Wallis (1995), noting sharp contrasts in the diversity and expediency of image creation, has convincingly argued for a contemporary diversity of shamanistic practice within the Neolithic of Ireland. It is possible to take the diversity noted by Wallis, and the loose temporal trajectory above, to tell a more complete story of these practices, and account for the changing relationship between passage tomb and landscape art.

4.5   Loughcrew: A conflation of worlds

Thomas (1992:140) suggests, through the example of cairn T and a measure of complexity defined according to the number of images per orthostat, that the art of the Loughcrew cemetery becomes progressively more complex the deeper one proceeds into each tomb (figure 4.17). Although this definition of complexity raises the same concerns as Dronfield's diagnostic categorisations - raising questions as to how one distinguishes specific motifs amongst a body of art so heavily characterised by polyopia and integration - these observations only achieve a high level of consistency within cairn U. Significantly, the imagery of this cairn is rather at odds with the rest of the cemetery, demonstrates marked affinities with the Boyne passage tomb repertoire. In this respect, it should not be surprising to observe, that the changing spatial character of this art recalls the *intensity* of image deployment seen in the depths of the Boyne tombs. The absence of imagery around the kerb and outer passage of this cairn again implies an emphasis on depth. Comparable patterns are evident at cairn W. At this

48

tomb, there is a marked contrast between the three-cup-marked kerb stone, the concentric circles of the inner passage, and the passage tomb style motifs of the chamber. The correlation between image intensity and depth, however, cannot be sustained throughout the rest of the cemetery. Rather, very deliberate deployments linking the open-air context of landscape art and the imagery of the tomb interior are apparent.

Figure 4.17: The distribution of 'complex' imagery (filled stones 8-11 motifs) as defined by Thomas (1992) for Loughcrew cairn T.

The contrived relationship between interior and exterior space at Loughcrew is most clearly illustrated through Thomas' chosen tomb of reference, cairn T. In contradistinction to cairn W, the imagery of the outer passage orthostats of cairn T lies closer to the passage tomb repertoire than the open-air art. As such, the imagery of this tomb which is in closest physical proximity to the open air context, exhibits a significant adjustment of stylistic focus. On entering the inner passage, however, the art abruptly changes, becoming distinctly landscape-like in character. The extensively cup-marked, opposed orthostats of L/R 5 (see above and figure 4.8) are located at the junction of passage and chamber. These image characteristics continue into the chamber, where each decorated orthostat is not too dissimilar to much open-air rock art. The art again changes character within each recess, where many of the motifs particular to Loughcrew are found in conjunction with elements more familiar from the passage tomb corpus (figure 4.18).

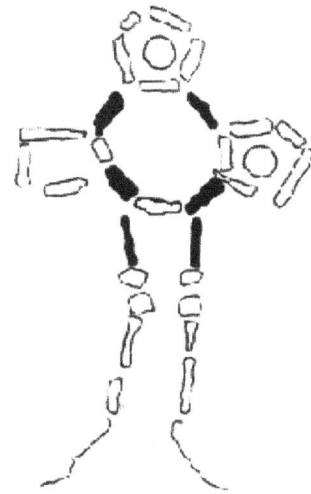

Figure 4.18: The distribution of landscape-like imagery at Loughcrew cairn T.

McMann (1994:532) notes how space explodes on entering the chamber, a sensation which recalls the outside world after the narrow confines of the passage. This change in the nature of space is accompanied by the deployment of imagery reminiscent of the landscape. It is as if one has left the outside world and passed through the confines of the passage, only to re-emerge in the 'open' environment. The same 'journey' that the content of the art makes.

Although deployments of landscape-like imagery predominates within the chamber, Dronfield's model suggests that 40 percent of the motifs located here are diagnostic in character. This figure is artificially high because of the methodological composition of the model. That is, it is the repetitive deployment of landscape-style imagery which gives the chamber its dominant characteristics: repetition which is under-represented in Dronfield's model. More informative, is the observation that 24% of all the diagnostic imagery of this cairn is located within the chamber, 36% in the passage (24.3% of all imagery here) and 40% in the recess (23.3% of all imagery found here). Lewis-Williams and Dowson (1993) have long suggested that the passages of the Irish tombs architecturally recreate the vortex of the trance experience: an interpretation enhanced by the concentration (30%) of diagnostic deployments in the outer passage of Loughcrew T. The art of the inner passage, has already been shown to be very different. Moreover, many of the cup-marks on orthostats L/R 5 show evidence of re-cutting (figure 4.6). As noted above, these are the last stones of the passage, immediately adjacent to the chamber, suggesting that their unusual composite character is intimately tied to their situation.

Drawing an analogy, numerous southern African Bushman engravings exhibit evidence of being hammered, rubbed, cut and flaked (see Lewis-Williams & Dowson 1989): a consequence of a belief that such pictures are reservoirs of potency, touched to enhance the trance experience. Ouzman (2001:237-41) contends that actions such as these may constitute attempts to "possess pieces of potent places". Applying Ouzman's interpretation to cairn T suggests that the re-cutting of the cupules - on orthostats L/R 5 - effectively renews them by "experientially and visibly maintaining contact between ... [interdigitating] ...ordinary and spirit worlds", and simultaneously drawing out potency.

Although opposing views are articulated regarding the use of henbane at Balfag (Long et al 2000 contra Barclay & Russel-White 1993), it seems improbable that some chemical means of inducing the altered state was not practised in the Neolithic (See Rudley 1993:24-30; Dronfield 1993, 1994, 1995, 1996; Sheridan 1999; Woodward 2000:133; Bradley et al 2001:112). If this is so, then it is not unreasonable to suggest that the induction of mild 'euphoria', through chemical means, was practised before entry to the tomb - facilitating passage through the vortex - and that the activities subsequently undertaken within its structure induced deeper levels of the altered state. The repetitive rhythms involved in re-cutting the cupules are likely to have facilitated the physical sensations of the altered state, encouraging the belief that through these actions the shaman were accessing the spirit world. Similarly, repetitive scoring and hammering, possibly accompanied by drumming and chanting, would affect the resonance of acoustic frequencies conducive to the induction of trance (*Secrets of the dead* 2001), again enhancing the physical sensations which provide these beliefs with a physiological reality. Opposed orthostats L/R 5 are also suggestive of more specific rites. The stone marbles characteristic of the passage tomb assemblage fit neatly into the cup-marks which cover the surface of these stones (McMann 1994:540). This suggests a correlative to the performative acts of re-cutting, analogous to the process of stone extraction and the breaking and reformulation of surface: practices which find resonance in the clearance of regrowth, or extraction of water, from the horizontal surfaces of the open-air art (see chapter 6).

The immediate, parallel proximity of alternative realms has already been noted (see chapter 3) and posited as intimately tied to beliefs in bodily transformation and trans-world passage: a commonly reported shamanistic experience, regardless of the specific form this is believed to take. Again, conceptions of bodily transformation are rooted in the physiological sensations of trance, including weightlessness, shortness of breath and bodily disassociation, which are subsequently interpreted as extra-corporeal experience. As such, the activities undertaken at the last passage orthostats of cairn T enabled the shaman to undertake their journey into the spirit world, in much the same

vein, but more directly expressed, as Wallis' (1995) suggestion that the narrow confines of the passage at Newgrange would cause initiate shaman to come into physical contact with the imagery of the passage-vortex. Having passed through the passage-vortex of cairn T, the shaman re-enters the 'outside' world of the chamber: only now, both they and this world are transformed. Transformation is evidenced by the content of the art, through the manifestation of diagnostic imagery at a level above that seen in the open air, whilst the latent dominance of landscape-style deployments serves to reiterate the immediate proximity, and daily reality, of the spirit world. As such, the chamber was understood as both real and spirit world, simultaneously of this world and the next. It is in this adjusted 'outside' world - on the other side of the vortex - that the shaman performed their socially sanctioned duties.

Conferring evidence comes from the other side of the Irish Sea. The imagery of the now destroyed Calderstones passage tomb (Merseyside) contains a number of depictions of feet. Significantly, those of stones Bi and Ei exhibit an unusual number of toes: indicative of the distorting effects of polymelia - sensations of 'extra' bodies, limbs and digits (see Lewis-Williams et al 1993:282; Lewis-Wiliams & Dowson 1989:78) - experienced in the altered state. Returning to the southern African analogy, many Bushman narratives refer to the spiritual significance of water-holes (Soloman 1998:294). Dia!kwain, for example, spoke of trancing shaman diving into water-holes to undertake subterranean, or subaqueous, journeys through the spirit world, and returning by the same route (Lewis-Williams 1980:472; Lewis-Williams & Dowson 1990:13). As such, these basins are believed to constitute cosmological break-through points (Lewis-Williams 1998:88), where the tiers of the shamanistic universe intersected. In this context, the depiction of spoor prints around the rim of water-holes appears as evidence for the transformed shaman-spirit helper, exiting the 'real' world and entering the spiritual domain of the watercourse, leaving their earthly traces behind them in the form of these prints (Lewis-Williams 1995a:16).

Within the chamber of cairn T, two carvings which loosely resemble depictions of feet are found on orthostat C15. The left foot is composed of natural rock markings with cup-marks in the place of toes; the right is ambiguously, but fully, carved. Although loose in their depiction, the visual ambiguity of these images is itself significant. Evans and Wallis (in prep) problematise the identification of stylised anthropomorphic figures within the passage tomb corpus. Rather than concerning themselves with the black and white confirmation, or refutation, of presence, these authors explore what it means to consume visual ambiguity. Asserting personalised comprehension within wider societal understandings, the fluidity of the altered state is drawn upon in suggesting that it was in such circumstances that the ambiguity of abstract carving was resolved into anthropomorphic forms. In this context, it is not unreasonable to suggest that the natural 'sole' of the left foot was construed into its representational form as hallucinations of entoptic dots were graphically fixed as cup-marked toes (figure 4.19). Given that these images can only be seen when looking out from the chamber - down the passage and into the open air - it is possible to suggest that they, like the southern African examples, indicate the departure of the shaman into the outside/spirit world.

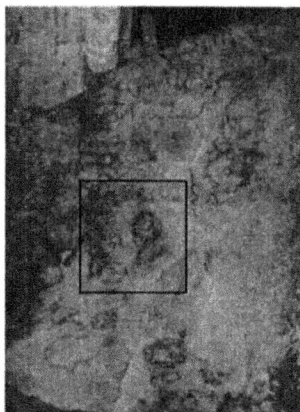

Figure 4.19: The construed left foot of Loughcrew cairn T.

Concomitant to all these artistic devices, the anomalous topographical placement of the Loughcrew tombs - on their series of mountain tops - locates these monuments at the highest local manifestation of the middle tier of the shamanistic universe: placing them in an arena where the transgression of spiritual realms was already most apparent. As such, imagery, architecture, topography and the altered state converge to suggest extra-corporeal travel. All this is not to posit some form of shamanic teleportation device, within which the shaman is said to materialise and dematerialise according to the location of rock art sites. Rather, it is to assert a form of practice that accounts for the appearance of landscape-like imagery within the chamber of cairn T and the re-focussing of the polysemous spectrum through the maintenance of particular in-out relationships (see chapter 6). Allowing for slight architectural differences, similar patterns (and practices?) are observed for cairns H, L and S. Even the most generalised observations made for these cairns, however, cannot be applied to tombs W or U. Clearly other concerns are at work here, suggesting a diversification of practice within this cemetery.

4.6i   Inside-out at Newgrange and Knowth: Newgrange

Like many of the cairns at Loughcrew, both Newgrangre and Knowth demonstrate a concern to connect internal and external space through the deployment of imagery. In contrast to cairn T, however, the art at Newgrange becomes more prolific - and moves further away from the landscape repertoire - the deeper it is located in the tomb. There are, of course, certain famous

examples that contradict this, notably kerbs 1, 52 and 67 (figure 4.20), but these have their own explanatory characteristics: characteristics which again centre around the relationship between imagery deployed within, and external to, the tomb (see below).

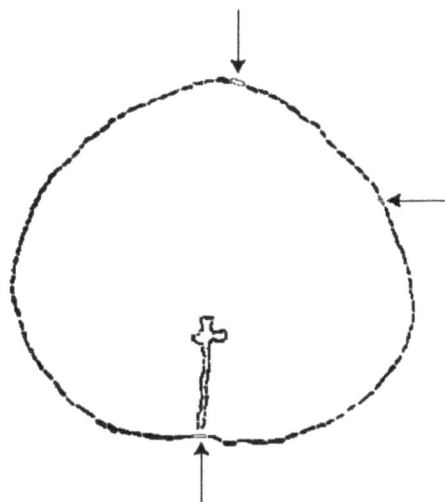

Figure 4.20: Key kerb stones at Newgrange (after O'Kelly 1982 with modifications).

It seems improbable that the concealed imagery of the passage roof stones at Newgrange was intended for ongoing human consumption. Despite this, these motifs are far from being outside the realm of human concerns. The highly specific relationship that these stones hold with the operation of the roof-box, and its associated lighting phenomenon, suggests that they played a significant role at this site. Hidden imagery is found at the very entrance of the passage and the passage-chamber interface, connected, almost literally, by the beam of light contrived by the roof-box around the winter solstice.

The relationship of this beam of light to the hidden art changes as it moves through the tomb (figure 4.21). At the front of the passage, the beam passes directly underneath the rear corbel and roof stone 3 of the roof box - both carry decoration on their upper surfaces - and between two similarly decorated corbels. Corbel 3/L5-6 (west) was laid with its decorated surface face down, the motifs concealed by lower stones, whilst Corbel 3/R4-5 (east), was arranged with its decorated surface uppermost and covered by roof stone 3. On reaching the passage-chamber interface, the light beam runs across the floor, rather than along the underside of the roof. Significantly, stone X is deployed in 'opposition' to the rear corbel and roof stone 3: its decorated surface face down towards the light beam, but concealed from it by the lower structural stones of the interface. It is as if some form of inversion has taken place in the relationship between art and light beam during its passage: a transgression of both space and orientation. Moreover, stone X

51

physically supports a further structural juxtaposition of difference. Immediately above this stone a massive lintel is found, which, in turn, supports the main body of the cairn. What is significant about this cairn mass is that it is composed of water-rounded boulders, which stand in stark contrast to the rest of the mound fill. The ambiguous connotations inherent in rock art materiality are thus juxtaposed against this structural juncture: a place of architectural and material disjunction which evokes the topographical connotations of the intermediate zone.

Retaining focus on the operation of the roof-box, it is possible to suggest that the passage of obliquely angled light, in close proximity to images reminiscent of the open air corpus, deliberately recreates the circumstances in which landscape art can most clearly be discerned: dawn or dusk. It is significant that given the impression of inversion connoted by the relationship between light beam and hidden roof imagery, and the materiality of the roof-box itself, it is the undecorated surfaces of these stones which are 'illuminated'. That is, in the blocking stones of the roof-box, quartz is actively manipulated into bringing its own connotative tergiversations to bear. Milky

quartz, such as that deployed at Newgrange, is almost translucent in character, exercising an ability to diffuse light without revealing the contours of an object. In this semi-transparent state, this 'stone' appears to be ambiguous and reactive: behaving in much the same way as water in its relationship to light. Again, like water, impurities in the quartz directly reflect sunlight, in effect it changes colour and becomes opaque. Significantly, this is only a temporary transformation, dependent on the direction and intensity of light, its very fluidity reinforcing the transgressive character of this substance. Moreover, and without drawing direct analogy, many New Age beliefs centre around the spiritual properties of quartz. This crystalline substance is widely believed to focus and direct energies (rockhounding 06/02/02): exactly what the roof box does to the sun's rays. Given the contradictory properties of quartz, it is not unreasonable to suggest that the passage of light through an architectural feature associated with this material brought about an inversion of the light beam, so that it was the hidden decorated surfaces of these carved rocks that were 'illuminated' by the sun.

Figure 4.21: The relationship between roof-box and hidden imagery at Newgrange (drawn from the data presented by O'Kelly 1982).

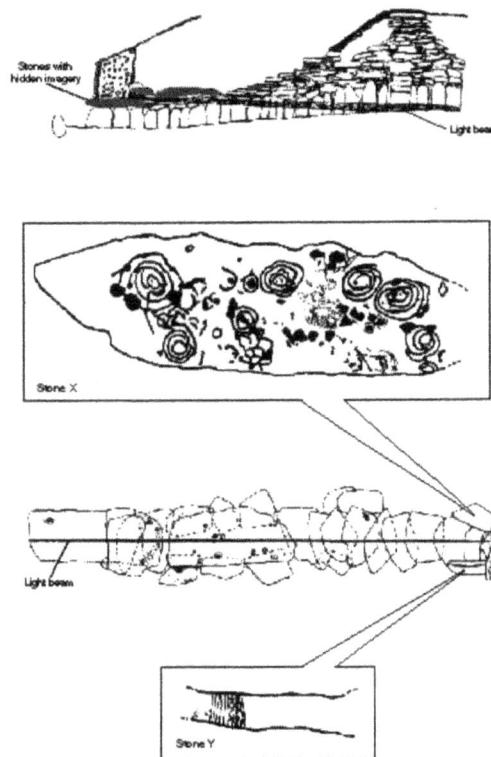

This interpretation of the relationship between art and roof-box is supported by consideration of stone X in its role as structural edifice. This stone is paired with stone Y: a slab supporting the opposing east end of the lintel, and embellished by more angular imagery along its forward-facing edge. The juxtaposition of circular and angular art, and disparate orientation, echoes the invisible differences between corbels 3/L5-6 and 3/R4-5. This juxtaposition has a direct bearing on the deployment of visible imagery in the passage. To the western side of the passage, stones X and Co3/L5-6 exhibit face-down landscape-like deployments. To the east, this relationship is inverted: stone Y displays angular imagery on its upward tilted forward edge, whilst Co3/R4-5 again orientates its imagery upwards. The orthostats of the western side of the passage are dominated by visible circular imagery, primarily deployed on the mid to lower sections of the stones (this is repeated in the west recess). By contrast, the orthostats to the east exhibit angular decoration, generally restricted to the upper reaches of the orthostats. As such, these visible patterns appear to correspond with the situation of the corbels, stone X and stone Y. Moreover, the imagery of the western side of the passage changes from loose deployments to intimately merged panels as one progresses into the tomb. Conversely that to the right (east), beginning with stone R3, becomes progressively less formalised. These patterns, however, are not exclusive but, rather, are indicative of general impressions. They are, however, both relevant and are open to explanation (see below).

O'Kelly's reconstruction of the facade at Newgrange exemplifies the theme of inversion as a mechanism for connecting internal and external space. This facade confronts the visitor with a massive wall of white quartz around the entrance to the tomb. Into this whiteness, large water-rolled granite boulders - taken from the from the beaches of the Cooley peninsula, near Dundalk (Co. Louth) (Eogan 1986:117) - are inserted. In its natural state, quartz is a crystalline intrusion of granite, occurring in small seams within this bedrock (Bradley 1976:25-6; Woolley 1976:48). If one accepts O'Kelly's reconstruction, with its emphasis on the predominance of quartz and minor intrusions of granite (see figure 1.4), this striking statement of inversion would be performatively evoked each time the tomb was entered and reinforced by the differential deployment of imagery to the eastern and western sides of the passage. Comparable quartz spreads have been recovered from Knowth and Loughcrew cairn T (Eogan 1986:46).

4.6ii   Inside-out at Newgrange and Knowth: Knowth

Although the art of every passage tomb group is clearly identifiable as a localised entity, that of Knowth I conveys the greatest difference. Within this difference, however, the same concerns to transgress the division between inside and outside worlds is retained: indeed, is perhaps at its most explicit.
Imagery which recalls the open-air art at Knowth is almost entirely absent. The compositional traits of kerb stones decorated with single, centrally positioned, circular motifs makes these stones unsuitable allegories for landscape art. The concentration of panels exhibiting Eogan's (1986:179) lavish style, in which some landscape elements occur, around both

entrances to this monument, however, may be taken as implying the passage of something familiar in the external world to the internal confines of tomb space. This contention, however, is subservient to a more convincing series of alignments.

Kerb stone 74, for example, is located immediately adjacent to the western passage entrance, directly aligned with the rear stone of the chamber, orthostat 42. The imagery of these stones is highly idiosyncratic, and yet these panels are virtually identical. Comparable alignment of curvilinear art occurs at the eastern tomb, but is slightly more problematic as the graphic convergence between kerb 11 and orthostat 47 does not approach the specificity of the western tomb (figure 4.22). This divergence, however, is countered through the idiosyncratic presence of curvilinear imagery in this section of the kerb.

The presence of a 'unifying' kerb at Knowth I suggests that it is appropriate to consider the two tomb structures not only independently, but also as part of a 'bigger' structure. Eogan (1986:184) interprets O'Kelly's (1982:65) suggested convergence between the art of the entrance stone and kerb 52 at Newgrange as evidence of a blind, or symbolic, entrance. If one follows the train of thought developed for this tomb, it is possible to suggest that the alignment of kerb 11 (east), orthostats 47(E) and 42(W), and kerb 74 (west) at Knowth, are indicative of a false passage through the axis of the cairn, linking internal and external space according to the cardinal points of the rising and setting sun. Indeed, a concern to emphasise this alignment is suggested by the pronounced kink towards the end of the western passage.

Turning explicitly to the internal art of these two tombs, Eogan (1986:178) contends that as one moves from entrance to chamber, the imagery takes on a greater intensity and intermixing of styles. On almost no occasion, however, does the curvilinear imagery 'unique' to Knowth share a panel with any other motif type. This allows distinct patterns of deployment to be distinguished within each tomb. Little curvilinear imagery is found within the chamber of the eastern tomb, where the single deployment on the rear chamber orthostat directly mirrors the 'isolation' of its opposed kerb stone. Although more common in the passage, curvilinear deployments in this architectural zone retain the characteristic alignment of kerb and chamber (figure 4.22). At the very end of the passage, for example, two pairs of adjacent curvilinear panels stand directly opposite each other. Similarly, towards the centre, this pattern is repeated in the concentration of five stones to the right hand side and three to the left. Such opposition appears to be an integral component in the meaning of the curvilinear imagery at Knowth. If 'metaphorical' passage through the long axis of the structure is suggested by the alignment of kerb and rear chamber stones, then it is also possible to propose movement into the main body of the mound, facilitated by these opposing passage orthostats.

53

Kerb 67 at Newgrange may have connoted a comparable effect. Indeed, given the significant qualities of the materials used in cairn construction, this interpretation is distinctly feasible: compatible with the idea of a tiered shamanistic universe (see below).

Figure 4.22: The distribution of curvilinear imagery at Knowth 1 (after Eogan 1986 with modifications).

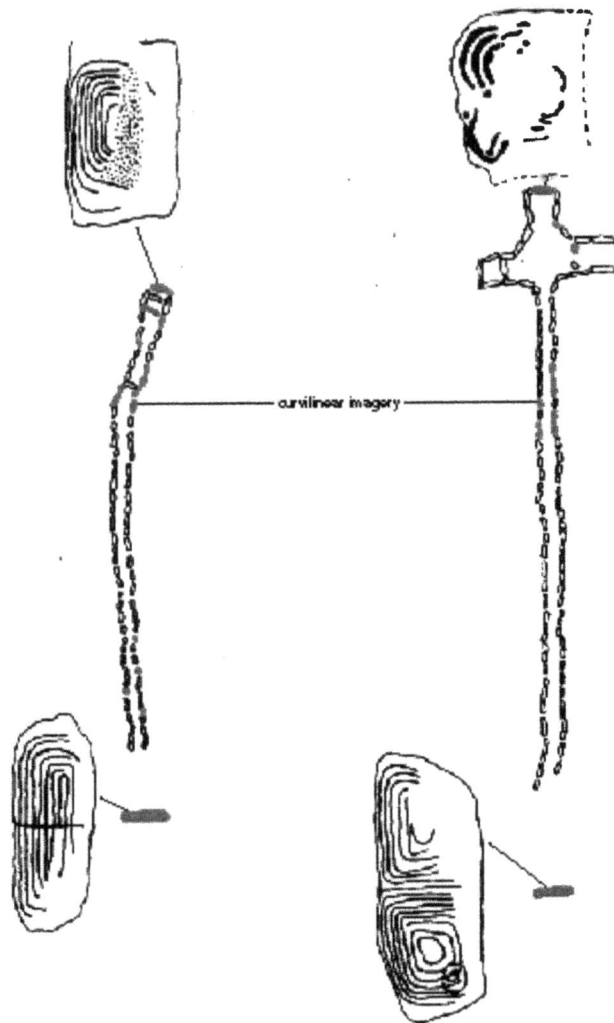

The remaining imagery of the eastern tomb lacks such direct associations. Patterns, however, do exist, but are more suggestive of penumbral concerns. Angular imagery, for example, although reasonably common to the right side of the chamber, is relatively rare in the passage. To the left-hand side the opposite arrangement is seen. This recalls the patterns of inversion noted for Newgrange, including the domination of angular art to the right side of the passage. In many ways, this deployment of imagery runs contrary to Eogan's (1986:184) suggestion that in both tomb structures at Knowth 1, angular art is almost exclusively restricted to the upper sections of the orthostats: facilitating communication in and out. By contrast, he sees the curvilinear imagery characteristic of the lower reaches of the stones as an art form associated with burials and the dead. The division of imagery into two categories, determined by their relative positions on each orthostat, has some currency. It is Eogan's allotment of subsequent attributes which is problematic. Rather than solely being an art of the dead, deployments of curvilinear imagery appear to operate as the focus for the in-out connotations of this monument and a concern to transgress the materiality of the structure.

4.7   Art and the 'dead'

The passage tombs were not only contexts for the deployment of imagery, but also held multiple associations with the dead and a series of recurrent 'grave goods'. Although few archaeologists have considered the relationship between the treatment of the dead and differential deployments of imagery, clear correlations exist. This section makes reference to

54

'angular', 'circular' and 'curvilinear' imagery. These are obvious reductions, and do not convey the full repertoire of the art; nor do they account for all the imagery on a given surface. Rather, these categories summarise the dominant characteristics of each panel.

Eogan's (1986:184) proposed correlation between curvilinear imagery and the dead at Knowth has been suggested as problematic. Simply to juxtapose this imagery and the remains of the dead is not explanatory, but descriptive (see Lewis-Williams 1990:133). What needs to be explored is how such patterns inform understandings of the effect and purpose of the art.

Amongst cruciform tombs, interment is generally a feature of the chamber recess: within undifferentiated structures, the central chamber (Eogan 1986:138). With the exception of the subtle variations inherent in a number of the Loughcrew cairns, these are the areas which exhibit the most intensive deployments of imagery. As a general rule, it is only angular imagery which holds a coherent cross-tomb association with burial deposits, as a virtue of both's preoccupation of with internal depth. Within specific tombs and cemeteries, the relationship between angular art and the dead persists, but is articulated alongside more localised concerns.

At Knowth I (east), both the rear and right recesses were found to contain cremation deposits (see Eogan 1986:42), they also exhibit a combination of angular and curvilinear imagery. This suggests that, in some respects, Eogan is correct to postulate a connection between curvilinear imagery and the dead. It is more significant, however, that this same imagery serves to connect internal and external worlds. Directly associated with the cremations of the right hand recess was a stone basin. Externally this was decorated with concentric circles, flanked by arcs and a series of horizontal bands, whilst a lip line, concentric circles and flanking parallel lines were carved on the inside. Similarly, from between the two 'door' jambs of this recess the famous Knowth mace head was recovered (figure 4.23). These two items constitute the only deployments of circular imagery within the chamber and recess area: art which finds its closest comparison in the external kerb stones of the monument. As such, these artefacts reinforce the connection between the dead, orthostat imagery and the conjoining of internal and external worlds.

Figure 4.23:The Knowth mace head (after Eogan & Richardson 1982).

Comparable associations are seen at both Loughcrew and Newgrange. Although cruciform in shape, the only burial recovered from cairn T came from beneath the flagstone of the central chamber with its landscape-type imagery and connotations of the outside/spirit world. This association is repeated at the other principal tomb, cairn L. This latter cairn, however, also contained a recess cremation which at one time may have been mirrored in the former monument. Regardless of recess deposits, the link between the dead and the tergiversation of inside and outside worlds is retained at both these monuments. Unfortunately, no burial evidence remains for cairns H or S, with their comparable image-chamber relationships.

At Newgrange, different burial rites appear to have been practised in different areas: rites which similarly involved the differential deployment of imagery. To the west, burnt bone and circular imagery are dominant, whereas to the east, inhumed remains are found in association with angular motifs. This cardinal bias in image type is repeated along the passage and, as noted above, provides one of the multiple means for the connotation of inversion and interconnection of space at this site. To explain the localised impetus behind these comparable, but divergent, rites one must look to the structure and associated practices of these different monuments.

4.8 From houses of the dead to embodiments of the spirit world

The passage tombs of Ireland have long been regarded as houses for the dead. This, however, is a rather passive assignation. At best, the tombs have been seen as stages for various ancestor rites, and bodily remains a series of associated props. By contrast, it is more profitable to view the passage tombs not as tombs at all but, rather, as active embodiments of the tiered spirit world. To conceptualise these monuments as embodiments of the spirit world, necessitates consideration of the means by which the component 'paraphernalia' of the passage tombs were mobilised to produced specific foci of connotative effect. Each tomb constitutes a venue where co-existing, and mutually reinforcing, understandings of spirituality were articulated through different combinations of imagery, deposition, architecture and the materiality of structure. The balance of these components varies over time and space, in turn emphasising shifts in societal engagement with the decorative strategies of the Neolithic in eastern Ireland

4.8i   Death and Identity

The correlation between certain attributes of passage tomb art and the deposition of the dead suggests that one should ask who was interred within these monuments. It is widely noted that very few bodily remains have been recovered from the passage tombs. Knowth I, for example, although 'open' for up to half a millennia, contained only 20 individuals. Clearly, interment was a matter of great exclusivity. This exclusivity can be bound in numerous ways to the social persona of the shaman and widespread understandings of the altered state as analogical to death. Wallis (1995:12-3) suggests the ongoing social-spiritual 'creation' of the shaman through repeated access to the passage tombs in a series of age - and experience - dependant rites. In this context it is possible to suggest that the remains encountered within the tombs are those of the biologically deceased shaman - now engaged in the ultimate condition of the altered state - whose societal position engendered a comprehensive understanding of the spirit realm which, in turn, was harnessed through interment. This would certainly account for the exclusivity of deposition, but the presence of child burial (see Eogan 1986), for example, suggests more is at work.

Although infrequent, inhumation appears as a passage tomb rite. Generally, it is child interments that are inhumed rather than cremated (Cooney 1992:134). Borrowing from Wallis' scheme, it becomes possible to suggest that initiation into the ranks of the shaman began at an early age, possibly birth. As a consequence of early death, these children were denied full access to the initiation sequence, 'disqualifying' them from the ultimate transformation to spirit provided by cremation. This is consistent with Cooney's (1992:141) suggestion that children were generally excluded from the full practices of death. The same line of reasoning can be applied to the occasional occurrence of adult inhumation. The presence of child cremations, most notably at Fourknocks, however, argues against this interpretation, although even at this site inhumed children considerably out number those cremated. Perhaps different individuals were being selected to perform different roles in the spirit realm, roles which reveal the diversity of practice undertaken at the passage tombs and which, in turn, impact on the creation of shamanic identity and its expression in death. This is an interpretation that can be further explored through consideration of the 'grave goods' recovered from the passage tombs.

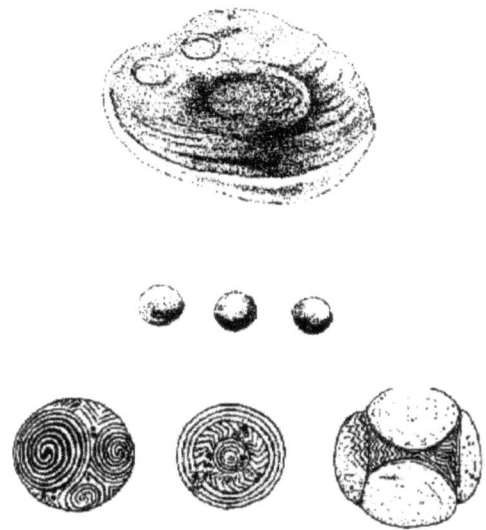

Figure 4.24: Passage tomb 'grave goods' (top and middle) and the carved stone balls (bottom) (drawn by Netty Galvin after Eogan 1986; Marshall 1977).

At Newgrange Z and Battinglass III cremations are found within large stone basins. Burial associated with similar 'vessels' is also seen at the principal tombs of Newgrange (four examples), Knowth (three examples) and Loughrew L (two examples), as well as at a number of satellite structures. It appears likely that, in these latter cases, cremations were again originally deposited in these basins. The placement of ancestral remains in such open vessels is not suggestive of containment but, rather, implies some form of engagement: possibly divination practice. Support for this suggestion comes from one of the basins recovered from Newgrange. This vessel has two cup-marks on its flattened rim, which Wallis (1995) suggests are receptacles for the polished marbles found within the passage tombs. Indeed, 11 such balls were recovered from beneath the basin which occupied the right-hand recess at Loughcrew cairn L (McMann 1994:540). Consistent with Lynch's (cited in Eogan 1986:183) identification of the passage tombs as oracles, and the preparatory rituals suggested for Loughcrew T, Wallis (1995) tentatively interprets these artefacts as scrying tools. [Such an interpretation is by no means incompatible with the use of these balls suggested by the re-carved orthostats at Loughcrew]. Analogy can also be drawn with the carved stone balls of Scotland. It is not unusual for these artefacts to be drawn into the same decorative range as the passage tombs and open-air rock art (e.g. Thomas 1999a:119). MacGregor (1999:267) notes, that when spun, the decoration on these artefacts becomes blurred and the various knobs on their surface take on the form of a solid, uniform boundary. When engaged in such motion, not only is an item removed from the Neolithic / early Bronze Age decorative repertoire, but it also takes on the form of an unworked stone:

crossing the boundary between finely crafted artefact and natural object in a temporary transgression of form which evokes familiar connotations of tergiversation. In these transformations, the manipulation of the carved stone balls recalls the inversions and adjustments of parallel realms evident in the passage tombs, making them eminently suitable scrying aids. Indeed, the worn condition of these artefacts is suggestive of regular handling (MacGregor 1999:265; figure 2.24).

Alternatively, but by no means incompatibly, the basins may have been receptacles for some kind of hallucinogenic preparation - recalling the ritual "stew" found at Barclodiad y Gawres (Powell & Daniel 1956:17) - consumed in the immediate presence of the cremated ancestor. The remains of this ancestor may have been ingested as part of this preparation, or later placed in the basin. Either way, such practice would reinforce the mutually sustaining transgressions of sensory adjustment, 'temporary' and biological death.

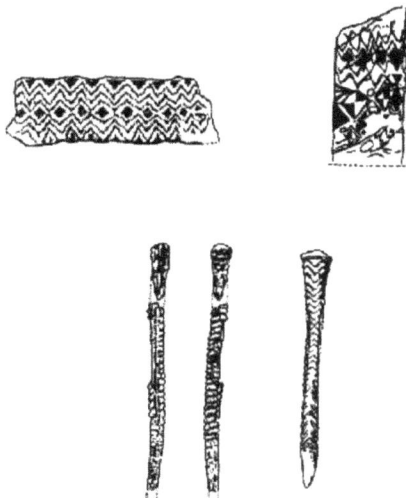

Figure 4.25: Angular Passage tomb imagery (Fourknocks left, Knowth right) and decorated pins (after Eogan 1986).

The presence of burnt bone pins, beads and pendants within cremation deposits suggests it was not only the body that was burnt, but also items of personal adornment. It is significant that the pins recovered from Knowth 3 and Fourknocks (Eogan 1986:140), for example, are carved with lines, chevrons and other angular motifs: image characteristics generally restricted to the depths of the tombs and associated with the dead (figure 4.25). These items may be closely tied to the shamans' social identity. Through the deployment of these items as personal markers, the shaman displayed this imagery within the world of the living where, beyond certain other specialised artefacts such as grooved ware (see Thomas 1996:149), such imagery was generally absent. As such, even in daily life the shaman continually articulated their special relationship with the spirits,

asserting a distinctive identity through atypical decorative strategies which proclaimed their ability to transgress realms. Again parallels can be drawn with the Scottish stone balls. The great majority of these 411 artefacts are found without secure archaeological provenance (Marshall 1976-7:55; Edmonds 1992:189). This has led to their identification as community, family or hereditary objects (Clarke et al 1985:59-62; Edmonds 1992:184). In the context of this chapter, however, it is significant that these balls are the only portable decorated media of the final British Neolithic and early Bronze Age which demonstrate persistent diagnostic characteristics (see Darwell-Smith 2002), suggesting that they are also part of the personal paraphernalia of the shaman (see chapter 6).

Figure 4.26: Rock art therianthropes (after Lewis-Williams & Dowson 1989 & Bahn 1997).

Although they may have asserted a distinctive identity in 'life', within the spirit world, the shamans' sense of separation from the self becomes pronounced, as their ego is subjected to dramatic change and considerable pressure. Indeed, ethnographic accounts suggest that the shaman has to exert considerable effort in maintaining their identity and purpose in the spirit world (see Ouzman 2001:244). Shamanic transformations associated with the greatest depths of the trance experience are widely expressed through the depiction of therianthropes - chimeric figures conflating the attributes of humans and animals - in rock art traditions around the world. Significantly, such figures are entirely absent from the rock art of the British and Irish Neolithic. What is seen, however, is the recurrent intermixing of human and animal bones, which often show evidence of lengthy curatorship (Gosden 1994:159; Edmonds 1995:33; Barclay & Hey 1999:71; Richards 1999:13; Thomas 1999b:15). The frequency with which this association is seen suggests that perhaps these are the 'therianthropes' of the British and Irish Neolithic. If this is the case, then the so-called 'head-and-hoof' burials of this time take on greater significance. Woodward (2000:34) suggests that these deposits "are probably the surviving elements from [entire] leather hides". The disproportionate emphasis on heads and hooves, however, immediately recalls the dominant characteristics of the wider therianthrope phenomenon. On a global scale, it is invariably the head and feet of the shaman which are transformed into corresponding animal body parts (figure 4.26), bodily areas indicative of the sensory inflections of the altered state and feelings of disassociation.

4.8ii   Life after death and the materiality of the spiritual

Neolithic post-mortem transformation of the human (shaman's?) body was often conducted within the tomb itself. Many deposits were kept at alternative locations in these monuments prior to 'interment' in the recess (Eogan 1986:181). At Lanhill (Wiltshire), for example, fully articulated corpses were found close to the entrance, whilst disarticulated arrangements of skulls and long bones occupied the chamber. This suggests the introduction of complete bodies into the passage, which become progressively more disarticulated as the corpse was moved towards the chamber. In this context, the tomb may be seen as a conduit through which the corpse undergoes transformation to the spirit as it transgresses internal divisions of space (see Thomas & Tilley 1993; Thomas 1999b). This is not too dissimilar to the connotations of tergiversation articulated by the distribution of imagery at Newgrange and Knowth - particularly the former with its contrasting spatial patterning of image formalisation - and the bodily transformations associated with the passage-vortex.

Rites undertaken within the tomb structure suggest that biological death alone did not affect the transformation to ancestral shaman. The ultimate transgression from the realm of the living to that of the dead may only have been possible with concomitant bodily decay, architectural permeability and artistic passage. Moving out from the tombs, however, the lengthy curating of bodily remains infers that the dead were often not immediately placed within these funerary structures. Indeed, given a life expectancy of twenty-something they were likely to be 'ever-present', experienced in the arena of living sites (Oram 1997:35; Bradley 1998a:53; Pollard 1999:84; Thomas 1999b:9). Evidence for the continuing involvement of the dead in the affairs of the living is abundant. A wide range of secondary burial strategies is likely to have been practised in the Neolithic, ranging from initial interment with select body parts subsequently removed, to ex-cairnation at alternative sites prior to 'burial' (see Baxter 1999). This suggests that the activities undertaken at the passage tombs were part of a wider system of performative practices, locating these monuments in a currency of post-mortem circulation which included deposition at other monumental locations.

Cooney (1992:129) suggests that the circulation of body parts may have been analogous to the medieval use of saints' bones, relics which held currency as insignia of office, battle talismans

and tribute. It also, however, suggests that the biologically deceased, or even ancestral, shaman were not released from their obligations to the living. This is most clearly illustrated through reference to Knowth. The alignment of eastern and western passages at this monument has lead Eogan (1986:178) to propose two sets of rites performed at the vernal and autumnal equinoxes (see also Wallis 1995). The primary activity is envisaged as a form of procession which unites morning and evening rituals: a convergence of both seasonal and daily liminality. Although procession for its own sake has been critiqued in the previous chapter, the architecture of this monument suggests that at Knowth procession may have involved the transportation of the remains of the dead between tombs, a specific performance of a more widespread practice.

Dronfield (1996) suggests that one of the fundamental tasks of the Neolithic shaman was to act as guide to the souls of the deceased. Procession at Knowth may have been a performative occasion where not only was guidance visibly demonstrated, but the deceased were regarded as actively contributing: guided by the living, and continuing their shamanic travels and tasking in the 'outside/spirit' world. In some respects, this implies the extension of personhood beyond the confines of biological life (see Gell 1998:223) which, in the case of child inhumations, may have enabled the individual to gain full access to the initiation rites which ultimately may have resulted in cremation. It also suggests connections to novel practices of following (circulating) herds and the chimeric 'figures' of head and hoof burials. Returning specifically to Knowth, during this passage the deceased shaman explicitly travelled from the ancestral realms, indicated by angular and curvilinear imagery, through the living-yet-transformed-world suggested by the circular imagery of the kerb which was both 'familiar' in the landscape and simultaneously of the other by virtue of its diagnostic content and stylistic affinities: before returning to the ancestral spirit world (figure 4.27), a performative evocation of the transgression of mound materiality implied by the monument's deployments of curvilinear imagery. This would explicitly assert the permeability and interdependence of these different worlds and the importance of the living shaman as intermediary.

Although there is no reason why cremated remains may not have been handled in the manner described above, the act of cremation itself suggests further levels of significance. This is a practice which transforms the solid body into something more ephemeral and intangible, perhaps 'equivalent' to the spirit (see also O'Brien 1999:205). It is significant that cremation did not take place within the tomb, but was conducted in the open air. This would allow the deceased shaman's body/spirit to diffuse into the ambience and transgress the tiers of the universe in a manner analogous to the extra-corporeal journeys undertaken during altered states of consciousness. As such, through the process of cremation, continuance of activity in the 'outside/spirit' world - the arena where the shamans had performed their duties when alive - was ensured. Subsequent to cremation it is likely that token deposits were placed deep within the tomb structure.

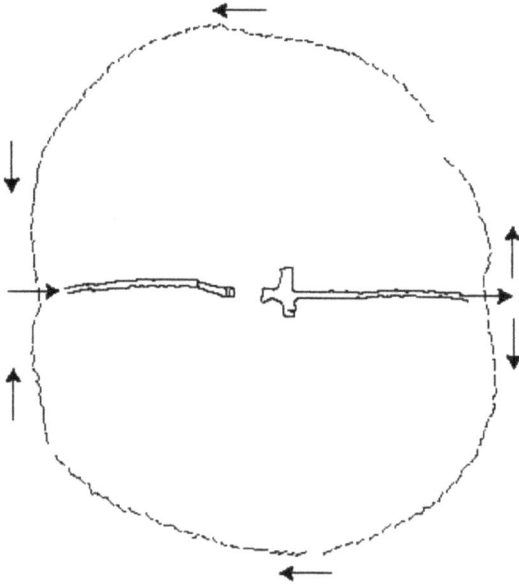

Figure 4.27: Possible processions at Knowth

In this context, it is interesting to note that the angular art - that which is primarily associated with the deceased - of Newgrange, Knowth and Fourknocks predominately occupies an elevated position within the recesses and chamber. As such, just as the essence of idolatry permits real physical interaction (Gell 1998:135), it is possible that the positioning of this imagery above the interred cremations in someway reworked the funerary process and facilitated the rising of smoke and spirit from the 'funeral pyre'. As such, within the Boyne tombs, the shamans exit their bodies and rise up through the tiers of the universe, itself embodied in the sky-like space of the chamber.

The positioning of a number of further interments support this contention. At Newgrange L, for example, a cremation was interred as a foundation deposit for the rear stone of the chamber (Eogan 1986:135), thus physically incorporating the remains of the deceased shaman into the structure of the tomb. Similar structural integration is seen in the intermixing of cremation deposits with sand and soil spreads, and deposition under flagstones. Evidence from the Isle of Arran suggests that the structural incorporation of human remains within the body of the tomb had a wide-reaching effect. At Clachaig, for example, human bones were jammed into the side walls of the chamber, as tomb and ancestor became one in the same entity (Jones 1999:347). What is significant about Clachaig is Jones' suggestion that the tombs of Arran, in their deployment of different stone types, brought together divergent topographical zones as, through construction, people drew upon the

possibilities of meaning associated with procurement and deployment locale - and the materiality of the substance itself - to negotiate meaning.

Amongst the Irish passage tombs, mound materiality was comprised by water-rolled stones, beach pebbles, mountain-top quartz, stripped turf and sand: all of distinctive provenance and particular landscape connotation. Briefly turning to Scandinavia, the great quarries of Aespriholmen and Stakaneset, situated on the Norwegian coast, are located near the important rock art sites of Vingen and Ausevich. Bradley (2000a:81-5) suggests that this imagery 'points' to significant special locations in the vicinity of the quarries, or even the quarries themselves. Concomitant to their materiality, the Boyne tombs have their own peculiar characteristics in which an inversion of Bradley's proposed relationship between quarry and art locale is seen. Bradley (1997a:119) observes that the concentration of rock art at Dundalk (Louth) is located in an area that provided a major source of stone for the Boyne monuments. Given that the deployment of landscape art has been presented as preceding the passage tombs, it is possible that the choice of stone selected for the passage tombs at Newgrange and Knowth was influenced by the location of this imagery. Although this does not constitute redeployment in the sense discussed above, it is again suggestive of a close relationship between the rock art and the passage tombs, indicating that Dundalk remained a location of, at least, historical significance to the passage tomb builders. Unlike at Loughcrew, these people would not have encountered the petroglyphs as part of their daily existence. Rather, this imagery would have been encountered as part of specialised quarrying and procurement visits, its significance grounded in the processes of stone extraction. The indirectness of this relationship can be seen in that it was predominantly uncarved rock, rather than the imagery itself, that was removed and taken to the Boyne and, once 'in situ', although carving exhibited some affinity with the imagery characteristic of the place of procurement, this relationship was deliberately obscured.

Comparable evidence is found in the Chambered cairn at Tullach an T-sionnach. Although located several miles from the sea, large quantities of marine shells and fish bones were recovered from the capping of this monument. Similar inclusions are seen in the mound at Quoyness and in the Knocklea passage tomb (Bradley & Mathews 2000:152-30), and throughout the distribution of both earthen and chambered long barrows (Woodward 2000:100). Bradley and Mathews (2000:153-4), drawing heavily on Bonsall's (1996) work in Oban, suggest that this practice incorporated symbolically charged memory threads into the structure of the tomb, connecting it to the massive cairn-like middens of previous generations and their associated burials. Bonsall's analysis, however, allows for interpretations which move beyond ancestral legitimisation. The location of these middens in a

59

liminal inter-tidal zone leads Bonsall to suggest that such 'structures' acted as conduits from one world - the land - to another - the sea: a gateway from the world of the living to that of the dead. O'Brien (1999:206) also favours a dominant practice of burial at sea throughout all prehistoric periods, at least in the southwest of Ireland, whilst the same liminal positioning is seen in the inter-tidal passage tomb at Roaringwater Bay on Ringarogy Island (Shee-Twohig 1995). In this context, the juxtaposition of animal bones, sea shells and human remains from the Lower Dounreay chambered cairn (Bradley & Mathews 2000:153), amongst others, immediately recalls the bodily transformations, extra-corporeal journeys and tiered universe of the shaman.

Supporting evidence comes from the passage tombs of Brittany; in this instance, however, it takes the form of art. Whittle (2000) presents an alternative interpretation of the axe-plough motifs as representations of whales. These motifs have an exclusively coastal distribution around the Gulf of Morbihan, broadly locating them amongst the connotations evoked by this juxtaposition of realms. In this context, it is particularly significant that at both Mané Rutual and Ile aux Moines, these images are located at the junction of passage and chamber - recalling the positioning of orthostats L/R 5 at Loughcrew T - suggesting that rather than being representations of mythical entities, these creatures are again indicative of the extra-corporeal travels of the shaman. Indeed, Whittle (2000:251), although citing the parallel to produce a very different argument, draws analogy with the widespread understanding of the whale as shamanic spiritual helper along the northwest coast of America.

Interpretation of this evidence suggests that the materiality of the Irish passage tombs is less about the reconstitution of place, as postulated for the tombs of Arran by Jones, than concerned with the values that these materials, and the locales from which they were procured, connote. The quartz for Newgrange, for example, had been quarried from the high mountain peaks of Wicklow - a location which conjoined the upper and middle tiers of the layered universe - and procured by a process which involved the breaking of surface and the conjoining of the middle and subterranean realms. The mound of the same monument was composed of a complex arrangement of turf and water-rolled pebbles, thought to have been recovered from the nearby river Boyne (O'Kelly 1982:92): a transmogrified substance (water) which was not only associated with the realm of the dead and trancing shaman, but also demonstrated just how intimate the relationship between interdigitating worlds was believed to be. Similarly, the deployment of water-rolled stones at Loughcrew brought upper and lower tiers together in a manner analogous to the juxtaposition of quartz and granite at Newgrange. These are only a few examples from a potentially endless list of particular contrivances common to a range of passage tombs, or peculiar to specific sites. But they suggest

that the materiality of these mounds brings together manifestations of water, earth, subterranean space and mountain top, in a material expression of the extra-corporeal effects of the altered state, widely held conceptions of a tiered universe and the transgression of parallel realms. As such, the passage tombs may be understood as venues where the tiers of the universe converged and could be manipulated. Consideration of the concealed imagery at Newgrange demonstrates how each site specifically utilised the common connotative devices of mound materiality to produce their own particular effect.

As noted above, Wallis suggests that concealed imagery of Newgrange stylistically resembles the actual visions of trance. Subsequent analysis reveals that 22.2% of hidden kerb art is diagnostic in character, the greatest concentration within the tomb. This value is closely followed by the diagnostic content of the chamber motifs. Consequently, burial deposits are not only found in an internal space defined by imagery clearly of the altered state, and the dead, but this in turn is 'contained' by motifs which demonstrate more immediate affinities to the same experiences and the outside world. This is consistent with Wallis' (1995) suggestion that the hidden art was made by the spirits (the transformed shaman undergoing the temporary death of trance?) for the spirits (the physically deceased shaman?), to be seen by them alone. Consequently, the inward orientation of the hidden kerb imagery suggests that the contradictory mass of the cairn is also of the transformed 'outside/spirit' world, and constitutes the venue for the transgressive tasking of the deceased shaman. As well as the properties discussed above, quartz is implicated in mechanisms of spiritual communication, magical journeying, interaction with other dimensions and spirit channelling (rockhounding 06/02/02). Bergh (1995:153) has suggested that "as a source of power ... quartz can been seen as giving the dead the power to undertake the journey to the other world". At Newgrange, however, quartz interacts with mound materiality, deployments of rock imagery, personal adornment and the inversion of light, to fulfil another of its recognised roles: that of "time link". That is, although angular imagery facilitates the entry of the dead to the spirit world, interaction between living and ancestral shamans takes place in conjunction with the operation of the roof-box and its intimate integration with deployments of hidden art: imagery characteristic of 'past' landscape deployments and indicative of a parallel realm in which the people from the past reside (see chapter 6).

4.9   Critical connections

As embodiments of the spirit world, the passage tombs do not become something metaphorical, but something imbued with its own reality: a living physical manifestation of parallel worlds and the means to manipulate them. How these worlds were controlled and manipulated varied on a case by case basis, suggesting a diversity of ritual and religious practice along the eastern side of Ireland. Moreover, within all these monuments engagement with the ancestral shaman was contrived through the imagery of the past: the imagery of the landscape with which the long-time-dead and ancestral figures would be familiar. This suggests that for the communities of eastern Ireland, the spirit world was history as much as 'geography'.

More generally, the effectiveness of critically theorising the relationship between open-air and monumental art has been demonstrated, suggesting that comparable analysis of other instances of image redeployment constitutes a profitable enterprise. Indeed, it is the recurrent redeployment of imagery in monuments of the final Neolithic and early Bronze Age that is the subject of the next chapter: a chapter that reveals a significant reworking of both imagery and spirit world.

CHAPTER FIVE
Tracing trajectories
Image redeployment in the final Neolithic and early Bronze Age of the British Isles and Ireland

Although initially a Neolithic phenomenon, the consumption of rock imagery continued into the early Bronze Age. This chapter explores the strategies through which such engagement was conducted through the redeployment of rock art in a range of monuments, and uses these to interpret the differential refocusing of the Neolithic spectrum of effect in different geographical locations.

5.1   Introduction

If stone rows were an enigma, then cup-marks, found primarily on Scottish stone circles .... were a riddle within an enigma (Hyman 1997:125).

Traditionally, the reuse of rock imagery in monumental structures has been used to provide a chronological context for British and Irish rock art. For generations, the association between carved slabs and early Bronze Age cist interments erroneously informed the dating and interpretation of the art. More recently, a number of authors (Simpson & Thawley 1972; Burgess 1990; Bradley 1995b:93, 1997a:138; Van Hoek 1997:14) have observed that the taphonomic features of these engravings suggest that the carvings could not have been primarily executed to decorate these monuments. In this reworked temporal frame, the practice of early Bronze Age re-use has become widely regarded as pointing to the last vestiges of a belief system which eventually "went out of use" (Beckensall 1998:8; Beckensall & Frodsham 1998:55). Physical interment has become equated with social death, and the imagery literally laid to rest in a funerary context. Early Bronze Age practice, however, provides clear evidence for ongoing strategies of redeployment: the placement of 'existing' imagery in a new place, to perform a new task, in new forms of social engagement. Rather than being laid to rest, consideration of these decorated monuments, and the relationship between the imagery of these structures and that left extant in the landscape, suggest that the art remained active amongst early Bronze Age communities.

Much of this chapter is targeted at a relatively high level of generality, the intention being to draw out recurrent patterns in the evidence from which to derive subsequent - and more specific - interpretations. Moreover, this chapter is also concerned with temporal patterns of continuity and change, and, as such, should be read as a continuation of the preceding chapter. Consequently, the observations made and the interpretations presented in forthcoming pages should be approached in this context, not viewed as standing alone, unsupported.

5.2   Spectrum continuity

Round barrows (figure 5.1), the dominant funerary monument of the early Bronze Age, have traditionally been associated with the emergence of the individual concomitant with the arrival of the Beaker folk (Barrett 1990:181; Last 1998: 43; Thomas 1999b:2). In a number of regions, however, these barrows were a feature of the early Neolithic, only coming to numerical pre-eminence during the early Bronze Age (Woodward 2000:36). Consequently, Bronze Age interments of this type, emerged "within traditional monumental contexts" (Thomas 1999b:16), suggesting a long history of development, which in turn implies some continuance in Neolithic structures of effect.

Figure 5.1: *Bronze Age barrows in the Stonehenge landscape.*

The association of round barrows with springs, stream lines and watersheds, or a structure which suggests partial acquiescence to the contours of valley spurs and knolls (Field 1999:6; Woodward 2000:63-74), for example, again suggest a concern to balance the connotative values of monument and landscape. This is also evident in the construction of barrows within regrown clearings, or around trees situated on low knolls (see Hewitt & Beckensall 1996:259; Mullin 2001:536). The appearance of 'continuity' is often mirrored in the materiality of many of these monuments. Although exhibiting considerable morphological variation, the cup-marked barrows of Cornwall, for example, contain many materials which juxtapose their contradictory connotations against those of the landscape. Taking the barrow cemetery located on the St Austell granite as an example, the recurrent use of yellow kaolinized granite, quarried from the single source of a nearby stream bed (Miles 1975:73), brings many of the transgressive connotations of Neolithic mound materiality to these monuments. More widespread practice is seen in the sealing of slate cairns with yellow clay, or an association with quartz spreads (see Christie1985).

The appearance of continuity is not restricted to barrow architecture. The cup-marked stone circles of Perthshire, for example, mirror the topographical associations of the barrows. Many of these circles, including the cup-marked monument at Croft Moraig (see Piggott & Simpson 1971, figure 5.2), were constructed on low knolls composed of water-rolled pebbles, whilst others, such as Lundin (Aberfeldy) (Stewart 1965-6:130; Walker & Ritchie 1987: 175) and the natural ring at Cromraror (Fortingall) (Coles 1909-10:126), straddle carved outcrops. Quartz is again common. White water-worn pebbles are abundant at Croft Moraig, as is quartz-tempered pottery (Piggott & Simpson 1971:8-9). Similarly, two dozen such stones were recovered from beneath the larger mass of water-worn pebbles at Lundin (Stewart 1965-6:131).

Figuree 5.2: The decorated stone circle at Croft Moraig.

Crossing the Irish Sea reveals comparable patterns. Although the wedge tombs of southwestern Ireland (figure 5.3) do not demonstrate any specific or recurrent topographical preference (O'Brien 1999:8), the juxtaposition of a highly erosive coastline and high mountain peaks characteristic of this area, broadly locate these monuments within a readily recognisable topographical zone. This is often complemented by an association with seasonally active springs and streams (see O'Brien 1999:80-3). More specific relationships are evident at the Altar and Toormore tombs (Mizen Peninsula). Both tombs are situated at the high tide mark, locating them on a fluctuating, and highly transgressive, boundary, reminiscent of the inter-tidal passage tomb at Roaringwater, whilst the former is also orientated towards the soaring crest of Mizen Peak (see O'Brien 1999:80-1). More commonly, these monuments are not located immediately on the coast, but set a little distance back,

recalling the association between rock imagery and prominent ridge systems. Extending the analogy, many are at once camouflaged and simultaneously revealed by the local topography: hidden in hillside basins and disguised by adjacent outcrops, but also 'elevated' and revealed by these same topographical associations (see O'Brien 1999:197 & 216).

Figure 5.3: The wedge tombs (drawn by Netty Galvin after an educational leaflet from the Lough Gur visitors centre).

Returning to round barrows as a generic group, there also appears to be some evidence of a 'continuity' in Neolithic practice in the rites conducted at these sites. The construction of barrows over pyre remains (McKinley 1997:137), for example, recalls the Neolithic building of stone, or earthen, monuments on sites formerly occupied by timber mortuary structures. Multiple interment, token deposition and the mixing of cremation and inhumation rites also persist, at least until the middle Bronze Age (Woodward 2000:23-5). Alongside this, one occasionally encounters head and hoof burials (Woodward 2000:34), whilst in 16% of cremations, animals were burnt along side the deceased (McKinley 1997:130). The Irish wedge tombs again demonstrate the intermixing of cremation and inhumation rites. Animal bones are also present, including the three fragments of whale bone recovered from Altar. In the context of chapter 4, rather than seeing this deposit as symbolising a "sea spirit invoked to protect the tomb" (O'Brien 1999:212), it may be more profitable to view it in terms of shamanic transformation, extra-corporeal travel in the subaqueous realm and the transgression of spiritual tiers. Similarly, deposits of animal bones - primarily fish and birds - found at a number of other wedge tombs, may also take on these metaphorical connotations. The same may also apply to the marine shells recovered from cist burials (see Bradley & Mathews 2000:153).

The suggestion of some form of continuity from the Neolithic into the early Bronze Age is further implied by the recovery of a recurrent suite of grave goods from many of the mortuary monuments of this time. In these grave assemblages, however, one can begin to detect the subtle inferences of change which also mark the social developments of the Bronze Age as significantly different to those of the Neolithic. Taken as a whole, the evidence from early Bronze Age grave-goods supports Piggott's interpretation of the rich Wessex barrows as the graves of shaman (see Shell 2000). This is particularly evident in the interment of a specific set of ritual equipment. Woodward (2000:113-21) suggests that miniature incense cups - decorated in geometric patterns and recovered from barrow sites throughout the British Isles - were used for the combustion of aromatic substance, releasing psychoactive smoke. The frequent association of these vessels with strike-a-lights and small bronze knives suggests a suite of artefacts for the preparation and consumption of such substances. Coloured beads make up the remainder of this recurrent assemblage. The small number of beads found in each interment argues against traditional interpretation as necklaces. Rather, Woodward suggests that these items may have been carried in a small pouch, and used as part of a shaman's ritual paraphernalia. Significantly, alongside objects of gold or silver, the colours most commonly taken by these beads are red, black and white: colours which immediately recall the differential deployment of stone types amongst the Clava cairns. Indeed, consideration of these cairns perhaps most clearly reveals how the Neolithic world view was subtly reworked through the architecture and decorative strategies of the early Bronze Age.

5.3   The Clava Cairns: A change of direction

Around the Moray Firth, a group of fifty stone-built passage graves, ring cairns and circles, are collectively referred to as the Clava cairns (figure 5.4). The central cairn of many of these monuments contains a chamber, breached by a passage, and is encircled by a ring of free-standing pillars. This composite architecture has traditionally been interpreted as the integration of passage tomb and stone circle traditions (Tabraham 1998:38; Bradley 1998e:111). Bradley (2000b:1), however, contends that the idiosyncratic character of these monuments is masked by allusion to these wider types, implying that the peculiar architecture of the Clava cairns suggests that they should be approached in ways which extend beyond conventional typology.

Like many monuments of the Neolithic, the distribution of the Clava cairns - along the coastal environs of the Moray Firth and the Nairn, Spey and Ness valleys - immediately locates them in the topographical contradictions of major river systems. Moreover, many of these monuments are located at the junction of valley and basin, in natural hollows, or - in rare instances of upland deployment - along spring lines (Bradley & Mathews 2000:131; Phillips 2000:172-180). The 'camouflaging' effect of the relationship between monument and topography within these settings allows Phillips (2000) to conclude, that the significance of these monuments did not extend beyond the immediately local. This topographical profile, however, is - in many ways - recognisable from the Neolithic. But, the manner

in which the materiality of structure interacts with this profile suggests that something very different is at work in these monuments.

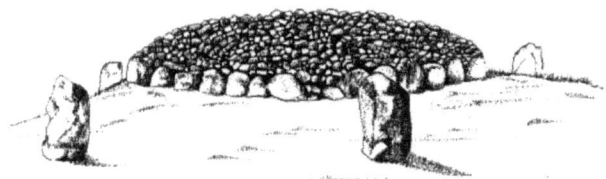

Figure 5.4: The Clava Cairns (drawn by Netty Galvin).

In their most famous manifestation, at Balnuaran, the relationship between the Clava Cairns and their gravel ridge appears to be one of 'seamless' topographical continuance and integration, each monument appearing as an enormous natural boulder set on end (Bradley 2000b:215); an effect enhanced by the construction of an outer casing composed of locally available glacial out-wash (Bradley 2000b:82). Almost all the monuments of the Clava group demonstrate comparable landscape sensitivity in their placement on glacial kanes and natural mounds (Phillips 2000:171-5). This effect, however, is somewhat misleading. At Balnuaran, for example, rather than suggesting an expediency in monument construction, this locally available material overlies that imported from some distance: sandstone quarried from the banks of the river Nairn, marine shells and layers of sand (Bradley 2000b:45, 166; Bradley & Mathews 2000:152). All of these latter materials are of pronounced contrary effect, and imply that, rather than being of the ridge itself - part of its very own materiality - glacial out-wash was used to conceal the connotations of tergiversation beneath the surface.

This deliberate, but 'imperfect', concealment is encountered throughout the architectural devices of the Clava cairns. Once again, this is most apparent in their recurrent concern to connect and transpose internal and external space. Rubble rays, for example, interconnect the central cairn mass and the external ring of monoliths (Bradley 2000b:63-73), in an alignment which emphasises the complementary grading of chamber, kerb and circle stones. Bradley (2000b:217) suggests that the idiosyncratic grading of the chamber - and its explicit, but concealed, connection to the surrounding ring of monoliths - implies "the translation of one building tradition into another": the conversion of stone circles into burial structures. Although this highlights the very deliberate ambiguities of monumental construction, like mound materiality, the subsequent concealment of this architectural statement suggests that greater significance is found in his concomitant suggestion that such an arrangement makes the monument appear as if it has been turned inside-out (Bradley 2000b:162).

This inversion of structure is typified by the differential valuation of material according to colour. Within the chamber of the northeastern passage tomb at Balnuaran, for example, changes in stone colour - from pink to red to white - follow the axis created by the transgressions of the passage. This alignment extends beyond the chamber and through the cairn mass, to re-emerge at a white band of kerb stones. As such, through the differential positioning of stone type and concentric arrangement of graded 'stone circles', the cairn mass becomes permeable: analogous to the encircling monoliths. Alien to the permeability of stone circles, these patterns demonstrate a pronounced directionality. That is, the idiosyncratic structure of the chamber brings the connotative values of the stone circle into the confines of the tomb interior: a significant reversal of the directionality evident in the Irish passage tombs and henge monuments, reinforced by the juxtaposition of stone type according to colour. The conjoining of architecture and prominent celestial events offers explanation for this change of direction.

Both passage graves at Balnuaran demonstrate the lunar alignments typical of the Clava cairns. They also, however, hold a significant relationship with the midwinter sunset. Most simply, the passage alignment of the northeastern monument contrives a beam of light from the setting sun which obliquely illuminates the outward-facing imagery of this architectural zone (Bradley 2000b:123), recreating the optimum conditions for the consumption of imagery in the landscape. By contrast, on entering the southwestern tomb, light passes between two prominent kerb stones positioned at either side of the passage entrance. One of these stones is decorated. Although highly eroded, Bradley (2000b:26) suggests that its partner, also, was once carved: possibly the same rock now split in two. At Newgrange, the operation of the roof-box was presented as facilitating the extra-corporeal movements of the trancing shaman out from the tomb, as they undertook their journeys through the outside-spirit world. At Balnuaran, however - given the connotations of tergiversation evident in landscape imagery - the breakage and outward orientation of the outcrop of the southwestern tomb, suggests physical passage through a conceptually transgressive media into the 'ground' beneath, giving this monument a pronounced out-to-in directionality which echoes that necessary for the recreation of optimum viewing conditions at its sister tomb. Having passed through the split outcrop, and down a passage characterised by distinctive stone types, the beam of light illuminates a row of low stones along the rear chamber wall, distinguishable from the remaining interior in terms of their high quartz content (Bradley 2000b:122-26). As such, moving from out to in, the midwinter sun exhibits an almost linear alignment with material which initially absorbs light (Bradley 2000b:128). On entering the

tomb's interior, this relationship is retained, but gradually reduces in coherency as light penetrates more deeply into the tomb. Interaction with different stone types suggests an incremental change in the nature of the light beam until it hits the rear wall, where the high quartz content creates an 'explosion' of brightness: effectively bringing the setting sun inside the chamber.

Positioned directly behind this band of quartz, a series of carvings are located in the rear wall of the southwestern chamber. These hidden cup-marks face into the repositioned sun which, in turn, 'illuminates' them. Consequently, although hidden, this art work is rendered 'visible'. Like the idiosyncrasies of architecture, however, it is not visible in the real world, but only in the now discrete and concealed realm of the dead: a world lit by the transmogrified power of the dying winter sun. Similarly, although outward facing, the kerb imagery of the Balnuaran cairns is again hidden, concealed by the conjoining of ray and kerb (Bradley 2000b:56). Given the apparent fluidity of material understandings, and the intimate relationship between sunlight and concealed image redeployments at this site, it is not unreasonable to suggest that these rubble rays were also conceptualised as transmogrified light sources, indicative of the material and conceptual differences between the actual and repositioned sun, and their very different worlds.

O'Brien's (1999:196) interpretation of the wedge tombs as "funnel-shaped opening[s] to the other world" gives these monuments the same directionality as the Clava cairns. This suggestion finds resonance in the orientation of these monuments. Not only does the recurrent positioning of the tomb entrance to the west echo the cardinal alignments discussed above, but it also implies a series of evening rites, during which, the participants' shadows would be cast *into* the monuments (O'Brien 1999:217). Again, the correlation between inward movement, the dying sun of the west and deposition of the dead is apparent, which, in combination with the architecture of the monument, suggest that these monuments were portals which lead to a more discrete subterranean, or subaqueous, realm of the dead. The geographical link between strategies of image redeployment evident in southwest Ireland and Cornwall (see 5.13), suggest that the relationship between imagery, the dead and the setting sun amongst the Cornish barrows (see Christie 1985:74-83) effects comparable understandings of the spirit world.

Although few attempts have been made to interpret the patterns of image redeployment in cist burials, contrary to the analysis of Simpson and Thawley (1972:84; also Burgess 1990:164), the incorporation of rock art in these monuments was conducted in a highly structured manner. Consistently, roof slabs are set with the imagery facing inwards, towards the corpse (Bradley 1992:173; 1995c:123). Beckensall (1999:111) draws a contrast between sky-orientated landscape art and earth-orientated single grave art. Bradley (1992) offers a comparable interpretation, but is a little more expansive. Building on his postulated correlation between open-air rock art sites and viewpoints (but see chapter 3), he suggests that the messages, which once informed the living, now informed the dead: something which could only be seen from within the spirit world.

5.4   Spectrum change

Bradley (2000b:223) suggests that the morphological differences between the Clava cairns and the passage tombs of the Neolithic can be attributed to a radically different cosmological understanding and, as such, these monuments belonged "to a different world from the monuments of the third millennium BC". Moreover, the redeployment of rock art in the early Bronze Age suggests the existence of a more discrete and distant spiritual realm which, initially, appears in marked contradistinction to the interdigitating realms of the Neolithic. Precedent, however, does exist in the sealing of tomb entrances during the later Neolithic of western Britain (Thomas 1999b:17): a geographically significant distribution of activity which is implicated in the regional trajectories of Bronze Age image consumption (see below and chapter 6). This 'new' realm is accompanied by a directionality of rite common to virtually all monument types in which landscape imagery is redeployed at this time. The consistent emphasis of movement from out-to-in, from the world at large to a specific place, once more suggests a pronounced sense of separation. That it is the world of the dead with which the redeployment of rock imagery is concerned, is not only evidenced by the permanent interment of human remains, but also by the westerly orientation of the wedge tombs, the midwinter sunset of the Clava Cairns and earth-orientated slabs of cist burials.

The distance between these worlds is temporal, as well as spatial. The redeployment of rock imagery in this manner, immediately recalls the association between the dead, and art recognisably of the past, noted for the Boyne passage tombs. On this occasion, however, a greater depth of history is juxtaposed against a greater sense of architectural, spatial, and spiritual containment: and a specificity of interment location. How these monuments were embroiled in new ways of living, and the significance of their image redeployments, is discussed more fully in chapter 6.

The practice of image redeployment, however, is not only concerned with the inclusion of rock imagery in monumental structures, but also involves the interaction of this imagery with that left extant in the landscape. It is this relationship which suggests that multiple strategies of image redeployment existed in the final Neolithic and early Bronze Age. Analysis of these strategies provides interpretative clues to the meaning and intent of this practice in the different areas in which the internment of landscape art is seen (see also Evans & Dowson 2003).

5.5   Strategies of early Bronze Age image redeployment

The instances of early Bronze Age artistic engagement discussed above are separated by considerable geographical distance. Despite this, clear patterning is evident in the strategies through which this imagery was consumed. Analysis of these strategies evokes the three-fold saliency of the open-air rock art - standard, elaborate and idiosyncratic - set out in chapter 2. At a national level, all three levels of petroglyph saliency (see chapter 2) are manifest in the corpus of early Bronze Age redeployment. Given the extent of variation in open air rock art, however, it is clearly inappropriate for studies which seek explanation for Bronze Age artistic strategies simply to juxtapose a single rock art repertoire against the entire monumental range. To be explanatory, monumental redeployments of rock art need to be considered in terms of their artistic relationship with local deployments of landscape art (figure 5.5).

5.6   Western Ireland

Although examples are found in the east, open-air rock art is primarily a feature of the western side of Ireland (Shee 1968:144; Lacy 1983:98; Van Hoek 1985:123, 1987:23-5, 1997:12; Johnston 1989:42; Harding 2000:341). Within this, the numerical balance of distribution is heavily weighted in favour of the Cork-Kerry group (Johnston 1989:19). This area is also home to a significant concentration of wedge tombs (Johnston 1989:295; O'Brien 1993; 1994; 1999; Walsh 1993, 1995). The open air rock art of southwestern Ireland is particularly elaborate, exhibiting strong regional characteristics and a high degree of innovation and idiosyncrasy. By contrast, redeployment in the wedge tombs is characterised by an extremely standardised range. The monument at Ballyvoge Beg, for example, contains only cup-marks, whilst that at Ballyhoneen - also in Kerry - consists of 12 cup-marks, one of which is encircled by a single broken ring (Johnston 1989:119; O'Brien 1999:209). The same restrictive repertoire also appears on the boulder burials andstone circles of the south and west (see Burl 1979:147; Johnston 1989:226; Burgess 1990:166; O'Brien 1999:218-23).

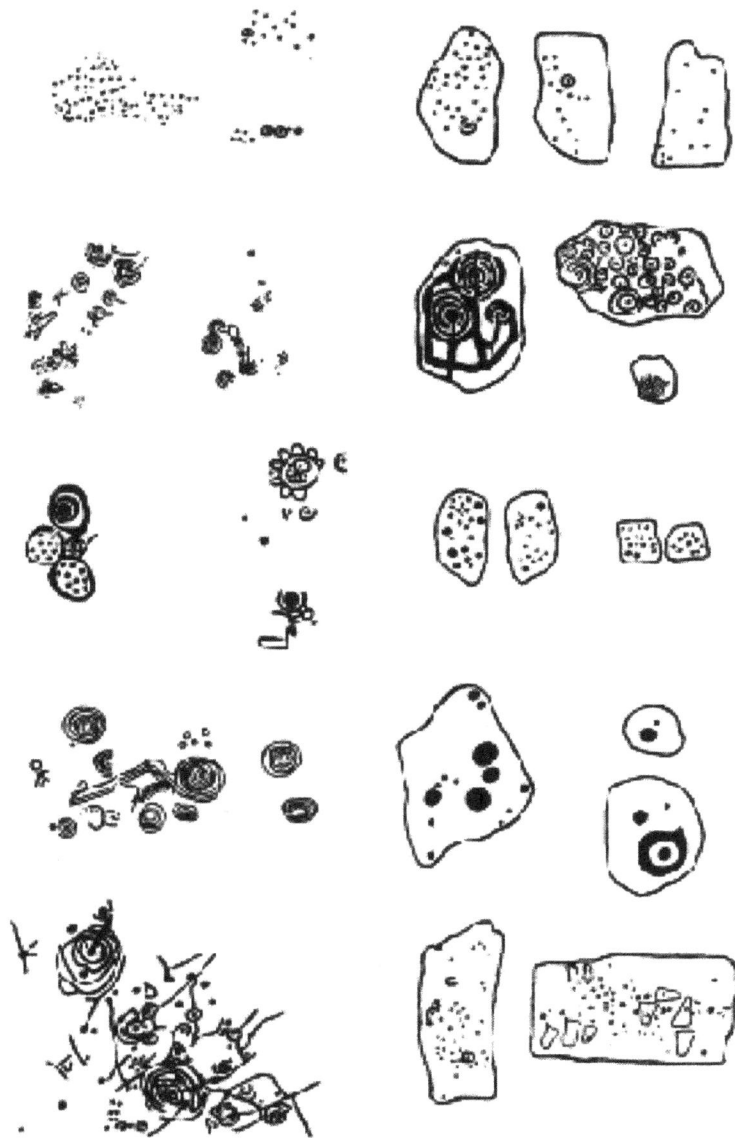

Figure 5.5: The redeployment of rock art in the British Isles. Left = landscape art, Right = redeployed imagery. From top to bottom: northeast Scotland, northeast England, the Peak District, Cumbria, Kilmartin (data after Barnatt & Reeder 1982, RCAHMS 1988; Frodsham 1989; Beckensall 1999).

5.7   Western Scotland: The Kilmartin valley, Argyll

Along the western coast of Scotland, the redeployment of rock art is evident in the cist burials of Ayrshire. This art, however, is highly idiosyncratic and very little imagery is found in the landscape (see Morris 1981). Although further fieldwork may help clarify the relationship between art of the funerary context and that of the landscape in this area, at the time of writing patterns derived from this evidence are somewhat tenuous. Kilmartin, in Argyll, however, offers greater opportunities for analysis. The Kilmartin valley is home to both an elaborate concentration of rock art and an extensive cist burial cemetery. Seven cairns are located along the valley floor, two of which - Nether Largie Mid and Nether Largie North - show evidence of

image redeployment drawn from the rock art corpus. Temporarily leaving aside the locally recurrent axe motif, a subsequent addition to the quarried outcrops (Oram 1999:139-40; Bradley 1997a; Beckensall 1999:111; Butler 1999:56), the imagery redeployed in these cists is again of a standardised range: very different to that encountered in the landscape. This range of redeployment extends to the cluster of standing stones located in the area, including Ballymeanoch, Nether Largie and Torbhlaran (see Burgess 1990:166; Beckensall 1999:123).

The Temple Wood stone circle is located in the same valley system as the Kilmartin cist burials. Although from the outset a pair of circles, only one is considered here: that which began its life as a stone, rather than a wooden, structure (see Bradley

67

1998a:136). The first phase of this monument comprised a ring of stone uprights, two of which were decorated: one with a double spiral, the other with a pair of concentric circles (Beckensall 1999:120): imagery immediately comparable with the rock art of the landscape (figure 4.2; Kinnes 1995:51). This immediately appears to contrast with the strategies of redeployment evident in the cist internments and standing stones. Significantly, however, this phase of building dates to the Neolithic. By contrast, during the early Bronze Age, a stone kerb was constructed and the monument began to be used for burial (Bradley 1998a:136). Amongst this secondary construction, Beckensall (1999:121) identified a slab decorated with two cup-marks, bringing this monument within the wider strategies of redeployment evident throughout the valley at this time.

Early Bronze Age image redeployment in the Kilmartin valley does extend beyond the standardised rock art range. Again, however, cist imagery from Badden and Carn Ban demonstrates a concern to avoid the locally dominant rock art repertoire, and, instead, places angular imagery - more characteristic of the later passage tombs - in burial structures of this date (see RCAHMS 1988; Beckensall 1999:122; below).

5.8   Northeast Scotland

Distributed some distance west of the Clava cairns, the recumbent stone circles echo many features of the former monument type (Bradley 2000b:3). Convergence is seen in the grading and number of orthostats, distinctive colour zones and an association with burial (Burl 1969-70:18; Bradley 2000b:7). Much of this correspondence is manifest in the recumbent stone itself, the same stone which is most commonly carved in the same standardised image range as the Clava Cairns (see Burl 1969-70:65, 1979:140; Bradley 1998e:111, 2000b:26-45). This disproportionate emphasis on cup-marking is replicated in the landscape. Although it is necessary to reposition the chronological focus of his argument - from the later Neolithic to the early Bronze Age - the predominance of cup-marking suggests that there is some merit to Burgess' (1990:160) suggestion that the "north-east [of] Scotland is one area where the ubiquity and context of cup marks makes clear their continuing importance". More productively, however, the multi-contextual emphasis of cup-marking points to a strategy of image redeployment immediately drawn from an established trajectory of rock carving.

Strategies of drawing image redeployment from the local landscape repertoire continue down the eastern side of Scotland. In Fife, for example, cist burials are accompanied by the inclusion of a standardised image range, whilst around Edinburgh and the Borders it is more elaborate motifs which fulfil both roles.

5.9   Central Scotland

Little in the way of cist imagery is found in the inland areas of Scotland between the Forths of Clyde and Firth. The only concentration of note can be found around Glasgow. Here, the cist imagery is as elaborate as the imagery of the landscape. In areas where there are no decorated cists, around Loch Tay in Perthshire, for example, rock with standardised imagery is used in the stone circle monuments generally accepted to be dated to the early Bronze Age (Morris 1981), emulating the standard character of art in the landscape. One can also tentatively suggest more subtle intricacies of patterning in the area around the Tay.

Along the northern shores of Loch Tay a number of undecorated stone circles are located in the same topographical zone as extensive rock art spreads. This pattern is repeated a little distance north, at the stone circle complex of Fortingall. Similarly, following the Tay valley east to Aberfeldy, an analogous situation is encountered in the four-poster and paired stones of Lundin (Stewart 1965-6:126-130).

Between these concentrations of monuments - indeed, 'central' to all three clusters - an inversion of pattern occurs around the confluence of the rivers Tay and Lyon (figure 2.29). Although this collection of cup-marked monuments, including the decorated circles of Croft Moraig (see Piggott & Simpson 1971) and Carse Farm (Barnatt 1989a:313-4), are constructed in an area in which cup-marking proliferates, their immediate locale is devoid of landscape imagery. In this context, it is perhaps significant that the presence of cup-marking at Croft Moraig corresponds to Barnatt's (1989b:179-182) identification of a regional centre, whereas the smaller undecorated circles - distributed to the west, east and north of this site - are closely allied to those sites he considers to be of local use.

Exceptions to this pattern exist, including the cup-marked circle of Colen - situated on a terrace above Loch Tay (Burl 1976:195) - and the undecorated Balhomais circle of the Tay-Lyon complex. These exceptions, and the possibility that many rock art sites around the Tay-Lyon complex have been destroyed by the improving agriculture characteristic of this area, suggest that this correlation should be treated with caution and, perhaps, the wider pattern of landscape emulation considered as representative of the entire area.

5.10   Northeast England

The full range of the rock art repertoire is redeployed in the cist interments of northeast England. Despite this, an elaborate image range predominates in both cist and landscape art, again suggesting strategies of redeployment consistent with the locally dominant artistic trajectory. The immediacy of this interconnection is most clearly illustrated on Weetwood Moor.

At Weetwood, a number of early Bronze Age cairns were constructed above previously carved outcrops. These monuments, however, were built in a manner which allowed most of the imagery to remain visible. Each in turn was also located in an area of extensive rock art distribution (Beckensall 1999:144-9), intimately connecting the imagery of the funerary rite to that of the landscape.

5.11   Northwest England

The two major valley systems of the Lake District are home to a limited distribution of landscape art (Beckensall 2002). Although occasionally resembling the standardised range of the cup-and-ring corpus, this imagery is more readily identifiable with the concentric circles, curvilinear sweeps and meandering linear motifs of the recently discovered Chapel Stile site (figure 5.6). This gives the rock art of this county a somewhat idiosyncratic character, which is repeated in a number of freestanding monuments, most famously the outlying stone at the circle complex of Long Meg and Her Daughters. The spirals, concentric circles and meandering lines of this massive block are thought to have stood originally as open air carvings in the red sandstone cliffs of the river Eden (Frodsham 1989:111-3), where they occupied the same vertical plane as the Chapel Stile motifs. The circle at Long Meg shares many architectural characteristics with the monuments at Kemp Howe, Grey Yauds and Castlerigg (Barnatt 1989(a): 344, 1989(b): 183). The imagery at Castlerigg is comparable with the elaborate imagery at Long Meg, as well as the stones recovered from the Neolithic burial monument at Old Parks.

Significantly, Burl (1976: 60) places Long Meg and Castlerigg amongst the earliest of British stone circles, locating them in the Neolithic; the same chronological horizon as the decorated burial structure at Old Parks (Beckensall1999). Because of comparable imagery Burl (1994: 7) argues that Little Meg is also Neolithic in age, while extending Burl's argument suggests the decorated cairn at Glassonby is the same age. Neolithic re-use of rock art in Cumbria is such that it is similar in character to the rock art in the landscape. Considering the three decorated stones at Little Meg, however, suggests an alternative interpretation of the age of this site. Two of these stones belong to the standardised cup-and-ring range whilst the so-called Maughanby stone has elaborate imagery, as in the landscape. Significantly, the two unnamed stones were associated with a cist-like structure, whilst the Maughanby stone retained the striking physical appearance it once had in the landscape (Frodsham 1996). Almost certainly the cist is a later structure. Evidence to support this suggestion comes from the Shap Avenue, a monument that according to Burl's scheme has a construction life that straddles the boundary of the Neolithic and the Bronze Age. Two of the few remaining stones of this monument, Aspers Field and Goggleby, have standard cup-and-

ring imagery, as is the case in the cist structure of Little Meg. This emphasis on standard imagery continues into monuments that are unequivocally dated to the early Bronze Age (including the ring cairn of Moor Divock, the double ring cairn of Hardendale, and cist covers at Redhills and Maryport). The carved rocks of Stag Stone Farm, Honey Pots, Dean and Penrith museum can also be added to this list (data from Frodsham 1989; Beckensall 1999). Although these rocks are not accurately provenanced, the material form and the truncation of motifs are reminiscent of early Bronze Age cist slabs encountered elsewhere.

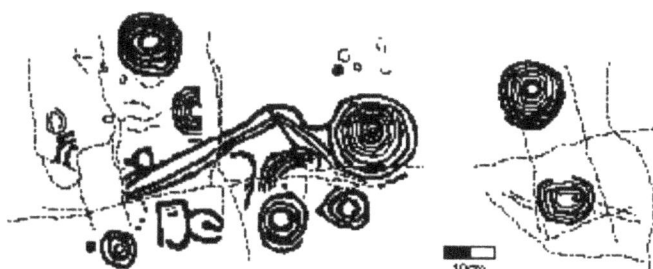

Figure 5.6: The engravings at Chapel Stile

When considered in totality, the redeployment of rock art in Cumbria suggest that strategies of image reuse appear to have undergone a dramatic reworking as the Neolithic passed into the early Bronze Age: turning away from visible redeployments of a locally dominant repertoire to the concealment of a standardised range of more 'alien' imagery in structures for the dead. The convergence between this pattern and the sequence at Temple Wood is self-evident.

The contrasting characteristics of landscape imagery and early Bronze Age monumental redeployments finds even more pronounced expression in the Peak District. The carving of living rock in this area is highly idiosyncratic, containing little standard imagery (see Barnatt & Reader 1981; Barnatt & Firth 1983). In contrast, imagery found in monumental contexts rarely extends beyond cup-marking, bringing these patterns of redeployment full circle and 'analogous' to the wedge tombs of southwestern Ireland (5.6).

5.12   Strategies of early Bronze Age image redeployment

Amongst early Bronze Age cist interments, it is widely believed that "the choice of motifs was influenced by conventions that were already well established": a deliberate selection policy which favoured the overemphasis on an elaborate image range above more standardised components (Bradley 1997a:139-52). This, however, masks much of the interplay which makes up two distinctive strategies of image redeployment: imagery drawn from immediately local bodies of pre-existing motif types and those strategies which eschew the dominant character of local landscape art in favour of a more standardised range. Rather than the existence of a set of selection criteria based upon the visual characteristics of a particular art site, what is seen in the practice of early Bronze Age redeployment are strategies which respond to the dominant characteristics of landscape imagery in different ways. it is this relationship which also accounts for the perceived dominance of elaborate imagery in early Bronze age cist art. That is, it is the numerical bias of decorated cist burials located in the northeast of England, coupled with the elaborate character of landscape art and a strategy of drawing redeployment directly from this repertoire, which produces an 'overemphasis' in the national corpus.

Evidence from Kilmartin and Cumbria further suggests that these early Bronze Age redeployments were the product of strategies which differed greatly from those extant in the Neolithic and, consequently, imply that the conventions which governed these decorative strategies were in many ways novel. Novelty, in turn, suggests active engagement with rock imagery during this later period of prehistory. This novelty is also apparent in the presence of passage tomb-like imagery in the cist burials of western Scotland. Somewhat paradoxically, it is from the other end of the British Isles, the southwestern peninsula of Cornwall, that insights into these idiosyncratic inclusions can be gained.

5.13   Cornwall and the southwest of the British Isles

The discovery of 12 cup-marked stones at Stithians reservoir - during an intense period of drought - was interpreted by Hartgroves (1987) as a probable incidence of landscape art. From this, and the records of the Cornish SMR, he tentatively proposed that the "fact that there is ... no recorded occurrence of ring markings or other more elaborate motifs ... suggests that the ... inhabitants of the south-west peninsula were pursuing ... their own tradition in respect of this branch of 'rock art'". Review of the gazetteer appended to Hartgroves' article, however, reveals only one unequivocal example of landscape art: the cup-marked stone of Tintagel Island. The remaining gazetteer is composed of carved stones situated in a monumental context, or examples without provenance, carved on loose slabs and of comparable form to those recovered from barrows. Indeed, Beckensall (1999:83-7) contends that there are no decorated outcrops in Cornwall, but 14 sites in which cup-marked rocks are interred in barrows dating to the early Bronze Age (see Bradley 1997a:148 and Christie 1985 for chronological evidence). This dramatic bias supports Christie's (1985) interpretation of the Stithians' stones as a denuded barrow. Consequently, during the early Bronze Age on the southwestern extremity of the British Isles, one is confronted by the carving of the most standardised range of the rock art repertoire for inclusion in these mortuary monuments, rather than the reuse of landscape art.

5.14   Regional patterning in strategies of early Bronze Age image use

In his 1997(a) publication, *Signing the land*, Richard Bradley postulated the existence of two trajectories of early Bronze Age image re-use: a western tradition centring on the Cornish evidence and a northern trajectory taking in established areas of rock carving. The former he considered characterised by a standardised image range, and the latter dominated by more elaborate compositions. By contrast, Haddingham (quoted in Beckensall and Frodsham 1998:52), suggested that "the distribution of carved cists may confirm the assumption that complex cup-and-ring carving had died out in some western districts by Bronze Age times, but that in eastern areas its influence persisted". Extending the range of enquiry to encompass southwestern Ireland, and contexts other than cist interments, confirms that it is more profitable to speak of an east-west divide: but in terms of strategy, rather than both authors emphasis on image content and Haddingham's conjectural longevity of regionally specific trajectories of carving. That is, placing a line down the centre of the British Isles, redeployment strategies in the east are exclusively drawn from the local landscape repertoire. In contrast, those to the west are characterised by the emphasis on a standardised image range, at odds with the dominant landscape repertoire (figure 5.7).

In its absence of landscape imagery, and exclusive cup-marking of monuments, the evidence from Cornwall suggests a mimicking of the redeployment strategies characteristic of the western half of the British Isles. It is from the southwest of Ireland, with its comparable strategies of image redeployment, however, that explanation is found for the 'appearance' of rock imagery in the Cornish Bronze Age. The wedge tombs of southwestern Ireland were constructed on the metalliferous peninsulas of Cork and Kerry, at about the same time as a rapid expansion of metal production was witnessed. Although copper was common to this area, a lack of tin provided a significant incentive for exchange with other metal-using communities. There is no evidence for the exploitation of tin in Ireland at this time, suggesting that the rich alluvial deposits of southwestern England were the most likely source of this raw material for the tomb builders of these peninsulas (O'Brien 1994:241-9; O'Sullivan & Sheehan 1996:74-7; Harding 2000:200). As such, explanation for the cup-marking of Cornish barrows is found in the convergence of Cornish tin and Irish copper in the production of bronze. The same route, and motivation, have been suggested by O'Brien (1994:249) to account for the appearance of stone circles in the southern extremities of Ireland, whilst the provenance of a series of artefacts, deposited either side of the Irish Sea, lends weight to the argument.

Figure 5.7: *Redeployment strategies in the British Isles and Ireland.*

Legend:
- Redeployment of standard imagery
- Redeployment of local landscape repertoire
- Unclear redeployment strategy

Similarly, in Perthshire, the axe procurement site of Creag na Caillich (Killin) also conforms to Cooney's (1997b:110) identification of a common profile. Not only are many of the petroglyphs of this area located in positions which reveal the profile of this mountain top, particularly given the uphill bias of viewing, but the stone obtained from this site demonstrates a similar petrology to that of Langdale (Ritchie & Ritchie 1981:46).

The connection between rock carving and stone procurement expands if one considers the many decorated monuments of Neolithic Cumbria. Like the large stone circles of Scotland (see Ruggles 1999:206), those of Cumbria were designed to encapsulate significant astronomical alignments (Burl 1994:8). Burl (1976:77-8, 1994:10) also suggests that the outliers of the Cumbrian circles further operated as direction markers, and the monuments themselves as staging posts, where visitors came to acquire axes from Langdale.

The deposition of artefacts procured from Langdale supports Burl's contention. Long Meg, for example, is located in the catchment area of a great many group VI products: most directly the Hunsonby rough-out group (Burl 1976:68-9). Similar relationships are evident for the decorated stone circles of Glassonby and Castlerigg (Bradley 1988:206; Burl 1994:10; also Cummins 1980; Bradley 1988; Darvil 1996a:211). Quoting Collingwood (in Burl 1994:10), but wary of cultural-historic implications, it appears as if "the stone circles and the axes thus hang together and seem to demand explanation as relics of a single people". To this list, in certain circumstances, rock art can be added.

The range of these Cumbrian associations extends beyond the stone circles, with a number of authors (Burl 1976:57; Cummins 1980; Bradley 1988; Darvill 1996a:211) proposing a correlation between axe production and major henge monuments. The grinding floors at Clifton and Belmont, for example, are thought to be connected to the three Penrith henges. Again, the Chapel Stile petroglyph site suggests an affinity with the henges. As one approaches the primary rock face at Chapel Stile, from north to south, the lower reaches of the Pike O' Sickle disappear, creating an optical illusion not dissimilar to that of many henges. As such, it is not too surprising that the arrangement of these stones recalls the internal settings of a number of such monuments (figure 5.8).

Similar mechanisms offer explanation for the depiction of metal axe heads in the cist interments of Kilmartin. Needham (1988; see also Bradley 1998b) suggests that these later depictions show greater affinities with hoard deposits than grave assemblages, implicitly linking them to cycles of procurement and deposition, rather than attributing exclusive use as 'artefacts' for the dead. In this context, the carving of a cup-mark and metal axe on the Drombeg stone circle takes on additional significance.

Precedent for this interconnection between the carving of cup-and-ring imagery and the procurement of material for the production of axes can be found in the Neolithic. The engravings of Chapel Stile, for example, are located in close proximity to the Pike O' Sickle (Langdale) axe factory. Visual consumption of this imagery reveals the distinctive profile of this prominent procurement site: a significant observation given Cooney's (1997b) suggested commonality of profile amongst the major stone sources of the Neolithic. The huge erratics on which the imagery of this site is carved resemble quarried blocks, displaced from the mountainside above (Beckensall 2002:69), implying an immediate allusion to the elevated location of stone procurement and act of extraction itself.

71

Figure 5.8a: The 'cove-like' arrangement of the Chapel Stile rock art site.

Figure 5.8b: An example of the internal settings at Avebury.

Wider connections between stone axes, their places of procurement and rock carving are seen in the recurrent Neolithic practice of depositing artefacts in places reminiscent of their procurement. Stone tools, for example, are commonly deposited in rock fissures, whilst carved chalk is frequently recovered from chalk pits (Bradley 2000a:121). With regard to the passage tombs of the Boyne, it is rock imagery which provides the commonality between place of inception and deposition whilst, similarly, 53.8% of the Langdale axes crossed the Pennines and were deposited in Northumberland (see Waddington 1999), an area rich in landscape art.

Operative alongside the strategies of early Bronze Age image redeployment discussed above, a further level of saliency is evident in this practice. Although Irish cist art is rare, in contradistinction to the 'mutual' distribution of British cist and landscape art, decorated Irish cists occur away from major concentrations of rock carving. As such, where cist imagery is

encountered it again 'diverges' from landscape repertoires, in that no such imagery exists in the local landscape. More is at work here, however, as there are no cists "decorated in the Galician [cup-and-ring] style from Ireland" (Simpson & Thawley 1972). The few interments which are encountered, hail from the passage tomb repertoire (see MacWhite 1946:72; Shee 1972; Johnston 1989:114-5). Consequently, by the early Bronze Age, it is passage tomb-style art which is exclusively redeployed in single grave interments along the northern and eastern coasts of this country. In contrast, on the British mainland the pristine condition of a number of cist slabs, and the re-carving of quarried outcrops (Bradley 1997a:140; Beckensall & Frodsham 1998:58), suggest a continuing currency for landscape art. These patterns of redeployment suggest that in areas with a well-established tradition of carving living rock, including southwestern Ireland, this style of image making enjoyed great longevity. Alternatively, where this was not so well established, the use-life of a largely alien imagery was more short lived, superseded by the passage tomb repertoire (see chapters 4 and 6). Within this structure, the passage tomb-like inclusions of Kilmartin suggest the contemporaneous existence, and local manipulation, of divergent trajectories: pointing to both mimicry and more widely distributed strategies of image redeployment encountered in the west of the British mainland.

5.15   From Neolithic to early Bronze Age

Although much of the Neolithic spectrum of effect is retained into the early Bronze Age, there is a consistent concern to conceal visible expression of it. This concealment accompanies a re-conceptualisation of the structure of the universe away from the interdigitating realms of the Neolithic, towards understandings of the world of the dead as a more discrete entity. The existence of clear strategies of image redeployment in the mortuary monuments of this time, suggests that, in a number of areas, rock art played a significant role in reconstituting this realm. Moreover, although in all cases the active 'distancing' of the dead is apparent, the different artistic trajectories evident in each region suggests a local understanding and reworking of this central concept.

Contrary to suggestions that the redeployment of imagery is indicative of a dying belief system, these redeployment strategies suggests that the communities of the early Bronze Age continued to engage with rock art in the open air: and that this was consumed in different ways in different social situations. As such, imagery was interred not as the result of a lack of relevancy, but because it was of the past, an active and ongoing history which was used to inform the present through both its materiality and those who had lived it (see chapter 6).

CHAPTER SIX
Discussion
An interpretation of the rock art of the British Isles and Ireland

The ongoing interrelationship between rock imagery and architecture allows for the identification of a changing social role, through both time and space, for the rock art of the British Isles and Ireland during the Neolithic and early Bronze Age. This chapter explores how this role is implicated in the social persona of a series of religious practitioners and how this persona, in turn, is integrated in broader social developments.

6.1   Introduction

> *If all rock-art is Neolithic, if all cist slabs are reused, if all motifs are both specific and specifying, then horizons of date, correlation and inspiration - even the establishment of particular belief systems - could be established ... but we must not substitute a wished for prehistory for the attainable actuality* (Kinnes 1995:52).

From the very outset, the citing of Malmer and Duff positioned this thesis outside of the dominant discourse of British and Irish rock art research. Through subsequent pages the existence of a widespread connotative saliency has been identified, and mechanisms of focus and effect utilised to produce interpretations for many Neolithic artistic and monumental trajectories. This saliency is not the wished-for convergence of Kinnes, but a demonstrable 'entity' composed of identifiable patterns, whose subtle interplay can be used to address the significance of Malmer's and Duff's words in coming towards an understanding of this particular body of rock art, and the interpretation of its many recurrent characteristics. This chapter makes use of a range of synthesises to produce a broad context in which to interpret the patterns identified in preceding pages: a strategy that allows for the construction of a history for the neolithic through its art.

6.2   Cultural selection and the 'specificity' of carving

The juxtaposition of rock art materiality and landscape has been shown to connote, and balance, a paradoxical ambiguity in which what is emphasised is simultaneously alleviated; what is implied, obscured. This interpretation finds resonance in the apparently random distribution of local carving traditions and the intermixing of decorated stones with uncarved rock. Geology and significant topography, although operative at wider scales of analysis (see below), have little impact at the immediately local level, suggesting the cultural selection of suitable surfaces. Selection is often taken as implying that there is something special, even unique, about the choice of the locale singled out for carving. This is evident in Deacon's (1988) analysis of the distribution of /Xam imagery in northern Cape Province, and echoed in Bradley's (2000a:3-17) identification of "sacred places in the northern landscape".

Amongst the rock art of the British Isles and Ireland, however, carved and uncarved stones share the same materiality and topographical correlates: neither is obviously distinct until one is in a position to view the imagery itself. Given the ambiguity and paradox which imbues all other aspects of the imagery, it is not unreasonable to propose a situation opposed to the hypothesis of Deacon and Bradley and claim that, in the case of this rock art, it was the local ubiquity of surface which rendered it suitable for carving. In this way, the carvings are both present and absent, ambiguous in their existence and local distribution. This is not simply to reproduce the arguments made in preceding chapters, but to explain restricted distribution within substantial areas of exposed bedrock. Moreover, the emphasis on ambiguity and intermingling suggests that hindrance, searching and confusion were deliberately contrived: integral components in the consumption and meaning of this imagery, perhaps most clearly illustrated in the differing accessibility / visibility relationships of the carved ridges (see chapter 2). This produces an emotional engagement of far reaching saliency which finds analogy in the physiological and conceptual effects of associated rite (see below).

The saliency of a shared polysemous spectrum of effect brings a corresponding ambiguity to relationships between rock art and a wide range of monuments. The connotative values which make up this spectrum imbue Neolithic art and architecture with a conceptual hybridisation which transcends specific morphological type and functionality, suggesting the deployment of connotative value as a means to effect a fluid conception of world-view and cosmological organisation. Although the multiple functionality and cosmological manipulations of the rock art demonstrate greater specificity (see below), what emerges from the 'commensal' existence of art and architecture is a picture of Neolithic material effect in which a series of cosmological tensions are managed. Paradox acts as a common structuring theme, made manifest in the form of a desirable material tension. Through its ambiguous materiality and paradoxical connotative values, the rock imagery and architecture of the British and Irish Neolithic simultaneously manifest and deny the challenges inherent in early agricultural practice. Maintenance of this construct is achieved through a consistent concern to balance, to strike contrast in such a way that it is both obvious and concealed. Consequently, a superficial *wholeness* appears to infuse Neolithic material articulations. This, however, is not the totalisation of Hegel or Dithey (see Gosden 1994:40), but rather something approaching an expression of life lived as a "differential whole" (Bourdieu quoted in Gosden 1994:115): the œuvre of existence.

Conceptualisation as a differential whole provides explanation for the clustering of rock art at a national level and patterns of image presence or absence. Primary deployments of rock art are almost exclusively restricted to the northern reaches of the British Isles, and much of the western side of Ireland. To the south of the British mainland, rock art is absent. Instead, one is confronted with the 'classic' monument types of Wessex and, in eastern Ireland, the decorated passage tombs. This is not to claim the simple substitution of one material expression for another, but to link architectural and artistic practice to specific ways of living.

In recent years, pictures of Neolithic settlement and subsistence practices have ascribed to strategies of mobility and ephemeral structures which leave little archaeological trace (Darvill 1996b:72). Within this, monuments are presented as fixed points in the cyclical seasonal rounds of pastoral communities (Edmonds 1997:105; Thomas 1999a:23-9). Although authors who propagate this model acknowledge that the British Neolithic was not composed of a single agricultural system (e.g. Edmonds 1997:100; Thomas 1999a:7), the popularity of the mobility model - and its successful handling of the evidence from southern Britain - implicitly informs understandings of subsistence strategy in other areas of the British Isles (but see Barclay 1997: 129; Cooney 1997a: 23-7, 1999: 49).

Settlement evidence from Ireland suggests some degree of sedentary existence built upon patterns evident from the early Mesolithic (Cooney 1991:126, 1997a:29; Cooney & Grogan 1998:462; Grogan 1996:59). Habitation sites are only one element of Irish settlement distribution, and themselves embody degrees of mobility and transience - derived from seasonal and specialist procurement strategies - centred around more stable home bases (Cooney & Grogan 1994:42; Grogan 1996:59; Cooney 2000:15). These home bases, however, often take the form of substantial timber, or timber and stone, buildings (Grogan 1996:41), whose very mass, phases of construction and multiple periods of occupancy suggest great longevity (Cooney & Grogan 1994:51, 1998:462). To the west of the island, evidence for settlement is complemented by a series of field systems (Caulfield 1983:197). Field boundaries, such as those of Céide (Co. Mayo), Valentia Island (Co. Kerry) and the Burren (Co. Clare), are found in areas which were capable of sustaining a year-round growing season (Cooney 1997a:28, 2000:46). Rather than extensive arable farming, these plots are more consistent with intensive animal husbandry, grass crops and semi-permanent tillage plots (Caulfield 1983:197; Cooney 1991:127, 2000:46). Although not suggestive of large scale arable cultivation, but cattle management, these boundaries are a particularly significant feature of the Irish landscape as, until the advent of the Neolithic, Ireland lacked large mammals and

any precedent for herd management (Cooney 1997a:26). Further field boundaries, of comparable date and westerly distribution, have been found in Donegal, Dingle and Inveragh (Cooney 2000:46), areas where the greatest concentrations of Irish rock art are also apparent. Consequently, along the western coast of Ireland, a relatively sedentary existence, complemented by strategies of specialist mobility, was lived within a tightly structured landscape, throughout which rock carvings were distributed.

To the east, in the area around the Boyne Valley, Woodman (cited in Cooney 1991:127) has proposed a situation analogous to the great monuments of Wessex, in which mobile communities orientated their existence around the passage tombs. Pollen evidence, however, places the passage tombs in an open landscape of pastoral practice and tillage, bounded by a series of hedgerows (Cooney & Grogan 1994:40-1; Cooney 1991:130-4; 1997a:28, 2000:47). In some respects, this landscape approaches the structural characteristics and long-term occupancy of the west, but it also suggests a marked difference between these two areas which is implicated in the differential distribution of open air and monumental art works in Ireland (see 6.5). What is most significant at this stage, however, is the spatial-chronological relationship of these subsistence patterns to deployments of rock imagery. The initial carving of landscape art has been suggested as taking place during the early Neolithic, a time span which more closely corresponds to the field systems of the west (3700-3200 BC (Cooney 2000:27)), than the passage tombs (3200-2900 BC) to the east, with their own distinctive image types and redeployment of pre-existing landscape art. The dating of the Raigmore pit slab suggests that it is likely that some instances of carving predate the construction of these boundaries, suggesting that rather than being a cause of carving, the enclosure of land and rock imagery are both symptomatic of wider concerns.

Barclay (1996, 1997; also Cooney 1997a, 2000) suggests varying degrees of sedentary existence for the Neolithic of Scotland, for which, like Ireland, Mesolithic precedence is found in the communities of Oban (see Bonsall 1996). Although fewer in number than in Ireland, early agricultural Scotland was not without its substantial domestic buildings. Houses such as those found at Auchantegan and Ardnadam provide evidence of settlement to the west, whilst the discovery of a number of house sites in Kincardshire (Galloway) again places these structures amongst substantial concentrations of rock art: a range of correlates extended by the houses of Inverness and fertile valley of the Tay (see Bradley 1997a:101; Cramb 2001). The high volume of cereal grain recovered from Balbridie (Kinnes 1985:27; Cooney 1997:27, 2000:38), for example, is also suggestive of some degree of sedentary existence, regardless of the use to which this product was ultimately put (see Thomas 1996 regarding the ritual use of cereals). These houses find useful counterparts in the extensive hedging of Machrie Moor (Kinnes 1985:28) and field systems of southwest Scotland (Cooney 2000:44), where, again, convergence with significant concentrations of rock imagery is apparent. In contrast, the very south of Scotland demonstrates a marked absence of both phenomena (see Kinnes 1985; Barclay 1996; Oram 1997 regarding the distribution of Scottish house sites and Barclay 1997; Cowie & Shepherd 1997; Whittle 1997 for corresponding characteristics of social organisation).

Taken as a whole, there appears to be evidence for a loose correlation between the carving of living rock and areas of more sedentary existence: a correlation which extends into the North of England. Sites such as Lismore fields and Willington (Darvil 1996b:90; Barnatt 1996) bring (semi-)sedentary ways of living to the rock imagery of the Peak District. Similarly, Waddington (1999:117) suggests patterns of year round occupancy and semi-mobility, concomitant with the imagery concentrated in the Milfield Basin (Northumberland). Again, however, in both Scotland and northern England, many of these strands of evidence are likely to have post-dated the initial deployment of rock imagery, suggesting that a simple causal link is inappropriate.

By contrast, the monuments of southern England expressed the connotative values of the paradoxical Neolithic cosmos amongst the more mobile communities of this area. It is possible that this combination of subsistence strategy and material articulation accounts for the absence of rock carving amongst these communities. If so, it is significant that rock imagery remains absent from the south of the British Isles until its 'redeployment' in the early Bronze Age: a time of markedly increased sedentary settlement. Conversely, Oswald (et al 2001:123) attributes the lack of causewayed enclosures in Ireland to more sedentary ways of living, whilst the morphological idiosyncrasies of many enclosures located in the north of Britain - if those of the south are taken as normative - suggests a corresponding adjustment of monumental focus concomitant with image deployment and more fixed ways of living. These are not absolute patterns, but the evidence suggests a flowering of rock carving amongst communities with a tendency towards sedentary life.

6.3   Conceptual ambiguity and image formulation

The connotations of tergiversation, and the ambiguity inherent in the materiality of the rock art and architecture of Neolithic monuments, also inform interpretations of image content. Indeed, this imagery exemplifies the ambiguities of paradox. In the most general sense, the recurrence of the circle motif exudes fluidity and ambiguity, whilst the prevalence of concentricity alludes to the multiple levels of psychological saliency which sustain this connotative range. Although to cite this connotative interaction is not the same as analytically extracting certain

motifs at the expense of others, to view the art as such is to posit yet another, albeit relevant, interpretative generality which implicitly undermines the diversity of image production. These standardised themes, however, are tied to the other levels of connotation identified in chapters 2 and 5, and combined in a manner which creates a visual effect of "inter-connection [and] fluidity" (Beckensall 1999:7).

Comparison of the case studies presented in chapter 2 clearly demonstrates how the differential balancing of connoted paradox and ambiguity produces imagery of strikingly different content. Returning to the carvings of Glen Lochay 2, west of Loch Tay, and the massive carved outcrops of Cragganester and Craggantoul, on the northern shores of the same body of water, all three sites materially lie in sympathy with the prevailing topography. Each is camouflaged by the landscape by virtue of sharing its locally distinctive characteristics. Similarly, these outcrops are decorated in a repertoire range which is again of locally dominant character. In contrast, the ridge system of Kealduff stands in contradistinction to the local landscape and exhibits imagery which is notably more idiosyncratic than that of the surrounding vicinity. The same is true for the Glen Lochay 5 ridge system. This pattern recurs throughout the British Isles, where, generally, as the number of *different* transgressive features - a combination of rivers and hill slopes as opposed to two rivers, for example - acting upon a rock art panel increases, a corresponding emphasis is seen in the elaboration of imagery (see Evans 1999).

In this context it is possible to suggest that image content and materiality converge with a series of topographical associations to promote the extenuation of local difference. Inevitably, however, paradox involves more than one component, and it may be that the alleviation of topographical contrast, rather than the enhancement of image content, is being connoted at these sites. There is, however, another way to interpret this relationship which retains the ubiquity of cultural selection. That is, at Kealduff, for example, each stone associated with the ridge is carved with highly idiosyncratic imagery. Consequently, although markedly distinctive, these ridge systems remain internally ubiquitous. One might even go as far as to suggest that the ridges are less visible than other more typical surfaces, in that, if one is looking for rock imagery then attention is naturally drawn towards more typical location. Sustaining this interpretation on grounds other than speculation, however, is somewhat problematic.

This combination of ubiquity and distinction would certainly be consistent with suggestions that the "Neolithic witnessed the emergence of a series of contradictions .... that could not be accommodated within existing structure" (Edmonds 1993:125). As such, where topographical juncture and elaborate imagery converge, that which could not be accommodated was conceptually and cosmologically engaged with through the interaction of peculiar image types and topographical features which created a surmountable disruption in the landscape: features which also find allegorical counterparts in the field boundaries and structures of semi-sedentary ways of living. Support and image consequently inform each other. Both, however, also interact to provide a social role for the imagery which suggests why these patterns appear as they do.

6.4   Alternative strategies, parallel realms

Deduction of a social role for the rock art involves consideration of the deployment of imagery in the passage tombs of Ireland, and analysis of the architectural features of other monument 'classes'. This analysis not only informs understandings of the purpose of rock art in the landscape, but further advances interpretation of the artistic differences evident between regions.

Amongst the Irish passage tombs, a recurrent concern to connect the imagery of inside and outside worlds is evident: a connection which was instrumental in the interaction of living and ancestral shaman. In the areas of these tombs which were immediately associated with the interaction of ancestral spirits and tasking shaman, imagery recognisable as formerly 'from' the landscape is encountered in an adjusted form. The combination of image type and chamber at Loughcrew's cairn T, or the concealed kerb and passage art at Newgrange, for example, have subsequently been interpreted as indicative of interdigitating realms. Through the construction of the mound, these realms were brought close to each other in the creation of an ambiguous interface which, facilitated by the conceptual transgressions of material connotation and image content, allowed the tasking shaman to broach the tiers of the universe. This demonstrates how the passage tombs operated as a cosmological and conceptual adjunct to the functionality of trance, as much as a physiological enhancement of the altered state.

In chapter 3 the widespread saliency of these ideas was demonstrated through consideration of the material juxtapositions of landscape, morphology and internal settings of the henges, for example. Amongst many henges the effect of transgression is retained in the tenuous balance established between the local (reality?) and the more distant (spiritual?), creating an 'optical illusion' in which the immediate vicinity of the monument is overcome, but remains present in its obvious absence. The loss of hinterland suggests that this arrangement is as much about allusion as illusion. That is, it is the creation of an illusion, which implicates simultaneous presence and absence, that allows for allusion to be made to alternative realms. It is the inherent instability of these juxtapositions which suggests that not only were parallel realms linked by an obscured and adjusted familiarity, but that they could also be transgressed and manipulated.

Recognisable difference from, and simultaneous familiarity to the real world - coupled to persistent presence / absence relationships - is perhaps the most significant aspect of the interpretation of these monuments in terms of establishing an understanding of the open-air rock art. Most simply, the majority of petroglyphs occupy a horizontal plane which, particularly in the case of the larger panels, would necessitate the physical transgression of carved surface - with its associated connotations of material and conceptual ambiguity - for all the imagery to be consumed. Such performative use of this art, already transgressive in conception, would allude to the penetration of tiers made manifest at this setting. Left to stand alone, this suggestion appears somewhat tenuous. Other characteristics of rock art consumption, however, bring further strands of evidence, and greater specificity, to this interpretation.

The imagery of these rock art sites is often most effectively consumed when looking uphill. This direction of viewing has already been interpreted as a mechanism for ensuring that the connotations of topographical tergiversation are constantly reinforced in the mind of the viewer. It also, however, directs attention towards the juxtaposition of earth and sky: the conjoining of cosmological tiers and point of passage between parallel realms. The implicit verticality of the rock carvings deployed along the crest of the spur at Coomasaharn, for example, demonstrates that, on occasion, materiality directly alluded to the transgression of upper realms. More consistent evidence, however, comes from the northern shores of Loch Tay.

The massive outcrop at Craggantoul in its clearing location, for example, makes reference to the juxtaposition of upper tree line and mountains to the north and south. This embodies the 'same' allusions and illusions as the henge monuments, whilst the foreshortened perspective affected by the adjacent ridge of Cragganester, creates a visual effect more directly comparable to these monuments. When the imagery of this latter site is consumed, the transgressive features of the loch and the lower reaches of the southern mountains are obscured from view: they are effectively missing, as the crest of this massive outcrop is directly juxtaposed against mountain top. For the illusion to be sustained, it is necessary to move in a manner comparable to many henges. Such performative displays visually create the impression of a physical transgression of tiers. Viewed from the foot of these outcrops, an individual walking up the rock face - away from the lowlands and towards the top of the outcrop - disappears from view on surmounting the crest: transported to the higher ground of the mountain top beyond. That this person can no longer be seen suggests that, although the mountain summits are of the real world, they are also of the parallel spirit realm, and it is this realm which the individual has entered. This process is reversed when the return journey is made. In this instance, one magically reappears from the mountain/spirit world on broaching the crest from the opposite direction.

It appears as if transportation between lowlands and uplands, and the sky beyond, formed the central rite at many of the larger rock art sites. The same line of reasoning can be extended to a number of individual panels, including Kealduff 1 (figure 6.1), and comparable interpretation applied to a number of ridge systems. In all these cases, the imagery itself is transgressed, repeating the tergiversations evident in the horizontal plane of many sites, and suggesting that these art works facilitated the transgression of realms in much the same way as the passage tombs. Indeed, at Loughcrew, the two come together as one passes through the encircling 'ring' of rock art to approach the summit of Carnbane East.

Figure 6.1: Kealduff 1.

All case studies suggest that it is the juxtaposition of mountains and sky, the transgression of middle and upper tiers, that the rock art is primarily concerned with. They are, however, more analogous to the passage tombs, and the tergiversation of multiple realms, than is initially apparent. In a number of instances, the upward orientation of view takes in the distinctive profile of upland stone procurement sites. This suggests the conjoining, and transgression, of multiple tiers by alluding to the breaking of surface in an area of pre-existing cosmological juxtaposition. More consistently, the outcrops on which the imagery is carved are frequently described as living rock: surfaces which are part of the bedrock. As such, although they protrude into the middle tier of the real world, they are analogous to icebergs, the great majority of their mass concealed below the ground's surface: a further component of the layered universe.

Supplemental to connotations of topographical tergiversation, the transgression of tiers and conceptualisation of parallel worlds goes someway to accounting for the coastal bias, and views over the watercourse (see Morris 1979, for example), evident throughout rock art distribution. The transmogrification of water, and the implications of its location, in the many burial mounds of the Neolithic, has been postulated through the

presence of water-rolled boulders and marine debris at many tomb sites. Given the prevalence of these associations, and the low number of interments in such structures, it is not unreasonable to extend the connection between the transgressions of water and the dead by suggesting a widespread Neolithic funerary rite of burial at sea, or in inland water ways (see O'Brien 1999 for example). The disposal of the dead in this way suggests that large bodies of water may have been understood as a further 'ancestral' realm: one which was consistent with the subaqueous travels of the shaman and the physiological sensations of the altered state.

Often, as at both Duallin and Glen Lochay 2, views over water are orientated in the opposite direction to areas of higher ground. The situation is a little more contrived at the ridge system of Kealduff. When looking towards the cliff face - an angle of viewing which reveals the location of the rock art but hides the imagery itself - water occupies the same position as at Duallin and Glen Lochay 2. On surmounting the ridge - a position where the imagery becomes visibly but its precise location is now camouflaged by the materiality of the ridge - a view directly over the watercourse is attained. The same observations apply to Glen Lochay 5 (see below). When considered in the context of a wooded environment, however, these two contexts of consumption become more analogous. In such circumstances the water would again be obscured from view, but an aural presence would be felt through the crashing of waves or sounds of flow (see also Pryor 2001 regarding the siting of 'seahenge'); a further example of conspicuous absence reminding the viewer of the existence of multiple worlds, as they contemplated what was implied by the juxtaposition of mountain-top and skyline: a juxtaposition which emerged from the forest canopy in a manner analogous to the protuberance of the outcrop from the earth's surface.

Often, there would be a striking contrast between the calm of the upward-orientated view and the crescendo of the water. This, however, would not always be the case. Storms would frequently bring the sounds of the river to the mountain tops, particularly if one considers autumn or winter to be the time when the rock art was most frequently engaged with (see below). This is most evident in the movement of weather patterns above Teermoyle Mountain. These weather patterns reinforce the fluidity of worldly tiers, demonstrating the ambiguities between subaqueous and aerial extra-corporeal travel, and their interconnection in the physiological sensations of the altered state.

At other sites such as Cragganester and Craggantoul - and the ridge system of Glen Lochay 5 - absent water would lie between the rock art and the mountain crests. In such instances, the realm of the dead would have to be transgressed before one could enter the upper tiers, suggesting a different specificity of rite and intent at these locales. In all cases, however, the petroglyphs appear to be deployed as facilitators for the trancing spirit of the shaman. Such facilitation may account for the complexity of the motif deployments at Glen Lochay 3, the only example in any of the case study areas where water flows directly over the carved surface. The drainage of water through the ridge system at Kealduff is suggestive of a similar role.

The predominantly horizontal plane of this rock art has long been recognised as suggesting that obliquely angled sunlight provides the optimum conditions for image consumption (Morris 1979, for example). Oblique lighting conditions imply morning and evening rites, particular suited to the months between autumn and spring. This time span encompasses liminal times of day and year, as well as periods traditionally associated with death and rebirth. Prominent solar events have been posited as integral components of many Irish passage tomb rites, and, by virtue of the commonalities of effect evident between these monuments and the rock art, it is not unreasonable to extend these observations to encompass landscape art. It is in this context that the significance of regrowth, and its relationship to the act of carving, becomes salient. The accumulation of detritus is again suggestive of seasonal engagement, most notably following the autumnal shedding of leaves by the deciduous forests of the time and, thus, compatible with the relationship between winter solstice and the passage tombs. The loss of canopy is significant in imbuing the forest with a greater sense of permeability, allowing greater exposure to the oblique light of winter mornings, an increased depth of 'obstructed' view and enhanced transmission of sound. In turn, each of these amplifies the effect of the rock art.

In terms of the rite itself, in chapter 4 it was suggested that the flaking, polishing and re-carving of rock art provided a means through which the potency of the imagery could be manipulated. By extension, the removal of scrub to reveal 'fresh' art work could be conceptualised as creating much the same effect. Given that the rock art was associated with multiple connotations of tergiversation, it is not unreasonable to suggest that the material removed from their carvings would be imbued with comparable properties. The water recovered from these engravings, for example, could be consumed as part of hallucinatory preparations, the physiological effect of which would confirm the transfer of potency from the imagery to the shaman.

6.5   Diagnostic and undiagnostic expression: accessing the spirit world

Although the interpretation of rite presented in 6.4 incorporates practices which include the inducement of the altered state, addressed as a totality, the corpus of British and Irish rock art exhibits little in the way of diagnostic imagery (see chapter 4).

This initially appears to undermine this understanding of the rock art and the interconnection of this artistic media and the decorated passage tombs. It is possible, however, to provide an explanation which accounts for both these relationships.

Although occurring at a much lower frequency than amongst the passage tombs, the relatively consistent deployment of motifs diagnostic of the altered state, and therefore exclusively representative of it, is encountered in the rock art distributed along the western fringes of Ireland. Neither diagnostic nor undiagnostic images are exclusively more weathered than the other, suggesting contemporaneous deployment (but see section 4.2). Variability in the selection of diagnostic type suggests that deployments of imagery readily identifiable with subjective vision contributed to the parochial identity of the rock art located in this area. In Donegal, for example, the meander is emphasised, whilst on Inveragh selection favours the arc-spiral and small-arc. Consequently, regional *elaboration,* in these instances, is as much due to the inclusion of diagnostic types, as to any consistent compositional arrangement. Similarly, derivation from the altered state may account for the technical divergence of loose pecking encountered on Inveragh. In this context, these unusual images may be understood as 'construed' versions of the pick-dressing seen in the passage tombs: itself suggestive of the movement of entoptic dots. It is significant that often this pecking, like natural markings in the rock surface, performs a 'linking' role (see chapter 2): an integral component in the creation of ambiguity, tergiversation and transgression: analogous to the social role of the shamans themselves and the physiology of the altered state.

In addition to these regional patterns, the occasional isolated manifestation of diagnostic imagery, such as the loop-arcs of the Braes of Taymouth (Strath Tay) (see Stewart 1958-9:77 (figure 6.2)), appears throughout the rock art of the British mainland. Unlike the concealed imagery of the passage tombs, the stylistic characteristics of the British and Irish rock art do not immediately evoke the imagery of actual hallucinations. Consequently, although it is unreasonable simply to transpose the analytical divisions of Dronfield on to prehistoric artistic understandings, it is less problematic to suggest that image selection, at least amongst the ritual practitioners of the Neolithic, points to an ability to discriminate, visually and decoratively, between imagery clearly recognisable as being exclusively of rites of tergiversation which incorporated altered consciousness, and that which ambiguously straddled both subjective and normative vision. This suggests the differential valuation of imagery derived from the altered state, and points to an origin for the more standardised components of the rock art repertoire in the same rites of sensory adjustment (see below; also Poulter 2000). In turn, this implies the existence of a common image bank, selection from which not only accounts for variability in the record, but also for the 'consistency' of the corpus as a whole.

Figure 6.2: *The Braes of Taymouth (after Stewart 1958-9).*

Explanation for the comparatively consistent selection of diagnostic imagery in the west of Ireland can be found in the material and conceptual structures which accompanied the (semi)-sedentary ways of living evident in this area (see 6.1). The physical structures of sedentary existence were perhaps the most conceptually and cosmological challenging of all the novel material manifestations of the early Irish Neolithic. Depositional practice, strategies of redeployment, material juxtaposition with field walls or house structures and diagnostic image content, all suggest that the induction and depiction of the altered state was practised at times both prior to, and contemporary with, the construction of these new features. If such induction was utilised to facilitate the transgression of parallel realms, and the 'barriers' between them, then its greater representation in imagery closely associated with the creation of new physical boundaries suggests the disruption of traditional mechanisms for entering these worlds. The comparatively high manifestation of diagnostic imagery, therefore, suggests greater emphasis on passage through and facilitation. This marks an archaeologically visible adjustment of spectrum focus, necessitated by the enhancement of conceptual and cosmological barriers, which found their material correlates in the new structures of agriculture.

The rock art of Louth, the only major concentration of landscape imagery in the east of Ireland, lacks evidence for the deployment of the diagnostic repertoire. In this respect, image characteristics are analogous to the content and selection policy evident in the British Neolithic. In itself, the choice to avoid the depiction of imagery readily recognisable as of the altered state is suggestive of transgressive concerns. These motifs are of both the parallel world and the 'normative': an ambiguity which complements the materiality of the rock art and is integral to the key rites of allusion suggested in 6.4. Although present in these areas of carving, sedentary existence was less formalised than along the western coast. Hedging, for example, retains many of the connotations of forest edge absent from the walling of the west. The corresponding lack of diagnostic imagery suggests strategies which attempted to ameliorate and manage conceptual and cosmological challenge, rather than confront it in the same direct manner seen in the west.

Practitioners, or audiences, at all levels of involvement could experience almost all these images - both as they were represented and mentally - regardless of the induction of the altered state. As such, it was the specialist's ability to take this common imagery, and turn it into a device to facilitate the spiritual tergiversations which allowed for the transgression of realms, that was valued. Each end of the paradoxical spectrum, however, continued to be implicated by the very ambiguities which allowed for these performative displays of illusion and allusion. Ultimately, it was this paradoxical structure which brought about a re-valuing of the power of allusion and the role of the ritual specialist, leading to dramatic alterations in the content and context of image deployment in the east of Ireland. From this point, the historical trajectory of art-making on the eastern side of Ireland began to diverge from the British mainland.

Imagery immediately indicative of the altered state was already familiar to the Neolithic artist: what was new amongst the passage tomb builders was the choice to depict it in such quantities and in such a context. The diagnostic content of passage tomb art suggests rough analogy to the strategies of spiritual engagement along the western coast of Ireland. This analogy suggests that subsequent to the initial phases of carving in Louth, the authority of allusion in the east was undermined by the steady encroachment of agriculture to such an extent, that it was not only necessary to adopt a more dramatic version of the strategies seen in the west, but also to express these through a monumental context which - through the manifestation of multiple worldly tiers - announced the significance of the altered state in its own right. Although the impact of (semi)sedentary life is implicated in the artistic developments which occurred along the eastern coast of Ireland, the direct transfer of significance from one coast line to the other, amounts to little more than the positing of generic casual links. Moreover, as indicated above, to attribute direct causality to the pressures of sedentary existence is inappropriate.

These tombs also served as 'burial' structures, placing the dead - or at least the token remains of certain members of the ancestral community - into this cosmological breakthrough point. In this context, it is significant that much of the diagnostic content of visible imagery of the passage tombs was expressed through its angular components: the art form which was most directly associated with the deceased. This suggests that, contrary to the practices of the west, access to parallel realms contrived through these monuments required the direct engagement of the dead. More than this, however, is at work in these monuments.

In all the passage tombs discussed in chapter 4, interaction between the deceased and living shaman was undertaken in the presence of imagery which simultaneously asserted both local history and otherness: imagery that was familiar both to the ancestors - by virtue of its relationship to pre-existing landscape art - and to those who dwelt in, or visited, alternative realms, as suggested by its diagnostic content. That this art was of the past, and given the longevity embodied in stone, suggests that such decoration was deployed as a time link - in a manner analogous to the cursus monuments or quartz using strategies of Newgrange - and, as such, constitutes an active engagement with local material history and its connotative and cosmological values. Access to the past, however, could only be attained through penetration of the mounds' materiality and, in this role, it was the 'new' deployments of diagnostic angular imagery, and the dead, which acted as a stepping stone.

Although the ancestral shaman were 'interred' as tokens in the passage tombs, the majority of the dead - including the dispersed personage of the deceased shaman - were diffused through the ambience by cremation, the circulation of body parts, or burial at sea. Consequently, although the spirit world was embodied in the materiality of the passage tombs, this was only part of a larger entity. The concern to interconnect the body of these monuments with wider worlds, and the ancestors who dwelt therein, is evidenced by the in-out relationships of the imagery deployed amongst the principal passage tombs. The imagery which connoted this connection was again 'new', but in many ways, the practicable, but inferential, nature of these relationships suggests the reworking of established strategies of allusion, rather than a decline in the authority of this practice. Significantly, however, this art also announced the penetrative power of extra-corporeal travel more visibly than ever before: suggesting a refocusing of balance.

This discussion of the role of the passage tombs suggests a significantly different understanding of the cosmological world in eastern Ireland to the western coast. In the west, the location of parallel realms was conceptualised as a spatial relationship, the penetration of which was facilitated through the diagnostic content of the rock art. To the east, this relationship took on a more temporal dimension, and the disruptions of agriculture were managed through time and history. By contrast, in the north of the British mainland, neither decorated passage tombs nor the consistent depiction of diagnostic imagery is encountered. This suggests longevity in the basic strategies centred around the rock imagery, and the retention of established practices of tergiversation through the manipulation of illusion and allusion: strategies exemplified along the northern shores of Loch Tay (see section 6.4).

Analogous social adjustments, but of a different time frame and intent, are evident in the later phases of Stonehenge. In phases I and II, those roughly contemporary with the construction of the

passage tombs, the wooden settings of this monument articulated a relatively 'standardised' version of the connotative effects of tergiversation. At this time the pastoral communities of Wessex remained substantially mobile. The enhanced sedentism of the Bronze Age, however, witnessed the concomitant deployment of the stone settings with which this monument is most commonly associated. These settings allowed the monument to connote a greater emphasis on the facilitation of transgression through allusion to more distant geographies, and their associations with the increasingly alien, and hence also spiritual, realms. Following Pryor's scheme (see chapter 3), it is again the people and connotative values of the past that were redeployed in the remodelling of this monument.

6.6 The significance of final Neolithic-early Bronze Age image redeployment

During the early Bronze Age many of the connotative mechanisms of the Neolithic were subject to concealment, and the directionality of rite reversed, as the spirit world was re-conceptualised as a more discrete and distant entity. It is significant that, in almost all instances, decorated monuments exclusively drew on an artistic repertoire which was of the past and, consequently, also the dead. The lingering presence of rock art in the landscape, and the interaction between this imagery and that of the interment context, suggests that although more distant, this realm remained comparable to reality: or perhaps more accurately, the history of the real; and that early Bronze Age communities continued to engage with landscape imagery, albeit in very different ways. As such, during this time, Neolithic rock art cannot be said to be dying and irrelevant, but rather is part of an active material history through which the people of later times structured and defined their way of life. Again, this was not the appropriation of an ancestral past to legitimate the present, but part of a wider phenomenon taking place in the early Bronze Age.

In the shift from the ancestor rites of the Neolithic to the funerary rituals characteristic of the early Bronze Age, archaeological thought has moved far beyond the imposition of a new race of warriors, the naturalisation of the individual and the material expression of top-down power relations (see Thomas 1999b:1-3). Barrett (1990:184; also Last 1998; Thomas 1999b:8) has interpreted the single grave interments of this time as part of a process by which new social relationships were brought into being, as much as they provided venues for the disposal of the dead. Through directly referencing secondary interments to primary instances of burial, these new funerary rites not only fixed the location of a person's death in space - as opposed to the currency of 'relics' extant in the Neolithic - but also in time: placing each individual within a recognisable line of descent. At Barnack, for example, seven generations are represented in a 'single' structure, encompassing over 20 events spread across 200 years (Last 1998:46). In effect, these

80

funerary practices were instrumental in developing more directional conceptions of time, which facilitated increasingly tenurial relationships with the land as part of a move towards enhanced settlement stability and short fallow cultivation systems (Thomas 1999b:8). In so doing, personal identity began to centre less around the group affiliation characteristic of the Neolithic and became more about genealogy (Thomas 1999b).

The consumption of rock imagery undergoes social adjustments comparable to those evident in the treatment of the dead. The deployment of rock art during the Neolithic was practised by communities whose ancestor rituals invoked the presence of the dead in the transactions of the living (see Thomas 1999b:5). These communities carried their dead with them, and distributed their personhood throughout the cosmos as manifest in a tiered conception of the 'landscape'. Consequently, the dead, in whatever form - physically deceased or tasking shaman - remained mobile: active participants in social life, as evidenced by the ongoing tasking of the deceased shaman amongst the passage tomb builders. Amongst the communities who practised rock carving the mobility of the dead was mirrored by the distribution of rock art in the landscape: providing the context and mechanisms which allowed for such mobility.

During the early Bronze Age, rock imagery was no longer predominantly deployed in the landscape, but interred with burial: implicated in the reorganisation of social relationships which were worked out through the differential treatment of the dead. Consistent with the increasing sense of physical and spiritual separation evident in the '(en)closure' of many later Neolithic tombs (see Bradley 1998a; Thomas 1999b:17), the redeployment of landscape art in the funerary structures of the early Bronze Age manipulated past strategies of group affiliation into more directional conceptions of descent. History was effectively rewritten according to changing conceptions of the body and imagery alike, anchoring the strategies of 'contemporary' life in a readily recognisable and distinctively local history.

In this context, the exotic grave-goods included in early Bronze Age cist burials no longer appear as elite power symbols. Rather, these goods are indicative of wide-reaching trade networks (Last 1998:46) and, as gifts, take on the connotations of dispersed personhood evident in the Neolithic. Consequently, interment again places that which was formerly of the wider world into a more discrete and conceptually distant location: echoing both bodily and artistic trajectories. Although operative according to the same basic premise, the strategies through which these transformations were effected exhibit evidence of pronounced regional variation.

The strategy set out above is most readily identifiable in the northeast of the British mainland and the redeployment of the full range of the local rock art repertoire. To the south - and analogous to the contemporaneous stone deployments of Stonehenge - the motifs 'redeployed' in these monuments were themselves alien and insinuated great distance: replicating the conceptual adjustments implicated in the repositioning of spiritual realms. In the northwest, strategies of image redeployment consistently depart from the dominant landscape repertoire, and instead emphasise the most standardised range of the petroglyph spectrum. This marks a distinctive revaluation of the art's content, as well as its context, and suggests that re-conceptualisations of the body and the spirit world required a parallel re-conceptualisation of imagery. The emphasis on a standardised repertoire range, effectively gave these inclusions an alien appearance and, as such, they may be seen as evoking the same connotations of distance and separation evident in the south. It appears more than coincidence that the same westerly bias is evident in the closure of burial monuments during the later Neolithic (see chapter 5). The inclusion of passage tomb-like imagery in the cist interments of Kilmartin is again suggestive of the distant and the alien, supporting this interpretation of the dominant strategy extant in the west. These inclusions also, however, reveal a specifically local route to focus, which, in turn, suggests explanation for the carved stone balls of the extreme northeast.

The presence of angular passage tomb-like imagery in the Kilmartin cists does not necessarily denote a commonality of rite, either with contemporary Irish Bronze Age practice (see chapter 5) or that of the earlier passage tombs. With the exception of the circular diagnostics interred in the cists of Ayrshire, graphic indicators of the altered state are absent from Bronze Age burials in Scotland. The Kilmartin cists do, however, speak of the formalisation evident in later passage tomb art and, as such, a local origin in the altered state cannot be ruled out. The geographical patterning of redeployment strategies, however, suggests that, in the absence of additional evidence, the angular imagery of this valley appears more analogous with processes of mimicry, or even direct redeployment, than indigenous ritual practice involving the induction and immediate depiction of the altered state.

Kilmartin lies at the western end of the Great Glen, the great prehistoric thoroughfare which linked the opposing coasts of Scotland, and this area of the British mainland to Ireland. In this context, it is significant that substantial quantities of diagnostic imagery appear in the carved stone balls - dating to the later third and second millennium BC - recovered from the extreme northeast (Marshall 1976-7; MacGregor 1999). MacGregor's (1999) sensory analysis of these artefacts, in conjunction with their diagnostic content (see chapter 4), suggests that these objects played a significant role in rites of tergiversation which encompassed the physiological and material transgressions of the altered state.

Although evidence of direct association is lacking, this area of the Scottish mainland is also home to the Clava cairns, with their redeployments of landscape imagery. This suggests a commonality of material forms with the marbles and passage tombs of eastern Ireland. Significantly, the Irish marbles conspicuously lack decoration, leaving the carved orthostats of these tombs to act as adjuncts to rituals which embraced the altered state. Although the superficial convergence of material forms suggests the mimicry of earlier Irish rites in the Bronze Age of the northeast, the pronounced difference in decorative strategy suggests a switch in the mechanisms through which the spirit world was engaged with. That is, it was the carved stone balls, rather than orthostat imagery, that acted as adjuncts to the altered state in northeast Scotland As such, although the induction of the altered state was common to both areas, and its artistic representation of comparable stylistic and material range, two very different rites were practised, producing two distinctive sets of material culture.

6.7 Conclusion: history from art

Critical exploration of the interrelationship between rock art, landscape and architecture has allowed a multifaceted history of the British and Irish Neolithic to be written through its art. To write this history it has been necessary to think about the imagery in a different way to traditional engagements with the art. In many ways, this is to follow the research trajectory espoused by Yates (1993). Yates was concerned with the impasse he perceived in typological-chronological approaches to Scandinavian rock art. Reducing Malmer's identification of 522 types of human figure to four mutually informing characterisations, and rejecting the chronological impetus, Yates explored the ways in which sexual identity was expressed, particularly what it *meant* to be male, in the context of this imagery. Translating this theorisation into the preoccupations of this study involves approaching the art in a more emotional manner, considering how it 'felt'. This approach has not only revealed certain happenings in the artistic trajectories of the British and Irish Neolithic, but has also offered explanation as to how and why these things occurred. The main components of this history can be summarised as follows:

- The multivalent interaction of material, image and landscape informs interpretation at a number of successive scales. For example, the interpretation of dots on a distribution map, the intermixing of carved and uncarved surfaces, topographical juxtaposition, micro-topographical associations and the ambiguities of image production are all mutually sustaining in their ambiguous relationship with the central concept of tergiversation. Ultimately, it is how this concept is

reworked that brings both diversity and similitude to the corpus.

- Exploring how the rock art 'felt' gives interpretative access to that which had remained opaque through consideration of formal decorative characteristics alone: reasoned interpretations of purpose, meaning and significance. The materiality of the rock art embodies a series of connotative relationships whose differential balancing reveals particular understandings of a fluid and tiered universe, whose particular significance - and strategies of engagement - varied from locale to locale according to the specific combination of connotative values. Similarly, image content suggests an intimate relationship with the altered sate which demonstrably changed over time and space. Somewhat paradoxically, materiality and image content provoke a 'common' social role for the imagery. This is most obviously apparent in the ways in which the materiality of surface - boulder field, glacial pavement, ridge system or massive outcrop - could be engaged with at a multitude of levels to access, control and manipulate spiritual realms to achieve different, but cosmologically 'analogous', outcomes. Through the 'same' adjustment of balance and 'transmogrification' of material form (e.g. water manifest as river-rolled stones), this spectrum extends to encompass much Neolithic architecture. In turn, each of these different material expressions - art and monuments - can be demonstrably linked to particular ways of living.

- The deployment of rock art as a strategy for handling the conceptual and cosmological implications of agriculture and sedentary existence. In this context, the engravings act as a means of managing a whole range of contradictions which challenged established ways of doing things. The relevance of sedentary life is clearly evidenced by the way in which adjustments in the trajectories of rock art consumption coincide with the appearance, and development, of the social and material expressions of changing subsistence patterns: regardless of the particular geographical location or chronological horizon in which they appear (e.g. early Neolithic Ireland / early Bronze Age Cornwall).

- The redeployment of rock imagery - through a range of strategies and variety of contexts - help facilitate change in the interrelationships of people, the relationships between people and landscape, and cosmological understandings of the world during the early Bronze Age. As such, although increasingly specifically associated with the dead, the imagery of the Neolithic cannot be said to be dying, or lacking relevance. Rather, regardless as to whether it was imagery directly of the landscape, or that of a range which demonstrates a clear reaction to the presence of landscape art that was interred, it was because art of this type was associated with an active community history which marked it as relevant and appropriate for redeployment in a manner which was actively structuring and not passively appropriative.

- The construction of this history suggests, at the very least, that British and Irish rock art deserves parity with the other material expressions which characterise the time-lines produced for the Neolithic (figure 6.3). More importantly, it also suggests that these same strategies should be explored as a means of telling us things which archaeology alone cannot satisfactorily account for (see Evans & Dowson 2003).

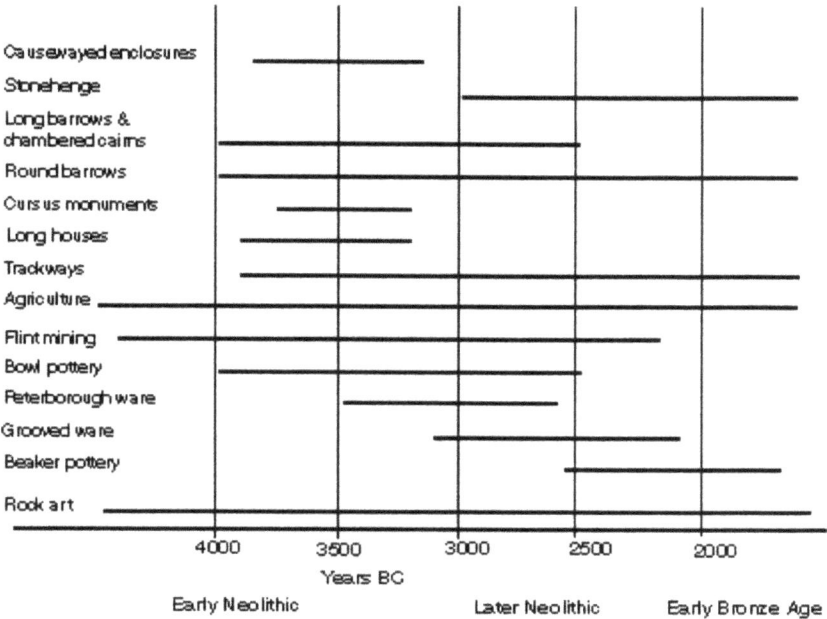

Figure 6.3: *Neolithic time-line (after Oswald et al 2001 with modifications).*

AFTERWORD

Over six years, and many thousand words, ago I began my investigation of British and Irish rock art with the somewhat naive expectation of coming towards a conclusion as to what the various components of the imagery meant; concentric circles would mean one particular thing, the addition of a meandering radial another and so on. The peculiar characteristics of this art, however, ensure that such understandings remain the most obscure element of these petroglyphs: as elusive now as they were six years ago, and, in all probability, prehistory. Early attempts to address the art in such terms consistently returned to the descriptive, an uncritical engagement which denies the complex abstract processes evoked by past peoples in the deployment and consumption of their art works. Such descriptive analysis has long characterised the study of British and Irish rock art. If progress was to be made, it was necessary to recognise that the questions of established discourse had "had their chance: it [was] time to experiment" (see Yates 1993:36). Experimentation led to the consideration of meaning as something that resided in matters other than image content alone, an understanding which suggests a further unfolding of Edmonds' (1995:15) own re-evocation of Levi-Strauss. For the archaeologist, like Edmonds' stone tools, and contrary to the dominant rock art discourse, this art can be 'good to think with'.

In some respects, this is to follow a particularly personal mantra, but one which is empowering rather than inhibiting. Reiterating the innovative work of Yates (1993), Thomas Dowson has been espousing the methodological imperative of 'theorising the art in its local and regional context' throughout the years I have been under his tutelage. Theorising the connotative balance evoked by the rock art has enabled the identification - and critical analysis - of a wide range of decorative strategies extant in the British and Irish Neolithic: strategies which ultimately comprise the building blocks of a history of the Neolithic written through its art. The writing of this history has inevitably been somewhat speculative, but it is speculation grounded in an empirical and theoretical base which bestows on it an intellectual integrity. Indeed, "a concern with the way in which objects contributed to the creation of people as social beings inevitably draws us into the realm of interpretation" (Edmonds 1995:19), and leads us at some point to come to terms with infinite difference and write a story (Thomas 1999a:5). Such stories, by their very nature, are always speculative and inventive but:

> *The data is available to allow us to explore*
> *the past with imagination* (Yates 1993:69).

REFERENCES CITED

Anati, E. 1963. New petroglyphs at Derynablaha, Co. Kerry. *Journal of the Cork Historical and Archeological Society* 68:1-15.

Anati, E. 1994. Valcamonica rock art: A new history for Europe. Valcamonica: Studi Camuni.

Anati, E. 1995. *Breacia Preistorica*. Valcamonica: Studi Camuni.

Arcá, A. 2000. Agricultural landscapes in Neolithic and copper age engravings of Valcamonica and Mt. Bego rock art. In, G. Nash (ed) *Signifying place and space: World perspectives in rock art and landscape*. Oxford: BAR (International series 902). pp. 29-40.

Ashbee, P. 1958. The excavation of Tregulland Barrow, Treneglos Parish, Cornwall. *Antiquities Journal* 38:174-96.

Ashmore,P. 1986. Neolithic carvings in Maes Howe. *Proceedings of the Society of Antiquarians of Scotland* 116: 57-62.

Ashmore, P. 1996. *Neolithic and Bronze Age Scotland*. London: B.T. Batsford Ltd.

Bahn, P. 1996. New developments in Pleistocene art, 1990-1994. In, P. Bahn & A. Fossati (eds) *News of the world: Recent developments in rock art research*. Oxford: Oxbow Monograph 72. pp.1-14.

Bahn, P. 1997. *Journey through the ice age*. London: Weidenfeld & Nicolson.

Barclay, A & G. Hey. 1999. Cattle, cursus monuments and the river: The development of ritual and domestic landscapes in the upper Thames Valley. In, A. Barclay & J. Harding (eds). *Pathways and ceremonies: The cursus monuments of Britain and Ireland*. Oxford: Oxbow. pp.67-76.

Barclay, G. 1989. Henge monuments: Reappraisal or reductionalism? *Proceedings of the Prehistoric Society* 55: 260-3.

85

Barclay, G. 1996. Neolithic buildings in Scotland. In, J. Thomas & T. Darvil (eds) *Houses in north-western Europe and beyond*. Oxford: Oxbow. pp.61-75

Barclay, G. 1997. The Neolithic. In, K. Edwards & I. Ralston (eds) *Scotland: Environment and archaeology, 8000 BC - AD 1000*. Chichester: John Wiley. pp.127-49.

Barclay, G et al. 1998. *The Cleaven Dyke and Littleour*. Edinburgh: Society of Antiquarians of Scotland Monograph 13.

Barclay, G. 2001. Neolithic enclosures in Scotland. In, T. Darvil & J. Thomas (eds) *Neolithic enclosures in Atlantic north-western Europe*. Oxford: Oxbow Books. pp.144-54.

Barclay, G & S. Halliday. 1982. A rock carving from Westerton, Angus District. *Proceedings of the Society of antiquarians of Scotland* 112: 561-2.

Barclay, G & C. Russel-White. 1993. Excavations in a ceremonial complex of the fourth to second millennium BC at Balfarg and Balbirnie, Fife. *Proceedings of the Society of Antiquarians of Scotland* 123: 43-210.

Barfield, L & C. Chippindale. 1997. Meaning in the later prehistoric rock engravings of Mont Bégo, France. *Proceedings of the Prehistoric Society* 63:103-28.

Barnatt, J. 1989a. *The stone circles of Great Britain*. Oxford: BAR (British Series 215(i)).

Barnatt, J. 1989b. *The stone circles of Great Britain*. Oxford: BAR (British Series 215(ii)).

Barnatt, J. 1990. *The henges, stone circles and ring cairns of the Peak District*. Sheffield: University of Sheffield.

Barnatt, J. 1996. Moving beyond the monuments: Paths and people in the Neolithic landscape of the Peak District. *Northern Archaeology* 13/14: 43-60.

Barnatt, J & P. Reeder. 1982. Prehistoric rock art in the Peak District. *Derbyshire Archaeological Journal* 102: 33-44.

Barnatt, J & P. Firth, 1983. A newly discovered 'cup and ring' carving in Ecclesall Wood, Sheffield. *Derbyshire Archaeological Journal* 103: 41-2.

Barnatt, J et al. 2001. A time and place for enclosure: Gardom's Edge, Derbyshire. In, T. Darvil & J. Thomas (eds) *Neolithic enclosures in Atlantic north-western Europe*. Oxford: Oxbow Books. pp.111-31.

Barrett, J. 1990. The monumentality of death: the character of Early Bronze Age mortuary mounds in southern Britain. *World Archaeology* 22(2):179-89.

Barrett, J. 1994. Defining domestic space in the Bronze Age of southern Britain. In, M. Parker-Pearson & C. Richards (eds) *Architecture and order: Approaches to social space*. London: Routledge. pp.87-97.

Barrett, J. 1997. Stone Age Ideologies. *Analecta Praehistorica Leidensia* 29:121-9.

Barrett, J. 1999. Chronologies of Landscape. In, P. Ucko & R. Layton (eds) *The archaeology and anthropology of landscape*. London: Routledge. pp. 21-30.

Barrett, J et al. 1991. *Landscape, monuments and society: the prehistory of Cranbourne Chase*. Cambridge: Cambridge University Press.

Baxter, G. 1896-7. Notice of a cup-marked stone recently found at Gallow Hill, Parish of Cargill. *Proceedings of the Society of Antiquarians of Scotland* XXXI: 290-2.

Baxter, M. 1999. Dancing with the dead in a mass grave. *British Archaeology* 50: 6-7.

Beckensall, S. 1995. Recent discoveries and recording of prehistoric rock motifs in the north. *Northern Archaeology* 12: 9-34.

Beckensall, S. 1996. Symbols on stone: The state of the art. *Northern Archaeology* 13/14: 139-46.

Beckensall, S. 1997. Prehistoric rock art: Progress and problems. *At the edge* 8: 10-15.

Beckensall,S. 1998. An ideology that faded into a new age. *British Archaeology* 37: 8-9.

Beckensall, S. 1999. *British prehistoric rock art*. Stroud: Tempus.

Beckensall, S. 2002. British prehistoric rock art in the landscape. In, G. Nash & C. Chippendale (eds) *European landscapes of rock art*. London: Routledge. pp. 39-70.

Beckensall, S & P. Frodsham. 1998. Questions of chronology: The case for Bronze Age rock art in northern Britain. *Northern Archaeology* 15/16: 51-69.

Beckensall, S & T. Laurie. 1998. *Prehistoric rock art of County Durham, Swaledale and Wensleydale*. Durham: County Durham Books.

Bednarik, R. 1990. On neuropsychology and shamanism in rock art. *Current Anthropology* 31(1): 77-83.

Bednarik, R. 1992. The stuff legends in archaeology are made of: A reply to critics. *Cambridge Archaeological Journal* 2(2): 262-5.

Bednarik, R. 1993a. Who're we gonna call? The bias busters. In, M. Lorblanchet & P. Bahn (eds) *Rock art studies: The post stylistic era or where do we go from here*. Oxbow monograph 35. pp.207-11.

Bednarik, R. 1993b. European Palaeolithic art: Typical or exceptional? *Oxford Journal of Archaeology* 12(1):1-8.

Bednarik, R. 1994. The discrimination of rock markings. *Rock Art Research* 11(1): 23-44.

Bender, B. 1993. Stonehenge - contested landscape (Medieval to present day). In, B. Bender (ed) *Landscape: Politics and perspectives*. Oxford: Berg. pp.245-80.

Benjamin, A. 1994. Time and Task: Benjamin and Heidegger, showing the present. In, A. Benjamin & P. Osbourne (eds) *Walter Benjamin's philosophy: Destruction and experience*. London: Routledge. pp.216-50.

Bergh, S. 1995. *Landscape of the monuments: A study of the passage tombs in the Cuil Irra region*. Stockholm: Bureau for Archaeological Excavation.

Bevan, L. 2000. Women's art, men's art: Gender specific image selection in the rock art of Valcamonica. In, G. Nash (ed) *Signifying place and space: World perspectives in rock art and landscape*. Oxford: BAR (International series 902). pp. 103-09.

Bird-David, N. 1999. "Animism" revisited. *Current Anthropology* 40(s): 67-91.

Bolin, H. 1998. Ancient artefacts and ethnic archetypes. In, A-C Andersson et al (eds) *The kaleidoscopic past*. Göteborg: Götrborg University. pp.347-54.

Bonsall, C. 1996. The 'Obanian problem: coastal adaptation in the Mesolithic of western Scotland. In, T. Pollard & A. Morrison (eds) *The early prehistory of Scotland*. Edinburgh: Edinburgh University Press. pp.183-97.

Bradley, J. 1976. The crystalline state. In, M. O'Donoghue (ed) *The encyclopaedia of minerals and gem stones*. London: Orbis. pp.24-41.

Bradley, R. 1982. Position and possession: Assemblage variation in the British Neolithic. *Oxford Journal of Archaeology* 1(1): 27-38.

Bradley, R. 1988. Fieldwork at Great Langdale, Cumbria. *Antiquities Journal* 68: 181-209.

Bradley, R. 1989. Deaths and entrances: A contextual analysis of megalithic art. *Current Anthropology* 30(1): 68-75.

Bradley, R. 1991. Rock art and the perception of landscape. *Cambridge Archaeological Journal* 1:77-101.

Bradley, R. 1992. Turning the world - Rock carvings and the archaeology of death. In, N. Sharples & A. Sheridan (eds) *Vessels for the ancestors*. Edinburgh: Edinburgh University. pp.168-76.

Bradley, R. 1995a. Symbols and signposts: Understanding the prehistoric petroglyphs of the British Isles. In, C. Renfrew & E. Zubrow *The ancient mind*. Cambridge: Cambridge University Press. pp. 95-106.

Bradley, R. 1995b. After MacWhite. Irish rock art in its international context. In, J. Waddell & E. Shee-Twohig (eds) *Ireland in the Bronze Age*. Dublin: Office Of Public Works. pp.90-6.

Bradley, R. 1995c. Rock carvings and decorated monuments in the British Isles. In, K. Helskog *Perceiving rock art: Social and political perspectives*. Oslo: Institute for comparative studies in human culture. pp.107-29.

Bradley, R. 1995d. Making sense of prehistoric rock art. *British Archaeology* 31: 8-9.

Bradley, R. 1996. Learning from places: Topographical analysis of north British rock art. *Northern Archaeology* 13/14: 87-99.

Bradley, R. 1997a. *Signing the Land: Rock art and the prehistory of Atlantic Europe*. London: Routledge.

Bradley, R. 1997b. Death by the water: Boats and footprints in the rock art of western Sweden. *Oxford Journal of Archaeology* 16(3): 315-24.

Bradley, R. 1997c. Stone circles and passage graves - a contested relationship. In, A. Gibson & D. Simpson (eds) *Prehistoric ritual and religion*. Stroud: Sutton. pp.2-13.

Bradley, R. 1998a. *The significance of monuments: On the shaping of human experience in Neolithic and Bronze Age Europe*. London: Routledge.

Bradley, R. 1998b. Daggers drawn. In, C. Chippindale & P. Tacon (eds) *The archaeology of rock art*. Cambridge: Cambridge University. pp.130-45.

Bradley, R. 1998c. Ruined buildings, ruined stones: Enclosures, tombs and natural places in the Neolithic of south-west England. *World Archaeology* 30(1):13-22.

Bradley, R. 1998d. Interpreting enclosures. In, M. Edmonds & C. Richards (eds) *Understanding the Neolithic of north-western Europe*. Glasgow: Cruithre Press. pp.188-203.

Bradley, R. 1998e. A new investigation into the Clava Cairns. *Proceedings of the Society of Antiquarians of Scotland* 128: 1125-6.

Bradley, R. 2000a. *An archaeology of natural places*. London: Routledge.

Bradley, R. 2000b. *The good Stones: A new investigation of the Clava Cairns*. Society of Antiquarians of Scotland Monograph 17.

Bradley, R. 2002. The authority of abstraction: Knowledge and power in the Landscapes of prehistoric Europe. In, K. Helskog (ed) *Theoretical perspectives in rock art research*. Oslo: Instituttet for sammenkignende kulturforskning. pp. 227-41.

Bradley, R & R. Chambers. 1988. A new study of the cursus complex at Dorchester on Thames. *Oxford Journal of Archaeology* 7(3): 271-89.

Bradley, R & R. Valcarce. 1998. Crossing the border: Contrasting styles of rock art in the prehistory of north-western Iberia. *Oxford Journal of Archaeology*. 17(3): 287-308.

Bradley, R & M. Mathews. 2000. The Clava ring-cairn at Newton of Petty. In, R. Bradley (ed) *The good Stones: A new investigation of the Clava Cairns*. Society of Antiquarians of Scotland Monograph 17. pp. 131-54.

Bradley, R et al. 1993. A field method for investigating the distribution of rock art. *Oxford Journal of Archaeology* 12(2): 129-44.

Bradley, R et al. 1999. Excavation at Clava. *Current Archaeology* 161: 184-7.

Bradley, R et al. 2001. Decorating the houses of the dead: Incised and pecked motifs in Orkney chambered tombs. *Cambridge Archaeological Journal* 11(1): 45-67.

Braun, D. 1995. Style, selection and historicity. In, C. Carr & J. Neitzel (eds). *Style, society and person*. New York: Plenum Press. pp.123-41.

Breck-Parkman, E. 1994. California Dreamin': Cupule petroglyph occurances in the American West. In, J. Steinbring (ed) *Rock art studies in the Americas*. Oxford: Oxbow. pp.1-12.

Brennan, M. 1983. *The stars and the stones*. London: Thames & Hudson.

Brindley, A. 1999a. Sequence and dating in the grooved ware tradition. In, R. Cleal & A. MacSween (eds) *Grooved ware in Britain and Ireland*. Oxford: Oxbow. pp.133-44.

Brindley, A. 1999b. Irish grooved ware. In, R. Cleal & A. MacSween (eds) *Grooved ware in Britain and Ireland*. Oxford: Oxbow. pp.23-35.

Brophy, K. 1999a. The cursus monuments of Scotland. In, A. Barclay & J. Harding (eds). *Pathways and ceremonies: The cursus monuments of Britain and Ireland*. Oxford: Oxbow. pp. 67-76.

Brophy, K. 1999b. Seeing the cursus as a symbolic river. *British Archaeology* 44:6-7.

Brophy, K. 2000: Wet Drybridge: A cursus in Ayrshire. In, J. Harding & R. Johnson (eds) *Northern pasts: Interpretations of the later prehistory of northern England and southern Scotland*. Oxford: BAR (British Series 302). pp. 45-56.

Brophy, K. 2002: The searchers: the quest for causewayed enclosures in the Irish Sea area. Paper presented at the *Neolithic of the Irish Sea: materiality and traditions of practice colloquium*. University of Manchester.

Brown, T. 1997. Clearances and clearings: Deforestation in Mesolithic/Neolithic Britain. *Oxford Journal of Archaeology* 16(2): 133-46.

Browne, G. 1899 - 1900. Notice on a cup-marked boulder called the Saj di Gorone, or stone of the heel, nr Stresa, on the Lago Maggiore. *Proceedings of the Society of antiquarians of Scotland* XXXIV: 297-99.

Brück, J. 1998. In the footsteps of the ancestors: a review of Christopher Tilley's A phenomenology of landscape: Places, paths and monuments. *Archaeological Review from Cambridge* 15(1): 23-36.

Buckley, V. 1991. The stone of Cethern's delusion. *Archaeology Ireland* 5:16.

Buckley, V & P. Sweetman. 1991. *Archaeological survey of County Louth*. Dublin: Stationary Office.

Burenhult, G. 1973. *The rock carvings of Götaland*. Stockholm: Institute of Archaeology.

Burenhult, G. 1979. Comment. In, E. Fett & P. Fett *Relations west Norway - western Europe demonstrated in petroglyphs*. *Norwegian Archaeological Review* 12(2): 92-5.

Burgess, C. 1990. The chronology of cup-and cup-and-ring marks in Atlantic Europe. *Rev. archéol. Quest, Supplément No. 2*: 157-71.

Burl, A. 1969-70. The recumbent stone circles of Scotland. *Proceedings of the Society of Antiquarians of Scotland* 102: 56-81.

Burl, A. 1976. *Stone circles of the British Isles*. New Haven: Yale University Press.

Burl, A. 1979. *Rings of Stone*. London: Frances Lincon.

Burl, A. 1994. The stone circle of Long Meg and her daughters, Little Salkeld. *Transactions of the Cumberland and Westmoorland Archaeological Society* XCIV: 1-11.

Butler, R. 1999. *Kilmartin*. Kilmartin: Kilmartin House Trust. Callary, R. 1926. Loughcrew carns, Oldcastle, Co. Meath: An ancient pagan cemetery. *Lecture pamphlet*. Drogheda: Drogheda Independent.

Cannon, A. 1996. Trends and motivation: Scaling the dimensions of material complexity. In, D. Meyer et al (eds) *Debating Complexity*. Calgory: University of Calgory. pp.31-8.

Cassel, K. 1998. Structure of space and perceptions of time. In, A-C Andersson et al (eds) *The kaleidoscopic past*. Göteborg: Götrborg University. pp.387-94.

Caulfield, S. The Neolithic Settlement of North Connaught. In, T. Reeves-Smyth & F. Hamond (eds) *Landscape archaeology in Ireland*. Oxford: BAR (British Series116). pp.195-215.

Caygill, H. 1994. Benjamin, Heidegger and the destruction of tradition. In, A. Benjamin & P. Osbourne (eds) *Walter Benjamin's philosophy: Destruction and experience*. London: Routledge. pp.1-31.

Caygill, H. 1998. *Walter Benjamin: The colour of experience*. London: Routledge.

Champion, T. 1989. Introduction. In, T. Champion (ed) *Center and periphery: Comparative studies in archaeology*. London: Unwin Hyman. pp.1-21.

Chapman, J. 1997. Places as time-marks - the social construction of prehistoric landscapes in east Hungary. In, G. Nash (ed) *Semiotics of landscape: Archaeology of mind*. Oxford: BAR (International Series 661). pp.31-45.

Childe, V G & J. Taylor. 1938-9. Rock scribings at Hawthornden, mid-Lothian. *Proceedings of the Society of Antiquarians of Scotland* LXXIII:316-8.

Children, G & G. Nash. 1997. Establishing a discourse: The language of landscape. In, G. Nash (ed) *Semiotics of landscape: Archaeology of mind*. Oxford: BAR (International Series 661). pp.1-4.

Chippindale, C. 1985. What is prehistoric art: A definition and its consequences. *Archaeological Review from Cambridge* 4(2): 141-58.

Christie, P. 1985. Barrows on the north Cornish Coast: Wartime excavations by C. K. Croft Andrew 1939-1944. *Cornish Archaeology* 24: 23-121.

Christison, D. 1903-4. On the standing stones and cup-marked rocks, etc, in the valley of the Add and some neighbouring districts of Argyle. *Proceedings of the Society of Antiquarians of Scotland* XXXVIII: 123-48.

Clare, T. 1987. Towards a reappraisal of henge monuments: origins, evolution and hierarchies. *Proceedings of the Prehistoric Society* 53: 457-77.

Clark, G et al. 1996. Explaining art in the Franco-Cantabrian refugium: An information exchange model. In, D. Meyer et al (eds) *Debating Complexity*. Calgory: University of Calgory. pp.241-53.

Clarke, D et al. 1985. *Symbols of power at the time of Stonehenge*. Edinburgh: HMSO.

Clarke, J. 1982. Prehistoric rock inscriptions near Dundalk, Co. Louth. *County Louth Archaeological and Historical Journal* 72: 107-16.

Clottes, J . 1993. Post-stylistic? In, M. Lorblanchet & P. Bahn (eds) *Rock art studies: The post stylistic era or where do we go from here*. Oxford: Oxbow monograph 35. pp.19-25.

Clottes, J. 1995. Perspectives and traditions in Palaeolithic rock art research in France. In, K. Helskog (ed) *Perceiving rock art:*

Social and political perspectives. Oslo: Institute for comparative studies in human culture. pp.35-64.

Coles, F. 1894-5. A record of the cup-and-ring markings in the stewardry of Kirkculdbright. *Proceedings of the Society of Antiquarians of Scotland* XXIX: 67-92.

Coles, F. 1908. Report on stone circles surveyed in Perthshire, north east section. *Proceedings of the Society of Antiquarians of Scotland* XLII: 95-162.

Coles, F. 1909-10. Report on stone circles surveyed in Perthshire (Aberfeldy district). *Proceedings of the Society of Antiquarians of Scotland* XLIV: 117-68.

Coles, J & D. Simpson. 1965. The excavation of a Neolithic round barrow at Pitnacree, Perthshire, Scotland. *Proceedings of the Prehistoric Society* 31: 34-57.

Conkey, M. 1996. A history of the interpretation of European 'paleoart': Magic, mythogram, and metaphors for modernity. In, A. Lock & C. Peters (eds) *Handbook of human symbolic evolution*. Oxford: Clarendon Press. pp.288-349.

Conkey, M. 1997. Beyond art and between the caves: thinking about context in the interpretative process. In, M. Conkey et al (eds) *Beyond art: Pleistocence image and symbol*. San Francisco: Memoirs of the Californian Academy of Sciences. pp.343-68.

Cooney, G. 1983. Megalithic tombs in their environmental setting: A settlement perspective. In, T. Reeves-Smith & F. Hamond (eds) *Landscape archaeology in Ireland*. Oxford: BAR (British Series 116). pp.179-94.

Cooney, G. 1990. The place of megalithic tomb cemeteries in Ireland. *Antiquity* 64: 741-53.

Cooney, G. 1991. Irish Neolithic landscapes and land use systems: the implications of field systems. *Rural History* 2(2): 123-40.

Cooney, G. 1992. Body politics and grave messages: Irish Neolithic mortuary practices. In, N. Sharples & A. Sheridan (eds) *Vessels for the ancestors*. Edinburgh: Edinburgh University. pp.168-76.

Cooney, G. 1997a. Images of Settlement and the landscape in the Neolithic. In, P. Topping (ed) *Neolithic landscapes*. Oxford: Oxbow. pp. 23-30.

Cooney, G. 1997b. Breaking stones, making places: The social landscape of axe production sites. In, A. Gibson & D. Simpson (eds) *Prehistoric ritual and religion*. Stroud: Sutton. pp. 108-18.

Cooney, G. 1999. Social landscapes in Irish prehistory. In, P. Ucko & R. Layton (eds) *The archaeology and anthropology of landscape*. London: Routledge. pp.46-64.

Cooney, G. 2000. *Landscapes of Neolithic Ireland*. London: Routledge.

Cooney, G & E. Grogan. 1994. *Irish Prehistory: A social perspective*. Dublin: Wordwell.

Cooney, G & E. Grogan. 1998. People and place during the Irish Neolithic: Exploring social change in time and space. In, M. Edmonds & C. Richards (ed) *Understanding the Neolithic of north-western Europe*. Glasgow: Cruithre Press. pp.456-80.

Cormack, E. 1949-50. Cross-markings and cup-marks at Duncroisk, Glen Lochay. *Proceedings of the Society of Antiquarians of Scotland* LXXXIV: 169-72.

Cowie, T & I. Shepherd. 1997. The Bronze Age. In, K. Edwards and I. Ralston (eds) *Scotland: Environment and archseology, 8000 BC - AD 1000*. Chichester: John Wiley. pp.152-68.

Cowling, E. 1938. Cup-and-ring markings to the north of Otley. *Yorkshire Archaeological Journal* XXXIII: 291-7.

Cowling, E &C. Hartley. 1959. A ring marked rock: The Grey Stones, Harewood Park. *Yorkshire Archaeological Journal* XL: 215-6.

Cramb, A. 2001. British Neolithic farmhouse 'older than the pyramids'. *Daily Telegraph* (7/9/01).

Cummins, W. 1980. Stone axes as a guide to Neolithic communications and boundaries in England and Wales. *Proceedings of the Prehistoric Society* 46: 45-60.

Curran-Mulligan, P. 1994. Yes, but it is art. *Archaeology Ireland* 8(1): 14-5.

Damm, C. 1998. Rituals: Symbols or action. In, A-C. Andersson et al (eds) *The kaleidoscopic past*. Göteborg: Götrborg University. pp.442-9.

Darvill, T. 1996a. *Prehistoric Britain from the air*. Cambridge: Cambridge University.

Darvill, T. 1996b. Neolithic buildings in England and Wales. In, J. Thomas & T. Darvil (eds) *Houses in north-western Europe and beyond*. Oxford: Oxbow. pp.77-111.

Darvill, T. 1997a. Ever increasing circles: the scared geography of Stonehenge and its landscape. In, B. Cunliffe & C. Renfrew (eds). *Science and Stonehenge.* Oxford: Oxford University Press. pp.167-202.

Darvill, T. 1997b. Neolithic landscapes: Identity and definition. In, P. Topping (ed) *Neolithic landscapes.* Oxford: Oxbow. pp.1-14.

Darvill, T & J. Thomas. 2001. Neolithic enclosures in Atlantic north-western Europe: some recent trends. In, T. Darvil & J. Thomas (eds) *Neolithic enclosures in Atlantic north-western Europe.* Oxford: Oxbow. pp.1-23.

David, B & H. Lourandos. 1998. Rock art and socio-demography in north-east Australian prehistory. *World Archaeology* 30(2): 193-219.

Davidson, R. 1950. Rock Scribings in Co. Down. *Ulster Journal of Archaeology* 13: 39-42.

Davies, J. 1959. A new engraved rock from Wharfedale. *Yorkshire Archaeological Journal* XL: 622-6.

Davis, W. 1993. Beginning the history of art. *Journal of Aesthetic and Art Criticism* 51: 327-50.

Darwell-Smith, T. 2002. *Grooved ware and the altered state.* Unpublished BA dissertation: University of Southampton.

Deacon, J. 1988. The power of place in understanding southern San rock engravings. *World Archaeology* 20: 129-40.

Donta, C. 1992. Incised images and the development of social and political complexity in southern Alaska. In, A. Goldsmith et al (eds) *Ancient images, ancient thoughts: The archaeology of ideology.* Calgary: University of Calgary. pp.11-8.

Douglas, M. 1995. Forgotten knowledge. In, M. Strathern (ed) *Shifting contexts.* London: Routledge. pp.13-30.

Dowson, T. A. 1994: Reading art, writing history. *World Archaeology* 25(3): 332-44.

Dowson,T . A. 1998a. Rock art: Handmaiden to studies of cognitive evolution. In, C. Renfrew (ed) *Cognation and material culture: The archaeology of symbolic storage.* Cambridge: MacDonald Institute. pp.67-76.

Dowson, T. A. 1998b. Like people in prehistory. *World Archaeology* 29(3): 333-43.

Dowson, T. A. 1999a. Interpretation in rock art research: A crisis in confidence. *The ley hunter* 133: 21-3.

Dowson, T. A. 1999b. L'art rupestre a la fin du millennium. Unpublished manuscript.

Dowson, T. A. 2002. Queer theory and feminist theory: Towards a sociology of sexual politics in rock art research. In, K. Helskog (ed) *Theoretical perspectives in rock art research.* Oslo: Instituttet for sammenkignende kulturforskning. pp.312-29.

Driscoll, S. 1998. Picts and prehistory: Cultural resource management in early Medieval Scotland. *World Archaeology* 30(1): 142-58.

Dronfield, J. 1993. Ways of seeing, ways of telling: Irish passage tomb art, style and the universality of vision. In, M. Lorblanchet & P. Bahn (eds) *Rock art studies: The post stylistic era or where do we go from here.* Oxford: Oxbow monograph 35. pp.179-93.

Dronfield, J. 1994. Subjective vision and the source of Irish Megalithic art. *Antiquity* 69: 539-49.

Dronfield, J. 1995. Migraine, light and hallucinogens: The neurocognitive basis of Irish megalithic art. *Oxford Journal of Archaeology* 14(3): 261-75.

Dronfield, J. 1996. The vision thing: Diagnosis of endogenenous derivation in abstract arts. *Current Anthropology* 37(2): 373-91.

Duff, W. 1975. Images: A way of seeing and a way of thinking. In, W. Duff *Images stone B.C.* Washington: University of Washington Press. pp.12-26.

Dutton, D. Tribal art and artefact. *Journal of Aesthetic and Art Criticism* 51(1): 13-22.

Editorial. 2000. Major new rock art discovered in Cumbria. *British Archaeology* 51: 7.

Edmonds, M. 1992. "Their use is wholly unknown". In, N. Sharples & A. Sheridan (eds) *Vessels for the ancestors.* Edinburgh: Edinburgh University. pp.179-93.

Edmonds, M. 1993. Interpreting causewayed enclosures in the past and present. In, C. Tilley (ed) *Interpretative Archaeology.* London: Berg. pp.99-142.

Edmonds, M. 1995. *Stone tools and society.* London: Batsford.

Edmonds, M. 1997. Taskscape, technology and tradition. *Analecta Praehistorica Leidensia* 29: 99-110.

Edmonds, M et al. 1992. Survey and excavation at Creag na Caillich, Killin, Perthshire. *Proceedings of the Society of Antiquarians of Scotland* 122: 72-112.

Edwards, A.1934. Rock sculpturings on Traprain Law, east Lothian. *Proceedings of the Society of Antiquarians of Scotland* LXIX: 122-37.

Edwards, G & R. Bradley. 1999. Rock carvings and Neolithic artefacts on Ilkley Moor, west Yorkshire. In, R. Cleal & A. MacSween (eds) *Grooved ware in Britain and Ireland.* Oxford: Oxbow. pp.76-7.

Edwardson, A. 1965. A spirally decorated object from Garbolisham. *Antiquity* 39: 145.

Eogan, G. 1986. *Knowth.* London: Thames & Hudson.

Eogan, G. 1992. Scottish and Irish passage tombs: Some comparisons and contrasts. In, N. Sharples & A. Sheridan (eds) *Vessels for the ancestors.* Edinburgh: Edinburgh University. pp.120-7.

Eogan, G. 1995. Ideas, people and things: Ireland and the external world during the late Bronze Age. In, J. Waddell & E. Shee-Twohig (eds) *Ireland in the Bronze Age.* Dublin: Office Of Public Works. pp.128-35.

Eogan, G. 1999. Megalithic art and society. *Proceedings of the Prehistoric Society* 65: 415-46.

Eogan, G & H. Richardson. 1982. Two maceheads from Knowth, Co. Meath. *Journal of the Royal Society of Antiquarians Ireland* 112: 123-38.

Evans, C. 1993. Digging with the pen: archaeologies and literary traditions. In, C. Tilley (ed) *Interpretative Archaeology.* Oxford: Berg. pp. 417-47.

Evans, C et al. 1999. Life in woods: Tree-throws, settlement and forest cognition. *Oxford Journal of Archaeology* 18: 241-54.

Evans, E. 1998. A question of appropriation: The rock art of Northern Britain. BA dissertation: University of Southampton.

Evans, E. 1999. Its just an illusion: Diversity versus homogeneity in the rock art of the British Isles and Ireland. Unpublished MA dissertation: University of Southampton.

Evans, E & T. A. Dowson. Forthcoming. Rock art, identity and death in the early Bronze Age of Ireland and Britain. In, C. Fowler & V. Cummings (eds) *The Neolithic of the Irish Sea colloquium conference proceedings*

Evans, E & R. Wallis. in prep. A vision thing? Neuropsychology and the passage tombs of Ireland.

Feather, S. 1964-5. Galician deer carvings: A Scottish parallel. *Proceedings of the Society of Antiquarians of Scotland* XCVIII: 315-7.

Fett, E & P. Fett. 1979. Relations west Norway - western Europe demonstrated in petroglyphs. *Norwegian Archaeological Review* 12(2): 65-107.

Field, D. 1998. Round barrows and the harmonious landscape: Placing early Bronze Age burial monuments in south-east England. *Oxford Journal of Archaeology* 17(3): 300-24.

Field, D. 1999. Bury the dead in a sacred landscape. *British Archaeology* 43: 6-7.

Fleming, A. 1999. Pheomenology and the megaliths of Wales: a dreaming too far? *Oxford Journal of Archaeology.* 18(2): 119-25.

Firth, R. 1992. Art and anthropology. In, J. Coote & A. Shelton (eds) *Anthropology, art and aesthetics.* Oxford: Clarendon. pp.15-39.

Forde-Johnston, J. 1957. Megalithic art in the north-west of Britain: The Claderstones, Liverpool. *Proceedings of the Prehistoric Society* 23: 20-39.

Franklin, N. 1993. Style and dating in rock art studies: The post-stylistic era in Australia and Europe. In, M. Lorblanchet & P. Bahn (eds) *Rock art studies: The post stylistic era or where do we go from here.* Oxford: Oxbow monograph 35. pp.1-14.

Frodsham, P. 1989. Two newly discovered cup-and-ring stones from Penrith and Hallbankgate, with a gazetteer of all known megalithic carvings in Cumbria. *Transactions of the Cumberland and Westmoorland Archaeological Society* LXXXIX: 1-18.

Frodsham, P. 1996. Spirals in time: Morwick Mill and the spiral motif in the British Neolithic. *Northern Archaeology* 13/14: 101-38.

Garwood, P. 1999. Grooved ware in southern Britain: Chronology and interpretation. In, R. Cleal & A. MacSween (eds) *Grooved ware in Britain and Ireland.* Oxford: Oxbow. pp. 144-57.

Geary, C. 1993. Art and political process in the kingdoms of Bali-Nyonga and Bamum. In, R. Anderson & K. Field (eds) *Art in small scale societies*. Englewood Cliffs: Prentice Hall. pp.84-102.

Gell, A. 1998: *Art and Agency: An anthropological theory*. Oxford: Clarendon Press.
Gazin-Schwartz, A & C. Holtorf. 1999. 'As long as I've known it ...'. In, A. Gazin-Schwartz & C. Holtorf (eds) *Archaeology and folklore*. London: Routledge. pp.3-25.

Gibson, A. 1998. *Stonehenge and timber circles*. Stroud: Tempus.

Giddens, A. 1984. *The constitution of society*. Cambridge: Polity press.

Gillberg, A. 1998. Biography in the history of archaeology. In, A-C. Andersson et al (eds) *The kaleidoscopic past*. Göteborg: Götrborg University. pp.294-301.

Gosden, C. 1994. *Social being and time*. Oxford: Blackwell.

Gosden, C. 2001: Making sense: Archaeology and aesthetics. *World Archaeology* 33(2): 163-7.

Gosden, C &G. Lock. 1998. Prehistoric histories. *World Archaeology* 30(1): 2-12.

Graham, A.1936. Two cup-marked stones from Claonig, Kintyre. *Proceedings of the Society of Antiquarians of Scotland* LXXI: 409-11.

Graves, J. 1876-8. On cup and circle sculptures as occurring in Ireland. *Journal of the Cork Historical and Archeological Society* 4: 283-96.

Green, M. 2000. *A landscape revealed: 10, 000 years on a chalkland farm*. Stroud: Tempus.

Groenman-Van-Waateringe, W. 1983. Early agricultural utilisation of the Irish Landscape: The last word on the elm decline? In, T. Reeves-Smyth & F. Hamond (eds) *Landscape archaeology in Ireland*. Oxford: BAR (British Series116). pp.217-232.

Grogan, E. 1996. Neolithic houses in Ireland. In, J. Thomas & T. Darvil (eds) *Houses in north-western Europe and beyond*. Oxford: Oxbow. pp.41-61.

Haggart, D. 1894. Notice of the discovery of cup-and-ring sculpturings at Duncroisk, near the falls of Lochay, in Glenlochay. *Proceedings of the Society of Antiquarians of Scotland* XXIX: 92-3.

Haley, S. 1996. Dead, buried but not gone. In, D. Meyer et al (eds) *Debating Complexity*. Calgory: University of Calgory. pp.122-6.

Harding, A. 2000. *European societies in the Bronze Age*. Cambridge: Cambridge University Press.

Harding, A & G. Lee. 1987. *The henge monuments and related sites of Britain*. Oxford: BAR (British Series 175).

Harding, J. 1996. Reconsidering Neolithic round barrows in east Yorkshire. *Northern Archaeology* 13/14: 67-78.

Harding, J. 1997. Interpreting the Neolithic: The monuments of north Yorkshire. *Oxford Journal of Archaeology* 16(3): 279-96.

Harding, J. 1998. The architecture of meaning: The causewayed enclosures and henges of lowland England. In, M. Edmonds & C. Richards (eds) *Understanding the Neolithic of north-western Europe*. Glasgow: Cruithre Press. pp.204-30.

Harding, J. 1999. Pathways to new realms: Cursus monuments and symbolic territories. In, A. Barclay & J. Harding (eds). *Pathways and ceremonies: The cursus monuments of Britain and Ireland*. Oxford: Oxbow. pp.30-8.

Harding, J & A. Barclay. 1999. An introduction to the cursus monuments of Neolithic Britain and Ireland. In, A. Barclay & J. Harding (eds). *Pathways and ceremonies: The cursus monuments of Britain and Ireland*. Oxford: Oxbow. pp.1-10.

Hartgroves, S. 1987. The cup-marked stones of Stithians reservoir. *Cornish Archaeology* 26: 69-84.

Hayman, R. 1997. *Riddles in Stone*. London: Hambledon Press.

Helskog, K. 1987. Selective depictions. A study of 3,500 years of rock carvings from Arctic Norway and their relationship to Sami drums. In, I. Hodder (ed) *Archaeology as long term history*. Cambridge: Cambridge University Press. pp.17-30.

Helskog, K. 1999. The shore connection: Cognitive landscape and communication with rock carvings in Northernmost Europe. *Norwegian Archaeological Review* 32(2): 73-94.

Hensall, A. 1970. Long Cairns of eastern Scotland. *Scottish Archaeological Forum* 2: 29-46.

Herity, M. 1975. *Irish passage graves: Neolithic tomb building in Ireland and Britain 2500 BC*. New York: Barnes & Noble.

Herity, M & G. Eogan. 1977. *Ireland in Prehistory*. London: Routledge.

Hesjedal, A. 1995. Rock art, time and social context. In, K. Helskog (ed) *Perceiving rock art: Social and political perspectives*. Oslo: Institute for comparative studies in human culture. pp.200-6.

Hesse, M. 1992. Archaeology and the science of the concrete. In, T. Shay & J. Clottes (eds) *The limitations of archaeological knowledge*. Liege: Etudes et Recherches Archeologiques de l'Universite de Liege. pp.107-14.

Humphrey, C. 1995. Chiefly and shamanistic landscapes in Mongolia. In, E. Hirsch & M. O'Hanlon (eds) *The anthropology of landscape*. Oxford: Claredon Press. pp.135-58.

Hewitt, I & S. Beckensall. 1996. Excavation of cairns at Blawearie, Old Bewick, Northumberland. *Proceedings of the Prehistoric Society* 62: 255:74.

Heyd, T. 1999. Rock art aesthetics: Trace on rock, mark of spirit, window on land. *Journal of Aesthetic and Art Criticism* 57(4): 451-8.

Hobsbawn, E. 1983. *The invention of tradition*. Cambridge: Cambridge University Press.

Hodder, I. 1994. Architecture and meaning: The example of Neolithic houses and tombs. In, M. Parker-Pearson & C. Richards (eds) *Architecture and order: Approaches to social space*. London: Routledge. pp.73-86.

Holtorf, C. 1998. The life histories in the Mecklenbury-Vorpommern (Germany). *World Archaeology* 30(1): 23-38.

Jackson, P. 1995. A continuing belief system? Irish passage grave art and the cup-and-ring engravings of the British Isles and Eire. In, K. Helskog (ed) *Perceiving rock art: Social and political perspectives*. Oslo: Institute for comparative studies in human culture. pp.396-406.

Jacobstahl, P. 1938. Celtic rock carvings in north Italy and Yorkshire. *Journal of Roman Studies* 28: 65-9.

Johnson, R. 1999. An empty path? Processions, memories, and the Dorset cursus. In, A. Barclay & J. Harding (eds) *Pathways and ceremonies: The cursus monuments of Britain and Ireland*. Oxford: Oxbow. pp 39-48.

Johnston, S. 1989. *Prehistoric Irish petroglyphs: Their analysis and interpretation*. Ann Arbor: University microfilms.

Johnston, S. 1993a. The utility of 'style' in the analysis of prehistoric Irish rock art. In, M. Lorblanchet & P. Bahn (eds) *Rock art studies: The post stylistic era or where do we go from here*. Oxford: Oxbow monograph 35. pp.143-50.

Johnston, S. 1993b. The relationship between prehistoric Irish rock art and Irish Passage tomb art. *Oxford Journal of Archaeology* 12(3): 257-79.

Jolly, W. 1881-2. On cup-marked stones in the neighbourhood of Inverness. *Proceedings of the Society of Antiquarians of Scotland* XVI: 300-401.

Jonaitis, A. Hierarchy in the art of the northern Tlingit. In, R. Anderson & K. Field (eds) *Art in small scale societies*. Englewood Cliffs: Prentice Hall. pp.105-17.

Jones, A. 1999. Local colour: megalithic architecture and colour symbolism in Neolithic Arran. *Oxford Journal of Archaeology* 18(4): 339-50.

Jones-Bley, K. 1992. The sun in image and thought. In, A. Goldsmith et al (eds) *Ancient images, ancient thoughts: The archaeology of ideology*. Calgary: University of Calgary. pp.83-90.

Karlenby, L. 1998. The accumulated landscape: The definition of continuity and discontinuity from an archaeological point of view. In, A-C. Andersson et al (eds) *The kaleidoscopic past*. Göteborg: Götrborg University. pp.404-11.

Kinnes, I. 1985. Circumstance not context. The Neolithic of Scotland as seen form the outside. *Proceedings of the Society of Antiquarians of Scotland* 115: 15-57.

Kinnes, I. 1995. An innovation backed by great prestige: The instance of the spiral and 20 centuries of Stoney sleep. In, I. Kinnes & G. Varndell (eds) *Unbaked urns of rudely shape*. Oxford: Oxbow. pp. 49-53.

Kirk, T. 1997. Towards a phenomenology of building: The Neolithic long-mound at La Commuee-Sèche, Colombiers-sur-Sealles, Normandy. In, G.Nash (ed) *Semiotics of landscape: Archaeology of mind*. Oxford: BAR (International Series 661). pp.59-70.

Lacy, B. 1983. *An archaeological survey of county Donegal*. Lifford: Donegal County Council.

Lacy, S. 1995. Introduction: Cultural pilgrimages and metaphorical journeys. In, S. Lacy (ed) *Mapping the terrain: New genre public art*. Seattle: Bay Press. pp.19-48.

Last, J. 1998. Books of life: Biography and memory in a Bronze Age barrow. *Oxford Journal of Archaeology* 17(1): 43-53.

Last, J. 1999. Out of line: Cursus and monument typology in east England. In, A. Barclay & J. Harding (eds) *Pathways and ceremonies: The cursus monuments of Britain and Ireland.* Oxford: Oxbow. pp.86-97.

Layton, R. 1999. Folklore and world view. In, A. Gazin-Schwartz & C. Holtorf (eds) *Archaeology and folklore.* London: Routledge. pp.26-34.

Layton, R & P. Ucko. 1999. Introduction: Gazing on the landscape and encountering the environment. In, P. Ucko & R. Layton (eds) *The archaeology and anthropology of landscape.* London: Routledge. pp.1-20.

Lewis-Williams, J. D. 1982. The economic and social context of southern San rock art. *Current Anthropology* 23(4): 429-48.

Lewis-Williams, J. D. 1983. The empiricist impasse in southern African rock art studies. *The South African Archaeological Bulletin* 39: 58-66.

Lewis-Williams, J. D. 1990: Documentation, analysis and interpretation: Dilemmas in rock art research. Review of Pager (ed) The rock paintings of the Upper Brandberg. Part 1: Amis Gorge. *South African Archaeological Bulletin* 45: 126-36.

Lewis-Williams, J. D. 1995a. Seeing and construing. The making and meaning of a southern African rock art motif. *Cambridge Archaeological Journal* 5(1): 3-21.

Lewis-Williams, J. D. 1995b. Perspectives and traditions in southern African rock art research. In, K. Helskog (ed) *Perceiving rock art: Social and political perspectives.* Oslo: Institute for comparative studies in human culture. pp.65-86.

Lewis-Williams, J. D. 1997. Agency, art and altered consciousness: A motif in French (Quercy) Upper Palaeolithic parietal art. *Antiquity* 71: 810-30.

Lewis-Williams, J. D. 1998. Quanto? The issue of many meanings in southern African San rock art research. *South African Archaeological Bulletin* 53: 86-97.

Lewis-Williams, J. D. & T. A. Dowson 1988. The signs of all times: Entoptic phenomena in upper Palaeolithic art. *Current Anthropology* 29: 201-45.

Lewis-Williams, J. D. & T. A. Dowson. 1990. Through the Veil: San rock paintings and the rock face. *South African Archaeological Bulletin* 45: 5-16.

Lewis-Williams, J. D & T. A. Dowson. 1993. On vision and power in the Neolithic: Evidence from the decorated monuments. *Current Anthropology* 34(1): 55-65.

Lewis-Williams, J. D. et al. 1993. Rock art and changing perceptions of southern Africa's past: Ezeljagdspoort reviewed. *Antiquity* 67: 273-89.

Llosas, M. 1999. Pigment analysis and absolute dating of rock paintings from Jujug, Argentina. In, M. Strecker & P. Bahn (eds) *Dating and the earliest known rock art.* Oxford: Oxbow. pp.67-74.

Long, D et al. 2000. The use of henbane (Hyoseyamus niger L.) as a hallucinogen at Neolithic 'ritual' sites: a re-evaluation. *Antiquity* 74: 49-53.

Loveday, R. 1997. Double entrance henges - Routes to the past? In, A. Gibson & D. Simpson (eds) *Prehistoric ritual and religion.* Stroud: Sutton. pp.14-31.

Lynch, F. 1967. Barclodiad Y Gawres. *Archaeological Cambrensis* 116: 1-22.

Lynch, F et al. 2000. *Prehistoric Wales.* Stroud: Sutton.

MacGregor, G. 1999: Making sense of the past in the present: A sensory analysis of carved stone balls. *World Archaeology* 31(2): 258-71.

MacKenzie, J. 1899-1900. Notes on some cup-marked stones and rocks near Kenmore, and their folklore. *Proceedings of the Society of antiquarians of Scotland* XXXIV: 325-34.

MacWhite, E. 1946. A new view on Irish Bronze Age rock scribings. *Journal of the Royal Society of Antiquarians Ireland* LXXVI:59-75.

Malmer, M. 1989. Principles of a non-mythological explanation of northern European Bronze Age rock art. In, H-A. Nordström & A. Knape (eds) *Bronze Age studies.* Stockholm: Statens Historiska Museum.pp.91-100.

Marshall, D. 1976-7. Carved stone balls. *Proceedings of the Society of Antiquarians of Scotland* 108: 40-72.

Martlew, R & C. Ruggles. 1996. Ritual and landscape on the western coast of Scotland: an investigation of the stone rows of north Mull. *Proceedings of the Prehistoric Society* 62: 117-32.

Marstrander, S. 1979. Comment. In, E. Fett & P. Fett *Relations west Norway - western Europe demonstrated in petroglyphs. Norwegian Archaeological Review* 12(2): 97-100.

Masters, L. 1973. The Lochill long cairn. *Antiquity* XLVII: 96-100.

Masters, L 1984. The Neolithic long cairns of Cumbria and Northumberland. In, R. Micket & C. Burgess *Between and beyond the walls*. Edinburgh: John Donald. pp.52-73.

McGrail, S. 1987. *Ancient boats in north-western Europe*. London: Longman.

McGrail, S. 1993. Prehistoric seafaring in the channel. In, C. Scarre & F. Healy (eds) *Trade and exchange in prehistoric Europe*. Oxford: Oxbow Monograph 33. pp.199-210.

McKinley, J. 1997. Bronze Age barrows and funerary rites and rituals of cremation. *Proceedings of the Prehistoric Society* 63: 129-45.

McMann, J. 1980. *Riddles of the stone age*. London: Thames & Hudson.

McMann, J. 1993. *Loughcrew: The cairns*. Oldcastle: After Hours Books.

McMann, J. 1994. Forms of power: dimensions of an Irish megalithic landscape. *Antiquity* 68: 525-44.

McGuire, R. 1996. Why complexity is too simple. In, D. Meyer et al (eds) *Debating Complexity*. Calgory: University of Calgory. pp.23-9.

Meredith, J. 1990. The aesthetic artefact. *Archaeological Review from Cambridge* 9(2): 208-18.

Miles, H. 1975. Barrows on the St Austell granite, Cornwall. *Cornish Archaeology* 14: 5-81.

Mithen, S. 1989. To hunt or to paint: Animals and art in the Upper Palaeolithic. *Man* 23: 671-95.

Moore, J. 1996. Damp Squib: How to fire a major deciduous forest in an inclement climate. In, T. Pollard & A. Morrison (eds) *The early prehistory of Scotland*. Edinburgh: Edinburgh University Press. pp.62-73.

Moore, M. 1987. *Archaeological inventory of Co. Meath*. Dublin: Stationary Office.

Morphy, H. 1994. The anthropology of art. In, T. Ingold (ed) *Compamori Encyclopedia of anthropology*. London: Routledge. pp.648-85.

Morphy, H. 1995. Landscape and the reproduction of the ancestral past. In, E. Hirsch & M. O'Hanlon (eds) *The anthropology of landscape: Perspectives on space and place*. Oxford: Clarendon. pp.184-210.

Morris, R. 1966. The cup and ring marks and similar sculptures of south-west Scotland. *Ancient Monuments Society's Transactions* 14: 77-100.

Morris, R. 1967. The cup and ring marks and similar sculptures of Scotland: A survey of the southern counties, Pt.II. *Proceedings of the Society of Antiquarians of Scotland* 100: 47-78.

Morris, R. 1970. The Petroglyphs at Achnabreck, Argyll. *Proceedings of the Society of Antiquarians of Scotland* 103: 33-56.

Morris, R. 1979. *Rock art of Galloway and the Isle of Man*. Poole: Blanford Press.

Morris, R. 1981. *The prehistoric rock art of southern Scotland*. Oxford: BAR (British Series 86).

Morris, R & D. Bailey. 1964. The cup-and-ring marks and similar sculptures of south-western Scotland: A survey. *Proceedings of the Society of Antiquarians of Scotland* XCVIII:1 50-7.

Morwood, M. 1992. Rock art in south eastern Cape York, Australia: An archaeological approach. In, A. Goldsmith et al (eds) *Ancient images, ancient thoughts: The archaeology of ideology*. Calgary: University of Calgary. pp.417-26.

Mullin, D. 2001. Remembering, forgetting and the invention of tradition: burial and natural places in the English early Bronze Age. *Antiquity* 75: 533-7.

Nash, G. 1997a. Monumentality and landscape: The possible symbolic and political distribution of long chambered tombs around the Black Mountains, central Wales. In, G. Nash (ed) *Semiotics of landscape: Archaeology of mind*. Oxford: BAR (International Series 661). pp.17-30.

Nash, G. 1997b. Dancing in space: Rock art of the Campo Lamerio Valley, Galicia, Spain. In, G. Nash (ed) *Semiotics of landscape: Archaeology of mind*. Oxford: BAR (International Series 661). pp. 46-58.

Needham, S. 1988. Selective deposition in the British early Bronze Age. *World Archaeology* 20(2): 229-48.

Neitzel, J. 1995. Elite styles in hierarchically organised societies: The Chacoan regional system. In, C. Carr & J. Neitzel (eds). *Style, society and person*. New York: Plenum Press. pp.393-418.

Nordbladh, J. 1995. The history of Scandinavian rock art research as a corpus of knowledge. In, K. Helskog (ed) *Perceiving rock art: Social and political perspectives*. Oslo: Institute for comparative studies in human culture. pp.23-34.

O'Brien, W. 1993. Aspects of wedge tomb chronology. In, E. Shee-Twohig & M. Ronayne (eds) *Past perceptions*. Cork: Cork University Press. pp.63-74.

O'Brien, W. 1994. *Mount Gabriel: Bronze Age mining in Ireland*. Galway: Galway University Press.

O'Brien, W. 1999. *Sacred ground. Megalithic tombs in coastal south-west Ireland*. Galway: National University of Ireland.

Odak, O. 1992. Cup-mark patterns as an interpretation strategy in some southern Kenyan petroglyphs. In, M. Lorblanchet (ed) *Rock art in the old world*. New Delhi: IGNCA. pp.49-60.

O'Kelly, M. 1958. A new group of rock scribings in Co.Kerry. *Journal of the Cork Historical and Archeological Society* 63: 1-4.

O'Kelly, M. 1982. *Newgrange: Art, architecture and legend*. London: Thames & Hudson.

Oram, R. 1997. *Scottish Prehistory*. Edinburgh: Binlinn.

O'Sullivan, M. 1989. A stylistic revolution in the megalithic art of the Boyne Valley. *Archaeology Ireland* 3(4): 138-42.

O'Sullivan, M. 1993. Approaches to passage tomb art. *Journal of the Royal Society of Antiquarians Ireland* 116: 68-83.

O'Sullivan, M. 1998. Retrieval and revisionism in the interpretation of megalithic art. *Archaeological Review from Cambridge* 15(1): 37-48.

O'Sullivan, A & J. Sheehan. 1993. Prospects and outlooks: Aspects of rock art on the Inveragh peninsula, Co.Kerry. In, E. Shee-Twohig & M. Ronayne (eds) *Past perceptions*. Cork: Cork University Press. pp.75-84.

O'Sullivan, A & J. Sheehan. 1996. *The Inveragh peninsula: An archaeological survey of south Kerry*. Cork: Cork University Press.

Oswald, A et al. 2001: *The creation of monuments: Neolithic causewayed enclosures in the British Isles*. Swindon: English Heritage.

Ouzman, S. 2001. Seeing is deceiving: Rock art and the non-visible. *World Archaeology* 33(2): 237-56.

Parker-Pearson, M & Ramilisonina. 1998. Stonehenge for the ancestors: The stones pass on the message. *Antiquity* 72: 308-26.

Parker-Pearson, M & C. Richards. 1994a. Ordering the world: Perceptions of architecture, space and time. In, M. Parker-Pearson & C. Richards (eds) *Architecture and order: Approaches to social space*. London: Routledge. pp.1-37.

Parker-Pearson, M & C. Richards. 1994b. Architecture and order: Spatial representation and archaeology. In, M. Parker-Pearson & C. Richards (eds) *Architecture and order: Approaches to social space*. London: Routledge. pp.38-72.

Peña Santos, A & J. Vazquez Varela. 1979. *Los Petroglifos Gallegas*. Sada: Ediciosdo Castro.

Phillips, T. 2000. The local siting of the Clava cairns. In, R. Bradley (ed) *The good Stones: A new investigation of the Clava Cairns*. Society of Antiquarians of Scotland Monograph 17. pp. 171-84.

Piggott, S. 1971-2. Excavation of the Dalladies long barrow, Fettercairn, Kincardshire. *Proceedings of the Society of Antiquarians of Scotland* 104: 23-47.

Piggott, S. 1973. The Dalladies long barrow, north-east Scotland. *Antiquity* XLVII: 32-6.

Piggott, S & D. Simpson. 1971. Excavation of a stone circle at Croft Moraig, Perthshire, Scotland. *Proceedings of the Prehistoric Society* 37: 1-15.

Pollard, J. 1995. Inscribing space: Formal deposition at the late Neolithic monument of Woodhenge, Wiltshire. *Proceedings of the Prehistoric Society* 61: 137-56.

Pollard, J. 1999. These places have their moments: Thoughts on settlement practices in the British Neolithic. In, J. Bruck & M. Goodman (eds) *Making places in the prehistoric world: Themes in settlement archaeology*. London: UCL Press. pp.70-93.

Pollard, J. 2001: The aesthetics of depositional practice. *World Archaeology* 33(2): 315-33.

Pollard, J & C. Ruggles. 2001. Shifting perceptions: Spatial order, cosmology and patterns of deposition at Stonehenge. *Cambridge Archaeological Journal* 11(1): 69-90.

Poulter, E. 2000. *An ethnology of psychedelic art*. Unpublished BA dissertation, University of Southampton.

Powell, T & G. Daniel. 1956. *Barclodiad Y Gawres*. Liverpool: Liverpool University Press.

Price, H. 1996. Regional variability in complexity, an Upper Palaeolithic case study. In, D. Meyer et al (eds) *Debating Complexity*. Calgory: University of Calgory. pp.212-23.

Price, S. 1989. *Primitive art in civilised places*. Chicago: University of Chicago Press.

Pryor, F. 2001. *Seahenge*. London: Harper Collins.

Purcell, A. 2002. The rock art of the Inveragh peninsula, Co. Kerry, south-west Ireland. In, In, G. Nash & C. Chippendale (eds) *European landscapes of rock art*. London: Routledge. pp. 71-92.

Raistrict, A. 1936. cup-and-ring marked rocks of west Yorkshire. *Yorkshire Archaeological Journal* XXXII: 33-42.

Rault, S. 1997: From Anneville to Zedea: A ritual seascape? Megaliths and long distance contacts in western Europe. In, G. Nash (ed) *Semiotics of landscape: Archaeology of mind*. Oxford: BAR (International Series 661). pp. 31-45.

RCAHMS. 1988. *Argyll: An inventory of the monuments, volume 6*. Edinburgh: HMSO.

Richards, C. 1990. The late Neolithic house in Orkney. In, R. Samson (ed) *The social archaeology of houses*. Edinburgh: Edinburgh University Press. pp.110-25.

Richards, C. 1992. Skara Brae: Revisiting a Neolithic Village in Orkney. In, W. Hanson (ed) *Scottish archaeology*. Aberdeen: Aberdeen University Press. pp.24-43.

Richards, C. 1993. Monumental choreograph: Architectural and spatial representation in late Neolithic Orkney. In, C. Tilley (ed) *Interpretive archaeology*. Oxford: Berg. pp.143-77.

Richards, C. 1996a. Henges and water: Towards an elemental understanding of monumentality and landscape in late Neolithic Britain. *Journal of Material Culture* 1: 315-36.

Richards, C. 1996b. Monuments as landscape: Creating the centre of the world in late Neolithic Orkney. *World Archaeology* 28(2): 190-208.

Richards, C. 1998. Centralising tendencies? A re-examination of social evolution in late Neolithic Orkney. In, M. Edmonds & C. Richards (eds) *Understanding the Neolithic of north-western Europe*. Glasgow: Cruithre Press. pp.516-32.

Richards, C. 1999. Rethinking the Neolithic of Orkney. *British Archaeology* 42: 12-3.

Ritchie, G & M. Harman. 1985. *Exploring Scotland's heritage*. Edinburgh: RCAHMS.

Ritchie, J. 1917-8. Cup-marks on the stone circles and standing stones of Aberdeenshire. *Proceedings of the Society of Antiquarians of Scotland* LII: 86-121.

Ritchie, R. 1992. Stone axeheads and cushion maceheads from Orkney and Shetland: Some similarities and contrasts. In, N. Sharples & A. Sheridan (eds) *Vessels for the ancestors*. Edinburgh: Edinburgh University. pp.213-20.

Ritchie, G & A. Ritche. 1981. *Scotland: Archaeology and early history*. London: Thames & Hudson.

Rockhounding:06/02/02. www.jewelrysupplier.com/2_quartz/quartz_spirituality.htm.

Roe, F. 1968. Maceheads and the latest Neolithic cultures of the British Isles. In, J. Coles & D. Simpson (eds) *Studies in ancient Europe*. Leicester: Leicester University Press. pp.145-72.

Roe, P. 1995. Style, society, myth, and structure. In, C. Carr & J. Neitzel (eds). *Style, society and person*. New York: Plenum Press. pp.27-76.

Romilly-Allen, J. 1881-2. Notes on some undescribed stones with cup-marking in Scotland. *Proceedings of the Society of antiquarians of Scotland* XVI: 71-143.

Root, D. 1996. *Cannibal culture: art, appropriation and the commodification of difference*. Boulder: West View Press.

Rozas, R. 1999. Prehistoric open-air rock art in Galicia, north-west Spain: Characteristics and principal iconography. *Rock Art Research* 16(2): 113-26.

Rudgley, R. 1993. *The Alchemy of culture: Intoxicants in society*. London: British Museum Press.

Ruggles, C. 1997. Ritual astronomy in the Neolithic and Bronze Age British Isles: patterns of continuity and change. In, A. Gibson & D. Simpson (eds) *Prehistoric ritual and religion*. Stroud: Sutton. pp. 203-8.

Russell, M. 2000. Flint mines in Neolithic Britain. Stroud: Tempus.

Sauter, M. 1976. *Switzerland: From the earliest known times to the Roman conquest*. London: Thames & Hudson.

Scarre, C. 1997. Misleading images: Stonehenge and Brittany. *Antiquity* 71: 1016-20.

Shee, E. 1968. Some examples of rock art from Co. Cork. *Journal of the Cork Historical and Archeological Society* 63: 144-52.

Shee, E. 1972. Three decorated stones from Loughcrew. *Journal of the Royal Society of Antiquarians Ireland* 102: 224-33.

Shee-Twohig, E. 1981. *The megalithic art of Western Europe*. Oxford: Clarendon Press.

Shee-Twohig, E. 1993. Megalithic tombs and megalithic art in Atlantic Europe. In, C. Scarre & F. Healy (eds) *Trade and exchange in prehistoric Europe*. Oxford: Oxbow Monograph 33. pp.87-100.

Shee-Twohig, E. 1996. Context and content of Irish passage tomb art. *Rev. archeol. Quest Supplement* No.8: 67-80.

Shell, C. 2000. Metalworker or shaman: Early Bronze Age Upton Lovell G2a burial. *Antiquity* 74: 271-2.

Sheridan, A. 1992. Scottish stone axeheads: Some new work and recent discoveries. In, N. Sharples & A. Sheridan (eds) *Vessels for the ancestors*. Edinburgh: Edinburgh University. pp.194-212.

Sheridan, A. 1999. Grooved ware from the links of Notland, Westray, Orkney. In, R. Cleal & A. MacSween (eds) *Grooved ware in Britain and Ireland*. Oxford: Oxbow. pp.112-124.

Sheridan, A. 2001. Donegore Hill and other Irish Neolithic enclosures: a view from outside. In, T. Darvil & J. Thomas (eds) *Neolithic enclosures in Atlantic north-western Europe*. Oxford: Oxbow Books. pp.171-89.

Shiner, L. 1994. "Primitive fakes", "tourist art", and the ideology of authenticity. *Journal of Aesthetic and Art Criticism* 52(2): 225-34.

Simmons, I. 1996. *The environmental impact of later Mesolithic cultures: The creation of Moorland landscapes in England and Wales*. Edinburgh: Edinburgh University Press.

Simpson, D. 1996. 'Crown' antler maceheads and the later Neolithic in Britain. *Proceedings of the Prehistoric Society* 62: 293-309.

Simpson, D & J. Thawley. 1972. Single grave art in Britain. *Scottish Archaeological Forum* 4: 81-104.

Simpson, D & R. Ransom 1992. Maceheads and the Orcadian Neolithic. In, N. Sharples & A. Sheridan (eds) *Vessels for the ancestors*. Edinburgh: Edinburgh University. pp.221-43.

Smith, C. 1992. Testing the information exchange theory of style: A structural/post-structural analysis of art from Arnhemland and the western desert in Australia. In, A. Goldsmith et al (eds) *Ancient images, ancient thoughts: The archaeology of ideology*. Calgary: University of Calgary. pp.397-406.

Soffer, O & M. Conkey. 1997. Studying ancient visual cultures. In, M. Conkey et al (eds) *Beyond art: Pleistocence image and symbol*. San Francisco: Memoirs of the Californian Academy of Sciences. pp. 1-16.

Soffe, G & T. Clare. 1988. New evidence of ritual monuments at Long Meg and her Daughters, Cumbria. *Antiquity* 62: 552-7.

Sognnes, K. 1996. Recent research in northern Europe. In, P. Bahn & A. Fossati (eds) *News of the world: Recent developments in rock art research*. Oxford: Oxbow Monograph 72. pp.15-28.

Sognnes, K & A. Haug. 1998. Searching for hidden images: Rock art geography in Stjørdal, Trødelag, Norway. *Rock Art Research* 15(2): 98-108.

Soloman, A. 1998. Ethnography and method in South African rock art research. In, C. Chippindale & P. Tacon . *The archaeology of rock art*. Cambridge: Cambridge University Press. pp.268-84.

Sondon, D. 1997. *Stonehenge: Mysteries of the stones and landscape*. London: English Heritage.

Spencer-Wood, S. 1996. Cultural complexity, non-linear systems theory and multi-scalar analysis. In, D. Meyer et al (eds) *Debating Complexity*. Calgory: University of Calgory. pp.54-63.

Staniszewski, M. 1995. *Believing is seeing*. New York: Penguin.

Steinbring, J & M. Lantelgine. 1991. The petroglyphs of west Yorkshire: Explorations in analysis and interpretations. *Rock Art Research* 8(1): 13-28.

Stewart, M. 1958-9. Strath Tay in the second millennium BC. *Proceedings of the Society of Antiquarians of Scotland* XCII: 71-84.

Stewart, M. 1965-6. Excavation of a setting of standing stones at Lundin farm near Aberfeldy, Perthshire. *Proceedings of the Society of Antiquarians of Scotland* XCVIII: 126-49.

Swartz, B & T. Hurlbutt. 1994. Space, place and territory in rock art interpretation. *Rock Art Research* 11(1): 13-22.

Tabraham, C. 1988. *Scotland BC*. Edinburgh: HMSO.

Tacon, P et al. 1997. Cupule engravings from Jinmium-Granilp (northern Australia) and beyond: Explorations of a widespread enigmatic class of rock markings. *Antiquity* 71: 942-65.

Taylor, T. 1994. The archaeologist as analyst and audience. In, Viewpoint 'Is there a place for aesthetics in archaeology?' *Cambridge Archaeological Journal* 4(2): 250-55.

Thomas, J. 1992. Monuments, movement and the context of megalithic art. In, N. Sharples & A. Sheridan (eds). *Vessels for the ancestors*. Edinburgh: Edinburgh University Press. pp.143-58.

Thomas, J. 1993a. After essentialism: Archaeology, geography and post-modernism. *Archaeological Review from Cambridge* 12(1): 5-27.

Thomas, J. 1993. Discourse, totalization and 'The Neolithic'. In, C. Tilley (ed) *Interpretative archaeology*. London: Berg. pp. 357-93.

Thomas, J. 1996a. *Time, culture and identity: An interpretative archaeology*. London: Routledge.

Thomas, J. 1996b. Neolithic houses in mainland Britain and Ireland - A sceptical view. In, J. Thomas & T. Darvil (eds) *Houses in north-western Europe and beyond*. Oxford: Oxbow. pp. 1-12.

Thomas, J. 1997. The materiality of the Mesolithic-Neolithic transition in Britain. *Analecta Praehistorica Leidensia* 29: 57-64.

Thomas, J. 1998a. Picts Knowe, Holywood, and Holm. *Current Archaeology* 160: 149-60.

Thomas, J. 1998b. Towards a regional geography of the Neolithic. In, M. Edmonds & C. Richards (eds) *Understanding the Neolithic of north-western Europe*. Glasgow: Cruithre Press. pp.37-60.

Thomas, J. 1999a. *Understanding the Neolithic*. London: Routledge.

Thomas, J. 1999b. Death, identity and the body in Neolithic Britain. *The Curl lecture*. University of Southampton.

Thomas, J. 2001. Neolithic enclosures: reflections on excavations in Wales and Scotland. In, T. Darvil & J. Thomas (eds) *Neolithic enclosures in Atlantic north-western Europe*. Oxford: Oxbow Books. pp.132-43.

Thomas, J & C. Tilley. 1993. The axe and the torso: Symbolic structures in the Neolithic of Brittany. In, C. Tilley (ed) *Interpretive archaeology*. Oxford: Berg. pp.225-326.

Thorpe, I. 1997. From settlements to monuments: Site succession in late Neolithic and early Bronze Age Jutland, east Denmark. In, G. Nash (ed) *Semiotics of landscape: Archaeology of mind*. Oxford: BAR (International Series 661). pp.71-9.

Thrane, H. 1995. Penultima Thule: The Bronze Age in the western Baltic region as an analogy to the Irish Bronze Age. In, J. Waddell & E. Shee-Twohig (eds) *Ireland in the Bronze Age*. Dublin: Office Of Public Works. pp.149-57.

Thrift, N. 1991. For a new regional geography 2. *Progress in Human Geography* 15(4): 456-65.

Tilley, C. 1991. Constructing a ritual landscape. In, K. Jennbert et al (eds) *Regions and reflections: In honour of Marta Stromberg*. Lund: Almqvist & Wiksell Internat. pp.67-80.

Tilley, C. 1994. *A phenomenology of landscape*. London: Berg.

Tilley, C. 1996. The power of rocks: Topography and monument construction on Bodmin Moor. *World Archaeology* 28(2): 161-77.

Tilley, C. 1999. *Metaphor and material culture*. Oxford: Blackwell.

Tipping, R. 1996. Microscopic charcoal records, inferred human activity and climate change in the Mesolithic of northernmost Scotland. In, T. Pollard & A. Morrison (eds) *The early prehistory of Scotland*. Edinburgh: Edinburgh University Press. pp.39-61.

Tolan-Smith, C. 1996. The Mesolithic-Neolithic transition in the lower Tyne valley: A landscape approach. *Northern Archaeology* 13/14: 7-15.

Tomaskova, S. 1997. Places of art:Art and archaeology in context. In, M. Conkey et al (eds) *Beyond art: Pleistocence image and symbol*. San Francisco: Memoirs of the Californian Academy of Sciences. pp. 265-88.

Topping, P. 1992. The Penrith henges: a survey by the RCAHME. *Proceedings of the Prehistoric Society* 58: 249-64.

Topping, P. 1997. Different realities: The Neolithic in the Cheviots. In, P. Topping (ed) *Neolithic landscapes.* Oxford: Oxbow. pp.113-24.

Tratebas, A. 1993. Stylistic chronology vs absolute dates for early hunting rock art on the North American plains. M. Lorblanchet & P. Bahn (eds) *Rock art studies: The post stylistic era or where do we go from here.* Oxford: Oxbow monograph 35. pp.163-77.

Trudgian, P. 1976a. Cup-marked stones from a barrow at Starapark, near Camelford. *Cornish Archaeology* 15: 49.

Trudgian, P. 1976b. Observations and excavation at Tichbarrow, Davidstow. *Cornish Archaeology* 15: 41-45.

Van Hoek, M. 1985. A new group of cup and ring marked rocks at Inisnown, Co. Donegal. *Ulster Journal of Archaeology* 48: 123-7.

Van Hoek, M. 1986. The prehistoric rock art of Galloway. *Transactions of the Dumfries and Galloway Natural History and Archaeology Society* LXI: 20-37.

Van Hoek, M. 1987. The prehistoric rock art of Co.Donegal (PtII). *Ulster Journal of archaeology* 51: 21-97.

Van Hoek, M. 1993. The spiral in British and Irish Neolithic rock art. *Glasgow Archaeological Journal* 18: 11-32.

Van Hoek, M. 1997. The distribution of cup-and-ring motifs along the Atlantic seaboard of Europe. *Rock Art Research* 14(1): 3-16.

Vatcher, F. 1969. Two incised chalk plaques near Stonehenge bottom. *Antiquity* 43: 310-1.

Viewpoint. 1994. Is there a place for aesthetics in archaeology? *Cambridge Archaeological Journal* 4(2): 249-69.

Voss, J & R. Young. 1995. Style and the self. In, C. Carr & J. Neitzel (eds). *Style, society and person.* New York: Plenum Press. pp.77-100.

Vyner, B. 1984. The excavation of a Neolithic cairn at Street House, Loftus, Cleveland. *Proceedings of the Prehistoric Society* 50: 151-96.

Vyner, B. 1988. The Street House Wossit: the excavation of a late Neolithic and early Bronze Age palisaded ritual monument at Street House, Loftus, Cleveland. *Proceedings of the Prehistoric Society* 54: 173-202.

Vyner, B. 2000. Lost Horizons: the location of activity in the later Neolithic and early Bronze Age in the northeast of England. In, J. Harding & R. Johnson (eds) *Northern pasts: Interpretations of the later prehistory of northern England and southern Scotland.* Oxford: BAR (British Series 302). pp. 101-10.

Waddell, J. 1970. Irish Bronze Age Cists. *Journal of the Royal Society of Antiquarians Ireland* 100: 91-139.

Waddell, J. 1990. *The Bronze Age burials of Ireland.* Galway: Galway University Press.

Waddell, J. 1991/2. The Irish Sea in prehistory. *Journal of Irish Archaeology* VI: 29-40.

Waddington, C. 1996. Putting rock art to use: A model of early Neolithic transhumance in north Northumberland. *Northern Archaeology* 13/14: 147-77.

Waddington, C. 1998. Cup-and-ring marks in context. *Cambridge Archaeological Journal* 8(1): 29-54.

Waddington, C. 1999. *A landscape archaeological study of the Mesolithic-Neolithic in the Milfield Basin, Northumberland.* Oxford: BAR (British Series 291).

Wainwright, G. 1969. A review of Henge monuments in the light of recent research. *Proceedings of the Prehistoric Society* 35: 112-33.

Walderhaug, E. 1995. Rock art and society in the Neolithic of Sogn og Fjordane. In, K. Helskog (ed) *Perceiving rock art: Social and political perspectives.* Oslo: Institute for comparative studies in human culture. pp.169-80.

Wallis, R. 1995. *'Tombs for living death': Irish passage tomb art and shamanism.* Unpublished manuscript: University of Southampton.

Walker, M. 1977. 'Schematised' rock markings as archaeological evidence. In, P. Ucko *Form in indigenous art.* Canberra: Australian Institute of Aboriginal Studies. pp. 452-69.

Walker, B & G. Ritchie. 1987. *Exploring Scotland's heritage: Fife and Tayside.* Edinburgh: HMSO.

Walsh, P. 1993. In circle and row: Bronze Age ceremonial monuments. In, E. Shee-Twohig & M. Ronayne (eds) *Past perceptions.* Cork: Cork University Press. pp.101-13.

Walsh, P. 1995. Structure and deposition in Irish Wedge tombs: an open and shut case? In, J. Waddell & E. Shee-Twohig (eds) *Ireland in the Bronze Age*. Dublin: Office Of Public Works. pp.113-27.

Watson, A. 2001: Composing Avebury. *World Archaeology* 33(2): 296-314.

Weigel, S. 1996. *Body-and-Image-Space*. London: Routledge.

Whittle, A. 1997. Moving on and moving around: Neolithic settlement mobility. In, P. Topping (ed) *Neolithic landscapes*. Oxford: Oxbow. pp.15-22.

Whittle, A. 2000. 'Very like a whale': Menhirs, motifs and myths in the Mesolithic-Neolithic transition of northwest Europe. *Cambridge Archaeological Journal* 10(2): 243-59.

Wolff, J. 1981. *The social production of art*. Basingstoke: MacMillan.

Woodward, A. 2000. *British barrows: a matter of life and death*. Stroud: Tempus.

Woolley, A. 1976. Geology for the collector. In, M. O'Donoghue (ed) *The encyclopaedia of minerals and gem stones*. London: Orbis. pp. 42-71.

Yates, T. 1993. Frameworks for an archaeology of the body. In, C. Tilley (eds) *Interpretative Archaeology*. Oxford: Berg. pp.31-72.

Young, A. 1937-8. Cup-and-ring markings on Craig Ruenskin, with some comparative notes. *Proceedings of the Society of Antiquarians of Scotland* LXXII: 143-49.

Young, R & T. Simmonds. 1995. Marginality and the nature of later prehistoric upland settlement in the north of England. *Landscape History* 17: 5-16.

Young, R & T. Simmonds. 1999. Debating marginality: Archaeologists at the edge. In, J. Bruck & M. Goodman (eds) *Making places in the prehistoric world: Themes in settlement archaeology*. London: UCL Press. pp.198-212.

Zilhão, J. 1995. The age of the Côa Valley (Portugal) rock art: validation of archaeological dating to the Palaeolithic and refutation of 'scientific' dating to historic or proto-historic times. *Antiquity* 69: 883-901.

Zilhão, J et al. 1997. The rock art of the Côa Valley (Portugal) and its archaeological context: First results of current research. *Journal of European Archaeology* 5(1): 7-49.

Zindel, C. 1970. Incisioni rupestri A Carschenna (Canton Grigioni, Svizzera). In, E. Anati et al (eds) *Valcamonica Symposium: Actes du Symposium International d'Art préhistorique*. Capo di Ponte: Edizioni del Centro. pp.135-42.

Zvelebil, M. 1997. Hunter-gatherer ritual landscape: Spatial organisation, social structure and ideology among hunter-gatherers of northern Europe and western Siberia. *Analecta Praehistorica Leidensia* 29: 13-7.

www.ingramcontent.com/pod-product-compliance
Lightning Source LLC
Chambersburg PA
CBHW051302270326
41926CB00030B/4702